Dynamics in Pacific Asia

Studies from the
International Institute for Asian Studies
LEIDEN AND AMSTERDAM

Edited by
Paul van der Velde, General Editor

Dynamics in Pacific Asia

CONFLICT, COMPETITION AND COOPERATION

Edited by

Kurt W. Radtke, Joop A. Stam,
John Groenewegen, Leo M. van der Mey
and Takuo Akiyama

KEGAN PAUL INTERNATIONAL
London and New York

in association with the

INTERNATIONAL INSTITUTE FOR ASIAN STUDIES
Leiden and Amsterdam

First published in 1998 by
Kegan Paul International
UK: P.O. Box 256, London WC1B 3SW, England
Tel: (0171) 580 5511 Fax: (0171) 436 0899
E-mail: books@keganpau.demon.co.uk
Internet: http://www.demon.co.uk/keganpaul/
USA: 562 West 113th Street, New York, NY, 10025, USA
Tel: (212) 666 1000 Fax: (212) 316 3100

Distributed by
John Wiley & Sons Ltd
Southern Cross Trading Estate
1 Oldlands Way, Bognor Regis
West Sussex, PO22 9SA, England
Tel: (01243) 779 777 Fax: (01243) 820 250

Columbia University Press
562 West 113th Street
New York, NY, 10025, USA
Tel: (212) 666 1000 Fax: (212) 316 3100

© International Institute for Asian Studies, 1998

Set in Times
Printed on Precision Fine acid-free paper
Printed in Great Britain
Jacket design by Jeremy Williams

British Library Cataloging-in-Publication Data
Dynamics in Pacific Asia: conflict, competition and cooperation
1. East Asia - Economic Conditions 2. East Asia - Politics and government 3. East Asia - Foreign Relations
I. Radtke, Kurt Werner, 1945-
330.9'5'0429
ISBN 0 7103 0598 2

Library of Congress Cataloguing-in-Publication Data
Dynamics in Pacific Asia : conflict, competition and cooperation /
edited by Kurt Radtke...et al
Includes bibliographical references. ISBN 0 7103 0598 2
1. East Asia—Politics and Government. 2. Asia. Southeastern—
Politics and government—1945. 3. East Asia—Economic conditions.
4. Asia, Southeastern—Economic Conditions. 5. National security—East Asia. 6. National security—Asia, Southeastern. 7. Asia—Foreign Economic economic relations—Europe. 8. Europe—
Foreign economic relations—Asia. I. Radtke, Kurt W. (Kurt Werner), 1945-
DS518.1.D96 1998
950—dc21   97-31320
CIP

Contents

Preface

The writing of this book started in earnest with the establishment of a joint research group that gathered at the Netherlands Institute of Advanced Study (Wassenaar, The Hague) between September 1995 and June 1996. The starting point was the question, to what extent and in what way the new dynamics in (South)east Asia would influence Europe's global position, and more specifically, how these changes should be conceptualized in order to assist in the formulation of new policies to deal with the new international environment. Most contributors to this book would agree that there is ample reason to view these changes as an opportunity for Europe, and not just as a threat. Understanding the structure of new dynamics might become a small contribution leading towards the formulation of better policies. In their joint contribution to this book Marini and Rood argue that this new environment requires the US to be both a European and an Asian power, and to accept the responsibilities which follow from the position of a great or global power. This also applies to Europe. Policy making towards Asia should not focus on Asia in isolation but set against the new global contest in which the rise of new great powers and a multi-polarization of the international system, a regionalization of economic activities and political responsibilities, and a further relative "decline" of the American capacity and ability to manage the international political and economic system, should be taken into account.

This, in the view of the editors of this book, should likewise become the setting in which European responses to the dynamic developments in (South)east Asia should be deliberated. Any change of global consequence is easily perceived by the existing great powers as a "challenge" to their current position. The dissipation of traditional power structures symbolized by the rise of new great powers, the simultaneous development of multipolarization and regionalization, and the reduction of the ability of any (super)power to dominate the international political and economic system exclusively also provide room and opportunity for middle powers such as the governments of a united Europe.

Our joint NIAS research group repeatedly discussed the question whether we should add another book to the by now seemingly unlimited number of tomes devoted to "new developments in Asia Pacific", or whether we should limit the visible output of our joint research to individual publications by members of the group. Eventually we opted for the publication of this book, for which we invited contributions from some members of the group as well as several other scholars who participated in the two international conferences we organized in spring 1996 on the "political" and "economic" dynamics in (South)east Asia and their consequences for Europe. We were greatly encouraged to commence work on this book by the moral and financial support of the International Institute of Asian Studies (IIAS), in particular the director, Prof. dr. Wim Stokhof, and Dr. Paul van de Velde, member of the IIAS. This is also the place to express our thanks to Nani Lei Stam who with great enthusiasm took part in editing this book.

In most volumes on Asia-Pacific researchers the theoretical focus is on the traditional mono-disciplinary approach, analyzing events from an economic, political, or cultural perspective. Although we certainly do not deny the validity of this approach, there always remains the danger of underestimating the fact that disciplinary theory is nothing but a tool to dissect one dimension of an essentially multidimensional reality, and confusing the results delivered by these one-dimensional tools with reality itself. Clearly, the time has come to deal with the rather philosophical question how these disparate methods of analyses might be combined to provide a multidimensional understanding of reality. Politicians instinctively understand that their decisions can never be based on "economics" or "politics" separately, and this may explain the rather natural inclination of practitioners of power to view academic analysis with some suspicion.

The aim of this volume remains very modest. Each individual contributor took up issues which, like the pieces of a mosaic, would eventually convince the viewer (reader) that behind the scattered pieces lies a more coherent picture to be discovered by the reader himself. The topics for our joint research group have been refined during several international workshops and conferences organized in the Netherlands by members of the joint research group between 1991 and 1996. We did not "order" members of our research group to tackle a particular aspect of "Asia Pacific" to fit in with a pre-set analytical framework. To do so, would have ignored a fundamental requirement of scientific research in the social sciences and the humanities, namely, the individual academic responsibility and freedom without which academic research is difficult, if not impossible, to imagine.

Core members of the joint research group and their fields of research were: Takuo Akiyama (Long Term Credit Bank, Tokyo), researching emerging financial markets in Asia; Dr. John Groene-wegen (Erasmus University, Rotterdam [EUR]), business networks in Asia; Dr. Leo van der Mey (State University Leiden, [RUL]), models for international and security relations in Asia; Dr. Kurt W. Radtke (RUL), China, Japan and the United States; Dr. Joop Stam (EUR), management and technology transfer in Asia. We also were joined by two short-term visiting researchers, Prof. Nakamura Sato, emeritus professor and dean, Faculty of Economics, Kyoto University (autumn 1995), and Prof. Igarashi Akio, Rikkyo University (Network Pacific Asia) (spring 1996). We are also grateful to the ambassadors to the Hague of China and Japan who joined us in informal and highly informative discussions, the ambassador of the People's Republic of China to the Hague, Mr. Wu Jianmin (28 November 1995), and the ambassador of Japan to the Hague, Mr. Ikeda Tadashi (28 June 1996). We should like to express our deep gratitude to the Netherlands Institute for Advanced Study (NIAS) at Wassenaar, The Hague, which provided an extremely congenial academic environment for our research, in particular to the current Rector, Prof. dr. Wesseling, and the previous Rector, Prof. dr. Van de Kaa whose support was essential in realizing this joint research project. We should also express once more our personal thanks to all the staff members of the institute, and in particular to Mrs. Anneke Vrins who assisted us in the organization of the two conferences mentioned above.

In the course of the project we organized two international conferences:

1. "International Relations and Security in Pacific Asia," 2-3 April 1996, held at the Institute for International Relations Clingendael, The Hague, and organized by L. van der Mey and K.W. Radtke. We should like to express our gratitude for the organizational and financial support given by "Institute Clingendael", and for the financial support by the NIAS, the CNWS (Center for Non-Western Studies, Leiden University), the IIAS and others.

2. "Asian Business Systems and Enterprise Strategies", 13-14 May 1996, held at the NIAS in Wassenaar. Organizers: J.P.M. Groenewegen and J.A. Stam. We should like to express our gratitude for the organizational and financial support of the NIAS, and the financial support of the IIAS, and the Rotterdam Institute for Modern Asian Studies (RIMAS) in Rotterdam.

A brief word on the genesis of this joint research group seems in order. The first beginnings of the project date back to the eighties when several researchers from Rotterdam and Leiden University studying current developments in Asia from their respective disciplines started cooperating, first on an informal basis. This resulted amongst others in the organization of two international symposia (Erasmus University Rotterdam 1991; Institute for International Relations, Clingendael, 1992). A meeting at Institute Clingendael in the presence of its then director, Prof. dr. J. Voorhoeve, and some members of the Ministry of Foreign Affairs encouraged us to set up a formal multidisciplinary research project on "East Asia as a region", followed by a three day Planning Seminar with participants from the Netherlands and abroad, at the NIAS in April 1994. The formal activities of the research group at the NIAS were carried by a core group of five researchers in the period September 1995 to June 1996, and two visitors (autumn 1995, spring 1996). In addition, we conducted numerous informal gatherings during this period in which researchers from various universities participated.

Kurt Radtke
Joop Stam
John Groenewegen
Leo van der Mey
Takuo Akiyama

Introduction

There are three main reasons for studying countries and economic regions in East Asia in their international settings, and not country by country:

1. The rapidly growing mutual dependence among countries and economic regions in (South)east Asia.
2. The interaction between economic developments, (domestic and international) politics, and security relations.
3. The necessity to approach specific regional problems, such as maritime disputes, the issue of "transparency" and mutual confidence building etc. structurally different from the approaches developed in Europe and the Americas.

Consequences for Europe are not limited to passively studying and tracing developments contributing to a new regional system in East and Southeast Asia. Following the increasing global role, new patterns of institution building developed in Asia will also influence the patterns of institution building worldwide. The formulation of those core issues demands an interdisciplinary and problem oriented approach. In the area of East Asian security we focus on the question of the relevance of European models of conflict resolution for issues such as "Korea" and "Taiwan", the considerable importance of "maritime security", and the prospects for greater auto-nomy of Southeast Asian countries in approaching security issues.

1

Commenting on the role of (external) great powers we assess the continuing performance of the US in maintaining stability, uncertainties about Russia's contribution to stability in East Asia, and increasing effects of developments in (South)east Asia on Europe. To give only a few examples, one may refer to the impact of newly developing financial markets ("emerging markets"), the demands made on global markets by gigantic investments in infrastructure, and the hunger for raw materials and food products. Europe clearly has a direct interest in the stability in this region, because economic instability in Asia (let alone military instability might threaten Europe's economic stability as well. Gatherings of Asian and European leaders such as the ASEM in Bangkok (March 1996) provide an opportunity to test the reaction to European policy initiatives. The role of organizations to promote (economic) integration, such as the ADB, APEC, ASEAN and its Secretariat are also undergoing dynamic changes. The establishment of European institutions served directly to develop a structural approach to reduce obstacles impeding peaceful integration, and promote an orderly solution of (peaceful) conflicts. Due to the huge asymmetries in Asia the European institutional approach cannot be transferred unchanged. This is one of the reasons why the functions of informal organizations, such as business systems, business networks, and patterns of market management have a particular role to play as a catalyst for integration in Asia. Interaction in Asia at all levels involves the "clash" of the many cultural traditions obtaining in (South)east Asia, a starting point for the building of a new Asian civilization now in the making. These issues cause us to rethink questions of theory in political science and economics.

Political and strategic issues
Maull opens the discussion by touching on the state-society nexus, the importance of regions, and misperceptions of unbalance of power. The first fallacy in analyzing regional security in East Asia consists in ignoring patterns of interaction between state and society. An analytical perspective focusing exclusively on the state will tend to overestimate the "China threat", but looking only at societal pressures may neglect problems posed by the state. Regions could become major stumbling stones for successful international governance, if they tilt against integrating themselves into broader contexts of cooperation and treat their own community as exclusive. "Balance of power" is often constructed as the "realistic" alternative to "institutionalist" approaches to international order. This

fails to recognize that "order" almost always result from a mixture of balance of power, hegemony, and voluntary association. Balance of power politics seems much more likely to define and pursue economic interests in mercantilist terms than to subdue its concern with military power, producing the risk of a reproduction of balance of power competition in the economic sphere. The dynamics propelling (South)east Asia into a "region" like Europe are the rise of intra-regional trade, technology and capital flows; the existence of intra-regional social institutions and networks tying together countries of the region; and the sense of identity and common destiny shared by people in the region. In terms of geopolitical structure Europe is basically a continental region, while East Asia is predominantly a maritime theatre. In East Asia, the most serious and potentially most violent international conflicts are the unresolved civil wars in Korea and China; the very centrality of these conflicts to global stability increases risks, but also induces great efforts to keep these conflicts under control. In spite of significant processes of convergence in foreign policy cultures, both in Europe and in East Asia fundamental incompatibilities exist, balanced in both cases by continued active US participation. In East Asia, multilateral political processes fostering integration get their dynamism from societal forces, above all from business. Yet as the transformation of balance of power politics still has to be achieved, conscious efforts have to be made to change the foreign policy cultures of key players, engaging all players in a peaceful learning process. Self-restraint will benefit all.

Radtke emphasizes that the interaction of economics and politics, history and culture, and security requirements creates dynamic patterns different for each of the participants in the international system. The individual "personality" of states may differ considerably, and keeps changing. China's rise as an economic great power is still accompanied by question marks concerning internal stability, and uncertainties concerning the implications for comprehensive security in East Asia. Japan wishes to reaffirm its security insurance by strengthening its security treaty with the United States, yet is aware that within less than two decades Sino-Japanese trade may be the dominating trade relation in global trade, by far surpassing the role of US trade.

Taiwan and Japan wish to prevent serious tensions between the United States and China, but at the same time agree to cooperate in long-term missile defense projects directed not only against North

Korea, but against perceived threats from China as well. Southeast Asia is less united internally than cooperating in ASEAN may suggest, but appears united in its policy of engagement with China without appeasement. The implications of the rise of Indian influence are as yet unknown. The security implications of integration processes pushed by APEC may be limited, but its role as facilitator for political and defense dialogue becomes increasingly important. The basic theme (or "contradiction") is the clear intention of the will of the United States to maintain global leadership well into the twenty-first century, including leadership in Asia, while China's growth may effectively undermine US influence in the region. Despite growing political economic and political interaction scarcity of resources, smoldering conflicts around Korea, Taiwan and the South China Sea, and certain disagreement on the delimitation of continental shelves and maritime economic zones require conflict management based on the resurrection of cooperation among the "great powers". New forms of deterrence, economic interdependence, the threat of unacceptable risks arising from the escalation of military clashes on even a minor scale force the participating great powers to engage in a pragmatic joint approach towards security, likely to evolve into a "Directorate of Asian Pacific Powers". The members of this "directorate" are not equidistant from each other, *vide* the close cooperation between the US and Japan. The importance of the rapid increase of the Sino-Japanese economic relationship will however qualitatively alter the chemistry of international relations by increasing the stakes of all parties in maintaining security. Security policies are being influenced by increasing economic interaction, also affecting the security role of the United States in East Asia, which has often been likened to that of a stabilizing power, or arbiter. The ability of the United States to act as a balancer is predicated on its overwhelming deterrent capacity and virtual absence of credible threats, a situation which may slowly change during the next one or two decades. US-China relations display a two-tier feature, in which manageable economic issues, including China's accession to the WTO, are conducted fairly independently from strategic long-term issues such as Taiwan, China's territorial claims in the South China Sea, and the expansion of US security relations with countries in Asia. At the same time, an increasing, but still very modest European presence may lower the threat of an increasing polarization between China and the United States.

Timmer stresses that Asia's, in particular China's rapid increase in energy requirements forces a new emphasis on secure energy links with South-West Asia and the Middle East, both along continental and maritime routes. He reviews other strategic ingredients for growth, and also presents an overview of economic and military strengths and weaknesses of the players important to stability in Asia. Future developments will not only depend on "objective" requirements and capabilities, but also on the way the players perceive themselves and others. If China sees itself as the next world power, classical balance-of-power policies by its neighbors and other Pacific states would obviously be an answer. This in turn might heighten China's apprehensions. The country directly faces on or near its borders eight of the most numerous or formidable armed forces in the world: those of the USA, Russia, India, Vietnam, Japan, the two Koreas and Taiwan. If Beijing's strategic think tanks really are charmed by geopolitical ways of thinking they probably are inclined to see the US dominating large parts of the Pacific Rim "counter coasts", as a result of the Second World War and the Cold War. Seen this way, the US is not a stabilizing force. Japan, however, is perceived with a mixture of ambivalence and distrust. China's strategic traditional thinking does not necessarily predispose it towards pure military deterrence and use of threats. Cao Cao, in particular, counseled against military adventures if one's own military technological and material base could not stand the comparison with one's main competitors. In the end, however, it is on the US alliances and security arrangements that the stability in the area hinges to a very large degree. Determining big power agenda-setting, however, is the fact that here nations with distinctive senses of the self-image and historic mission in the world meet. It is from this domain that gross misunderstandings and apprehensions could arise once more, increasing the urgency of multilateral frameworks for security in Asia to take off seriously. It is nothing short of amazing that the disappearance of the Soviet Union, the successor to the Russian colonial empire covering most of Central, North and a large part of Northeast Asia, seems to have had so little impact on the dynamics of power involving China, Japan, Korea, Southeast Asia and the United States.

Fritsche draws attention to the fact that Russia is currently reconsidering its "strategic partnership" with the West, and strengthening its links with China. Again, this development appears paradoxical in light of the fact that the main driving force behind the

break-up of the Soviet empire came from those political quarters
for whom Russia's future was closely bound up with its integration
in the Western "community of civilized nations", coupled with the
hope that through "strategic relations" with the US Russia could
secure for itself a role as a "global player" on the world stage. At
that stage there was a widespread feeling that the trouble with
Russia was that it was too Asian. This view was challenged by the
"Eurasians" who saw Russia as belonging to both Europe and Asia,
but at the same time as a "unique" entity that was distinct from
both continents. Disappointment about "the West" aiding Russia's
ability to act as a global player also led to a reconsideration of
another sort: a country aspiring to that status whose economic base
is weak must resort to military might. There also was a change of
emphasis in the importance of Asia. China was no longer just a
regional partner, but once more a global factor in the Russian-
American-Chinese triangle. Some in the Russian general staff call
for a strategic partnership not only with China, but also with India
and Iran. Like Timmer above, Fritsche emphasizes the often
neglected importance of continental Eurasia for decision makers in
Beijing and Moscow. At stake is not just the energy question, but for
some Russians the attempt to prevent the West gaining a foothold
in Central Asia and the Caucasus. Cooperation between Russia and
China has so far led to the conclusion of border agreements, and
attempts to increase economic and security cooperation. Of political
interest is the express wish of politicians in China and in Russia to
limit interference from abroad, which has repeatedly resulted in a
joint stance of both countries *vis-à-vis* countries pushing for further
"globalization". Both countries are also driven by a similar self-
identity, seeing themselves as a multi-ethnic state whose unity is
under threat. Russian support for Beijing's "one-China policy" is
reciprocated by Chinese understanding for Moscow's actions in
Chechnya. Both Moscow and Beijing regard "Islamic fundamentalism" as a threat not only to their own internal stability but also
to the stability of Central Asia. Both sides are unanimous in their
rejection of Western interference and aspirations to hegemony.
Despite such communality of interests, there is also a widespread
fear of a "threat" posed by China, in particular since Russia's
superiority has vanished at the same time as China's economy
started taking off. Sino-Russian relations are however not just of
bilateral importance. An intensification of Sino-American tensions
and a further deterioration in Russia's relations with the West
(NATO expansion) could result in a further rapprochement between

Moscow and Beijing at a level below that of a formal alliance. Yet even with better relations with the West China will remain a long-term priority for Russia. Fritsche argues that the eventual outcome - cooperation or confrontation - will largely depend on Russia's internal developments, while the consequences will be felt not only in Asia, but in the West, too. His argument is a timely reminder that geopolitics in the twentieth century is not just determined by the quadrilateral relationship between the United States, Japan, China and a united (Western) Europe.

This awareness may have implications in the search for solutions to crises in the regions. In his discussion of the situation on the Korean peninsula Manfred Pohl makes the case for a gradual unification, in which he emphasizes the active role of both North and South Korea in the unification process. Any solution imposed by the Great Powers is unlikely to be successful. Pohl agrees with other observers that as a state as well as a former model of self reliant development North Korea is already doomed, a judgment also based on his regular contact with North Korean representatives and his own visits to the country. The unavoidable demise of North Korea does, however, not preclude an active role for the current North Korean leadership in settling the crisis. Pohl points out that while the ordinary citizens are extremely ill-informed about the outside world, and Kim Ilsong and his clan may live in a world of their own, part of the elite is definitely aware of international developments in a fairly realistic way. The food crisis may nudge the North Korean representatives into dialogue with the US, Japan and South Korea, while China is probably able to play a role as intermediator. On the other hand, it cannot be in South Korea's interest to see the North collapse in an uncontrolled way, thus inducing all parties to look for a constructive approach to deal with the current crisis. Pohl then goes on to discuss in which way the governments concerned may use "carrots" (offers of economic assistance, e.g.) or the "stick" (pressure, political, economic or otherwise) to steer the complicated negotiations into a desirable direction.

Pohl argues that the process that led to German unification cannot operate as a model for Korea, but that there are still a few lessons to be learned - most of all, to learn from the negative experiences of the German unification process. On the positive side, South Korea should pay attention to the patience with which West Germany pursued its Ost-Politik, which eventually contributed vitally to the collapse of the East German government. At the same time the actors must be aware of the fact that unification is not simply a set plan, but from a certain stage onwards acquires a dynamism of its own. Despite all obvious difficulties, there is no practical alternative to gradual unification in Korea, Pohl argues, and suggests that South Korea take the following steps: increasing cooperation with the north without clamoring for early unification under South Korean conditions; strengthen domestic political reforms, despite opposition of vested interests; improve income distribution; and finally, to overcome regionalism as a basis for the distribution of power, a pattern nestled deeply in Korean political culture.

Despite some surprising success in stabilizing political power in North Korea, the government there will have to tackle first of all the food problem; the immense problem of restructuring the (communist) Korean Workers' Party (KWP) and its mass organizations in such a way that they will be able to operate within the organizational structure of a participatory democracy, However, once there is basic agreement on unification there can be no doubt that a unified Korea will quickly assert itself as one of the leading powers at least in Northeast Asia. For this reason, the whole process of unification will, as a matter of course, see the United States, Japan, China and a united (Western) Europe remain involved on the Korean peninsula.

Van der Mey takes up the issue of interaction between regional powers and the "Big Four" when he discusses the role of ASEAN and its contribution to an Asian security system through the ASEAN Regional Forum (ARF). The establishment of the ARF was in fact not the first attempt to find an "Asian" approach towards peace-making. It was preceded by India's efforts during the fifties to bring about a peace zone in Asia in collaboration with the People's Republic of China and other like-minded countries. The approaches at peace-making to be discussed in this chapter are characterized as Nehru's "zone of peace" and the "ASEAN way" to peace. The Indian Prime Minister J. Nehru was the architect of the security scheme in which a collaborative venture with China should help to shape a peace zone in Asia. Basis of this scheme was the declaration of the so-called "Five Principles of Coexistence" proclaimed by both countries in 1954. In essence, the five principles were guidelines for good neighborship. One year later, at the Bandung Conference (1955), in 1967, ASEAN was to mark a new beginning in cooperation in Southeast Asia. Despite some gloomy prophesies, ASEAN has prevailed and has found responses to internal and external challenges which it has been confronted with. Basis of this organization's functioning are self-restraint and accommodation. ASEAN has developed into a framework for national economic growth and sub-regional cooperation, politically as well as economically. In the nineties, ASEAN has expanded its scope by incorporating Vietnam as a new member and by setting up the ASEAN Regional Forum to initiate a security dialogue with the major powers and other states in the region.

The ASEAN way to peace has proven more successful than Nehru's approach. In order to explain the evolution of these attempts at peace-making, the following factors are taken into account: the international context, the institutional development and 'the rules of the game'. International system conditions provide the key explanation for the foundation and subsequent consolidation of ASEAN. In the mid-sixties there was a common perception of a communist threat, which gave a certain impetus to cooperation. This perception of external threat was complemented by a commonly felt need for 'resilience', thus making ASEAN less dependent on the great powers. With the advantage of hindsight, it can be that Nehru's aim of a peace zone for the whole of Asia which would be respected by the superpowers was too ambitious.

Another major reason for the success of ASEAN is to be found in the way its further design came about. As a sequel to the Bangkok Declaration, institutionalization gradually took place. This is in stark contrast with the pursued peace zone which was merely declaratory. An important drawback in the Nehru model was the fact that it got no further than underwriting general principles, which received no political follow-up nor any institutional imbedding. A final explanation for ASEAN's success involves its style of operation, namely, a general acceptance of the rules of the game. These rules can be captured by the concepts consensualism and pragmatism. This too is in contrast with the envisaged peace zone, where the countries involved were expected to promote the maintenance of this zone of their own accord. The weakest spot in Nehru's security scheme was the belief in the special relationship between India and China as a basis for the peace zone. The underestimated destructive dynamism of national antagonisms, regional rivalry and personal friction led to the war of 1962, as well as to the collapse of the peace zone in Asia.

All in all, the ASEAN countries knew how to make good use of the opportunities available to improve their mutual relations and to improve the position of the sub-region. They understood that they were partly dependent on the great powers to realize their policies. This is all the more true for their new aim to extend the security regime. If the ASEANization of Pacific Asia is to succeed, then the security dialogue instigated by the ARF must be constructively supported by the major Asian powers and the United States. Van der Mey adds a further aspect to this argument by pointing out the importance of the contribution ASEAN is making to the construction of a security regime through the ASEAN Regional Form (ARF). This, in fact, was not the first attempt to find an "Asian" approach towards peace-making. It was preceded by India's efforts during the fifties to bring about a zone of peace in Asia in collaboration with the People's Republic of China and other like-minded countries.

Issues of economic interdependency
The economic and industrial development process in Pacific Asia is characterized by a large degree of interdependence as well as differences in the level of development of each member state at a given time. Differential labor costs, for example, have contributed towards regional division of labor, followed by international specialization, technology transfer and diffusion of knowledge by way of local sub-contracting (Ohki, 1991). While Japan occupies an advanced, leading position, the respective other economies of the region follow in her path. Simultaneously we observe a regional economic integration. Berri and Ozawa (1996) refer to a process of "comparative advantage recycling", i.e. as the industrialization of the region progresses, a structural upgrading of technological sophistication, from low-tech labor intensive to hi-tech capital intensive, takes place. The recycling of comparative advantages assumes a strong interlinkage between economies and industries through trade and investment and foresees a spin-off for the host countries attracting direct foreign investment.

Closely related to this interlinked pattern of development we observe a clustering of economic activities at the borders between nation-states of Asia in so-called sub regional economic zones. Each of these new clusters has its own dynamics and is pushed along by one center. Developments in these subregional economic zones are fed by investment and industrial activities of international corporations utilizing factor differentials. Examples of subregional economic zones (SREZ) are: Singapore-Johore-Riau; Thailand-Laos-Cambodia (Baht zone); Taiwan-Hong Kong-Guangdong;

Kyushu-South Korea-Shandong; Japan Sea Rim Economic Zone (South Korea, North Korea, North(east) China, East Siberia, Japan).

These subregional economic zones do not have a special legal status but are part of the sovereign territory of countries involved. However, international economic activities initiated by multinational enterprises flourish irrespective the borderlines of nation-states. The emergence of the subregional economic zones exemplifies a further international division of labor in the region and the network building of companies in a hub and spoke structure. In the wake of these developments coordination between the headquarters of the multinational corporation and their (sub)regional Asian activities becomes a serious issue which increasingly requires attention.

Apart from the economic interrelations and patterns of development in Asia, the characteristics of "Asian Capitalism" draw our attention as well. Understanding economic systems can be undertaken from different perspectives such as the political, economic and cultural perspective. In the political approach the state has a central role with the danger of downplaying the role of other actors. To a certain extent economic structures do reflect the political power structures, but there is more. In the economic approach economic efficiency is the main explanatory variable with the disadvantage of considering power relations, history and culture irrelevant. In the cultural approach Asian capitalist systems are understood as the result of shared values with the disadvantage of being too general and not capable to explain big differences in economic organization within the same culture. It is our view that all three perspectives contribute to the understanding of Asian economic systems, but the one approach should not exclude contributions from the other. In a relevant theoretical approach economic rationality as driving force behind strategies of firms should be combined with factors of the institutional environment in which those economic actions are embedded. In a relevant theoretical perspective specific power relations are taken into account in order to understand the specific consequences of bargaining processes. In other words, understanding the complexity of recent developments in Pacific Asia and its consequences for Europe demands an analysis in which actors' behavior is embedded in a specific institutional environment, in which history and path dependent developments are explicitly taken on board.

Typically in Asia not the individual actor is the crucial actor, but the network in which the individual is embedded. Like individualism is institutionalized in Western societies, so are social relationships in Asian societies. The relational logic of Asia produces a society that rests on networks and economic and political actors should be understood in relation with their networks. This certainly does not mean that all Asian economies are alike. On the contrary, each one has its own specific history, institutions, structure of firms and role of government. In all Asian economies networks play a central role but the specific conditions of time and place have to be taken into account in order to understand the differences between the varieties of Asian organization and Asian capitalism.

Japanese capitalism is best characterized as relational, or organizational capitalism, to express the fact that both firms and government purposefully invest in relations (see Groenewegen). South Korean capitalism is of a different nature. Here history and culture resulted in "patrimonial, or political capitalism", in which hierarchical structures, both inside firms and industrial groups (*chaebol*), dominate. Networks certainly also dominate the Taiwanese scene, and both firms and government play an important, but fundamentally different role than their counterparts in Japan and Korea. The Taiwanese government first of all stimulated and enabled small and medium-sized family based firms to become competitive.

The contributions in this volume all take the interrelations between economic and political actors as point of departure and show the importance of taking specific institutions into account in order to understand the differences within Asian network capitalism.

Groenewegen focuses on Japan and discusses how the relationship between government and enterprises developed over time. He shows that especially the Ministry of International Trade and Industry (MITI) before the sixties had a strong guiding role; enterprises in Japan lacked the necessary technology and finance which made them very dependent on government. However, external and internal factors changed in such a way that government's role became more indirect. In addition to the trade balance problems (and the ensuing political pressure of the US) and the growing financial independence of firms, especially the developments in technology explain the change in the relations between government and business in Japan. The necessity to be at the forefront of technology demands another type of technology policy. MITI found the answer in the so-called research associations (RA's). Groenewegen analyzes the RA's and outlines the conditions under which government in a modern market economy like Japan, can effectively guide business.

In his contribution Stam analyses the spin-off of technology transfer of Japanese enterprises investing in Pacific Asia and focuses on the electronic industry in the ASEAN countries. Since the early 1980s the transfer of Japanese assembling activities to ASEAN has increased due to rising labor costs in Japan, the growth potential of the region but in particular the change in development policy in most of the ASEAN countries, namely, from an import substitution policy to an export-oriented industrialization program. Within a short period of time the nature of the Japanese assembling activities in the region changed from simple to sophisticated. However, the pace of local industrial development did not always coincide with the requirements of modern hi-tech production in terms of quality and quantity. Consequently, local industry has not always been able to provide the necessary products and services to the rapidly expanding Japanese (and other foreign) assembling enterprises. To compensate for this gap small and medium-sized Japanese part and component manufacturers have followed their Japanese masters to the region. Thus the Japanese mass-manufacturing industry has installed a "full-set" industrial infrastructure by using their networks with which they are familiar in Japan.

These inter-firm networks and linkages helped to lower the barriers for small and medium-sized Japanese companies to invest in Southeast Asia but also created serious competition for budding local industries. Only through long-term involvement and technological tie-ups can local industry benefit from the leading position of Japanese manufacturing industry. In reality technology transfer related to Japanese investment in production facilities and the spillover to local industry tends to decrease as the technological sophistication increases. Financial support and technological upgrading of small and medium-sized local enterprises by the Southeast Asian governments seems to be the best remedy for bridging the gap between local industry and foreign companies.

These observations and conclusions are corroborated by the survey of Mirza, Kee Hwee and Bartels among non-ASEAN transnational corporations (TNCs). In their report they analyze the motivation for investment, the major obstacles foreign companies encountered and the preferred investment policy. In order to attract and coordinate intra-ASEAN investment of transnational corporations it is important to know the relevant factors for investment decisions and the reactions to incentive schemes. From a historical perspective it is clear that investment attraction schemes of the respective ASEAN host countries proved to be a major factor for investment decisions, although availability of a suitable partner and a conducive regulatory environment ranked high as well. Future investment will be stimulated by these factors but also by low production costs and the prospect of developing markets. Political instability, economic restrictions, deficiencies of physical infrastructure as well as non-transparency of policies and measures were considered the main obstacles to foreign direct investment by non-ASEAN transnational corporations. In addition, foreign firms are looking at ASEAN as a region. It seems therefore appropriate to develop ASEAN wide investment incentive schemes and harmonize policy measures, for instance, as proposed in AFTA. Increasing competition for FDI with other developing regions and zones like China and India makes an explicit intra ASEAN FDI policy highly desirable. A regional division of labor and strengthening of intra-ASEAN economic activities increases trade and investment and creates income and prosperity. On the basis of this survey the authors construe a framework for strategic choices for ASEAN and non-ASEAN TNCs and conclude that considerable scope exists for ASEAN to pursue a FDI encouraging strategy which simultaneously facilitates the strengthening and internationalization of ASEAN TNCs and furthers development objectives of the region.

Akiyama describes the importance of capital markets in the developing economies of Asia. Supply of capital is crucial for investment and until recently the control of capital flows has been strongly government dominated. However, when emerging economies reach the stage of export-led growth or even domestic-demand-based growth, then firms show a growing need for risk capital. On the other hand investors looking for risk diversification become interested in investing in emerging markets. Government should then deregulate and make capital markets attractive for outsiders. The attractiveness of capital markets is also related to the structure of firms and business groups. The closer these groups are (due to family relations, bank relations or government ties), the more reluctant private investors are. Akiyama describes the situation in several

Asian economies and shows the enormous differences in liberalization between countries like Japan and Korea on the one hand and for example Indonesia and Malaysia on the other.

With the contribution of van Hoesel we direct our attention to the relations of Asia with Europe. Van Hoesel concentrates on South Korea, an interesting case in point because the South Korean economy is in a new period of transition. The limits of the Korean economic growth path became apparent in the mid 1980s when the currency, the Won, appreciated, wages rose and the need to advance to the next stage of industrialization, that of the development of high technology, was strongly felt. As a consequence of that transformation both the Korean government and the large industrial groups (*chaebols*) like Samsung and Hyundai, as well as the relation between these two needed fundamental changes. With respect to government the Ministry of EPB (Economic Planning Board), which had been the central coordinator of Korean industrial development, felt competition from the Ministry of Science and Technology as well as the Ministry of Trade and Industry. For the *chaebol* the burden of high debt became heavy, particularly when large investments in R&D were necessary. Moreover, the need to change the vertically integrated conglomerate structure into internationally competitive structures became strongly felt. Van Hoesel explains how firms were forced to invest outside South Korea, first in Asia and later in the US and Europe. He describes the two waves of investments of Samsung, Daewoo, Hyundai and LG in Europe and how the character of investments changed.

A serious issue related to the international division of labor is the coordination between headquarters and regional Asian activities, not only for Japanese enterprises but for European and American companies as well. As Schütte explains in his contribution on regionalization of global thinking and the strategy and organization of European MNCs in Asia, European multinational firms are seriously lagging behind in Asia for several reasons like disinterest, difficulties to enter Asian markets but also managerial underperformance. Japanese and Korean companies on the contrary generate cash in Asia for investment in Europe. If European firms want to improve their position in the newly emerging markets, regions or sub regions, an Asia strategy is called for. Such an Asia strategy should reflect a balance between regional integration and local responsiveness. In Schütte's vision a regional (or sub-regional) headquarters then can take a more headquarters oriented role in the sense of intelligence gathering or budgeting and control or be more directly involved in the regional activities of the company. Schütte strongly argues in favor of a strategic approach towards Asia as a region. This implies a clear delineation of the borders of markets and ranges of activities. Effective regional headquarters though are managed by board members of the company. While drawing up the strategic plan for Asia one has to keep in mind that only a few countries and economies are large and powerful like Japan and China, all others are small to mid-sized. Therefore, European enterprises should seriously determine the place and role of their regional headquarters commensurate with their Asia strategy.

In the last contribution Gioia Marini and Jan Rood focus on the impact these new developments have for the United States and Europe, also making it clear that a proper understanding of the Atlantic relationship requires a sharp awareness of the Asian impact on both the US and Europe. They argue that the collapse of the Soviet Union fundamentally altered the geostrategic realities underpinning post-World War II American foreign policy. This tectonic shift changed in particular the position of Western Europe, which until then was the main confrontation line of the bipolar world political system. It was only natural that the Europeans reacted with alarm to Secretary of State Warren Christopher's November 1993 statement to the Senate Foreign Relations Committee that "[no] are of the world will be more important for American interests than the Asia-Pacific region". It emphasized that in a world in which competition among nations had shifted from the political-military field to the field of technological sophistication and domination of markets, Europe was losing the battle. Without any exclusive relationship or political leverage of its own toward Asia, Europe was being pushed to the periphery of world affairs. Four years later, as a result of the conclusion of the Uruguay Round, the American participation in IFOR and the agreements about a new set-up of NATO, the worst fears about an American disengagement from Europe seem to have worn off. Marini and Rood cite Michael Cox to argue that the main changes in US policy goals are shifts in the relative weight of some of those aims, such as the pursuit of the global spread of democratic capitalism, underwriting the balance of power in Europe and Asia, and ensuring that the United States remain the dominant actor in the international system. The collapse of the Soviet Union, and the growth of US-Asian relations, therefore threatened the Transatlantic connection from two interrelated perspectives: the lack of a common security challenge, and the risk of an escalation of economic problems. The threat of a massive Soviet attack has disappeared, but the US still has a vital interest in preventing the rise of a dominant power on the European continent, and in maintaining peace and stability in this region. Secondly, NATO infrastructure is still vital for American operations in other parts of the world, especially in the Middle East. Thirdly, although the US-EU economic relationship is plagued by conflicts, crises and from time to time even (the threat of) trade wars, there is also a strong economic interdependence between both sides of the Atlantic. Both in terms of imports and exports Asia-Pacific has become more important to the US than trade with the European Community. Within the increasingly triadic pattern of trade flows between the US, Europe and Asia-Pacific, the Transatlantic trade relation has been relegated from first place until the beginning of the eighties to third position at present. But from a "qualitative" point of view, there still is a very strong, and according to some, more stable trade relationship between the US and Western Europe than between the US and the Pacific area.

Also, Western Europe is by far the most important investor in the US as is the US in Western Europe, and the degree of technological cooperation and participation in joint development programs is much more intense between European and American firms than between the US and Asia. Fourthly, European integration forces the US to stay involved in Europe, because not to do so may affect America's global position negatively. Finally, the US is the one and only remaining superpower. But in this ever more complicated and interdependent world political and economic system, even the US must depend on reliable allies in order to realize her goals and commitments. It is fair to assume that compared to other possible alliances, the US-EU relationship is a potentially "winning coalition", and that Western Europe is America's most stable and "natural" partner. Having provided a summary of the structure of America's relations with Asia, Marini and Rood proceed to put the question, whether the next American president has the choice between Europe and Asia? Their answer is no, if he wants to maintain the US position as a global power. In other words, her status as a global power requires her to be both a European and an Asian power, and to accept the responsibilities which

follow from the position of a great or global power. This has consequences for Europe's relations with both the US and Asia. While,
according to Richard K. Betts, in Europe "[o]ne of the reasons for
optimism about peace (...) is the apparent satisfaction of the great
powers with the status quo," the same cannot be said of Asia. For
these reasons the Asian demand for American engagement in security affairs may be stronger than in Europe. In this view, it even
might be in the European interest to support America's involvement
in Asia and to encourage American leadership in maintaining
stability in this region. For, in the end, a stable and prospering
Asia is also in the interest of Europeans.

Marini and Rood conclude that the following factors will determine whether the US will be able to maintain its position as a
global power, factors that can only be understood from a broader
systemic point of view that provides the setting for US external
policies. This setting is characterized by:

1. the rise of new great powers, and a multipolarization of the
   international system;
2. a regionalization of economic activities and political responsibilities;
3. a further relative "decline" of the American capacity and
   ability to manage the international political and economic
   system.

This, in the view of the editors of this book, should likewise become the setting in which European responses to the dynamic
developments in (South)east Asia should be deliberated. Any
change of global consequence is easily seen by the existing great
powers as a "challenge" to their current position. The dissipation of
power structures symbolized by the rise of new great powers, the
simultaneous development of multipolarization and regionalization, and the reduction of the ability of any (super)power to
dominate the international political and economic system exclusively also provide room and opportunity for middle powers such as
the governments of a united Europe.

After the end of the Cold War the Great Powers aspiring to exercise global leadership are nearly identical with the Great
Powers of the Nineteenth Century, with the only exception that
Japan has now replaced Russia, and that Europe is still in a transitional stage where the role of England and France may gradually
become supplanted by a United Europe in which re-united Germany

may increase its leverage. In the background lurks China, a potential Great Power that disintegrated in the nineteenth century but now is aiming to become part of a new global order. New patterns of global trade, new technologies, and revolutions in the way military power are constructed and used for military and political purposes. All imply that the new global order cannot simply be compared to the pattern of "Balance of Power" of the Nineteenth Century, in which the governments of the Great Powers appeared to be the main players on a chessboard, the design and rules of which they seemed to control. One of the points of our book is that developments taking place in (South)east Asia, and their inherent dynamics have consequences for global order which will influence the patterns of institution building and the exercise of power by the world's leader to a degree hardly anticipated by politicians only twenty years ago. Economic developments in that region have implications not only for the economies of Europe and the Americas but they also have influence on the organization of global politics; vice versa, political decisions taken in (South)east Asia regularly influence economic conditions in the rest of the world. Such interaction makes it imperative that analyses of current changes should employ as a matter of course the analytical tools of various social sciences, such as economics, politics, or history, and that practicing politicians should be aware of the indivisible nature of economic, political and historic processes in order to develop optimal policy choices.

In actual fact, however, scholarly analyses tend to address themselves to a strictly segmented audience, where US scholars tend to focus on either US relations with China or Japan, or on Sino-Japanese relations. European specialists tend to focus on Europe's relations with the US, or on Europe's relations with one or several countries in (South)east Asia. This book cannot pretend to provide an answer how the multi-focussed, multi-layered analysis that would eventually be required could be achieved, but we hope to have demonstrated that narrower approaches are clearly inadequate, not only from a scholarly point of view, but also for politicians who willy-nilly have to deal with complex issues nearly blind-fold: they resemble the navigator of a supertanker laying a course in thick fog without proper charts or radar, having to take into account simultaneously rocks and shallows hidden below the surface, unexpected currents, sudden storms, and harbors whose position he is only able to guess.

Our common research project at the Netherlands Institute of Advanced Study, of which this book forms an important part, started with the question about the consequences of the new dynamics in (South)east Asia for Europe. Our research group did not develop a set of specific policy choices open to the governments of Europe in order to promote the interests of Europe in a changing globalizing world. Our answer to the initial question is, to emphasize the need to understand the global parameters within which new European policies towards Asia should be formulated. Although most contributors to this book would agree that these dynamic developments harbor the danger of destabilization, there is ample reason to view these changes as an opportunity for Europe, and not just as a threat. Fear of change makes for bad policies. Understanding the structure of new dynamics might become a small contribution leading towards the formulation of better policies.

Chapter 1

Hanns W. Maull: "Enhancing Cooperation in International Institutions"

Cassandra, as you might recall, was cursed by the gods: her prophecies always came true (and they often seemed to have been prophesies of doom; witness her prediction of the imminent fall of Troy), but she was never believed. Cassandra's modern followers among experts on regional security in Asia Pacific are better off. They receive much attention for their dire warnings about the future of Asia Pacific security (though fortunately we still do not have any proof that their forecasts are always correct).(1) China's recent actions over Taiwan's presidential election have done much to help the stocks of modern Cassandras rise.

Like Cassandra, Narcissus was also cursed by the gods. His flaw was self-indulgence: he was so taken by his own, unique beauty that the gods decided to destroy him. There is also a school of modern followers of Narcissus among practitioners and experts on regional security in Asia Pacific. They hold that East Asia's unique experiences and characteristics will take it on its own course - the "Asian Way" (2) or "Pacific Way"(3) - towards a bright future, in which it will reign supreme in the world. The stocks of Narcissus' followers seem to have declined somewhat in recent times, but they have by no means become extinct. And, as with Cassandra's modern followers, we cannot be sure that the gods really will punish them.

Indeed, I hope they will be right with their forecasts of a bright and peaceful future for the region. Whose forecast for regional security in Asia Pacific is closer to the mark? And, more importantly, what could be done to prevent the fulfillment of the dire prophecies of the Cassandras? The title of my paper suggests that enhancing cooperation-operation in international institutions would offer such an opportunity. I share this conviction, with an additional observation that I will assume that more effective international cooperation in global institutions (such as the United Nations or the nuclear non-proliferation regime) will benefit, and may often even require, the ability to cooperation-operate effectively at the regional level. From this vantage point, I shall look at the ingredients of closer international cooperation-operation in East Asia, by using European experiences in a comparative perspective as analytical tools.

PART I: SOME CONCEPTUAL CONSIDERATIONS

The discourse about security in Asia Pacific often suffers from a lack of conceptual sophistication and clarity. Thus, several important recent studies on the prospects for regional security in Asia Pacific analyze patterns of international relations in the region in terms of balance of power and plead for a "moderate multipolar balance-of-power system" in the region.(4) Yet their prescriptions are probably incompatible with a predominance of balance-of-power politics. The assumption that balance-of-power policies and politics could produce the kind of benign security environment envisaged by those studies represents a leap of faith, rather than a logical conclusion.(5) The desired arrangements clearly involve more than balance-of- power politics, yet what this implies and how this "more" could arise is left open. What is missing in the conceptual framework of analysis are factors relating to societal conditions both within and beyond national borders. Yet both dimensions - that of politics, which is crystallized by the state as the most important political actor, and that of society - are relevant for a proper understanding of today´s international relations, which are characterized by a high degree of tension between dynamic social change and relatively rigid political structures.(6) This tension which produces strains and adjustments of political arrangements at all levels, gives rise to new political mechanisms and processes. Within states, one expression of this is a growth in regionalism and federalism; at the international level, this tension is reflected in the proliferation of international institutions and international regimes, but also in trends towards regionalism.(7)

Rapidly increasing interactions and patterns of interdependence across borders are adding substance and meaning to the concept of international society by the day. International society thus increasingly develops capacities to cope with problems autonomously, largely or completely bypassing governments. But states are trying to enhance their ability to control developments beyond their own boundaries through cooperation and integration with other states, both formally (i.e. through institutions) and informally.(8) Optimists about East Asia's regional stability either build their case on patterns of regional integration between societies, or on institutionalized interaction between states, while the pessimists (in good "realist" fashion) tend to dismiss the realities of international or regional society as irrelevant, and consider it highly unlikely that states could organize effective cooperation among themselves.

Fallacy No. 1: Ignoring the state/society nexus
The reality of future relations between state and society is likely to fall somewhere between the extremes of complete dominance by the state over society, or the marginalization or even destruction of the state by societal change. The first fallacy in analyzing regional security in East Asia consists of ignoring patterns of interaction between state and society. To take the example of China: an analytical perspective which focuses exclusively on the state will tend to overestimate the "China threat", while a perspective looking only at societal pressures may neglect real problems posed by the Chinese state.

Put simply, society produces the resources needed to play the power game, but also throws up problems of authoritative allocation and regulation which only politics can resolve. Conversely, the state can enhance and manipulate or even smash processes of wealth production, but it may also be outflanked by efforts at social self-organization. We must then understand not only how both games of power and wealth are conducted in the nations of Asia Pacific, but also how the two games interact. Clarifying relations between state and society will tell us whether we are dealing with "strong" or "weak" states.(9) This, in turn, will have important implications for international relations. Remember that the almost complete failure of analysts to envisage the implosion of Soviet power resulted from a bias in analytical perspective; the dimensions of societal change in the former Soviet Union were largely ignored or at least completely underestimated in their implications. Yet the interaction between society and politics has long escaped national boundaries. The "power game" and the "wealth game" are also played simultaneously at the international level, and the two games also interact. Again, the correlation of political and transitional forces at work will differ, resulting in what we might call "strong" and "weak" systems of international governance. Economic growth may foster political stability at home and internationally? But if so, under what circumstances, and through which mechanisms? Conversely, how much "state" is needed to sustain economic growth, both domestically and internationally? These are examples of the interaction between power and wealth games. These interactions may be patterned; they may form trends, or perhaps reflect the existence and effectiveness of institutions.

Fallacy No. 2: Ignoring the importance of regions
Strong systems of international governance will probably have a high degree of institutional density or at least of effective mechanisms of problem-resolution. And they may well be multi-layered: given the complexities of international relations, an intermediate level between the state and the international system at large will often be indispensable. Thus, the analysis of issues of international governance should not be confined to the conventional three-level analysis, which Kenneth Waltz in a classic book title once summarized succinctly as *Man, The State, and War*.(10) In both the economic and the political/security realms of international governance, regions may be crucial building blocks for peace, prosperity and stability by discharging some of the functions needed to sustain international governance.(11) This could facilitate the evolution of cooperation-operative patterns of behavior and reduce the burdens placed on global institutions and regimes. But regions also could become major stumbling stones for successful international governance, if they tilt against integrating themselves into broader contexts of cooperation-operation and treat their own community as exclusive. More specifically, it is thus not regionalism *per se* which may be needed for successful international governance, but "open" regionalism.(12)

Fallacy No. 3 : Misunderstanding balance of power

"Balance of power" is often constructed as the "realist(ic)" alternative to "institutionalist" approaches to international order. This view fails to recognize that "order" almost always results from a mixture of balance of power, hegemony, and voluntary association. Politics is always about power, and very often about "checks and balances" to prevent power from becoming absolute. Take domestic politics in a democracy, and you will find many elements of balance of power. The really interesting question is thus not whether or not balance of power exists - it will always play a role in politics - but to what extent, and how it is modified by other elements. Successful governance seems to involve a judicious combination of balance of power, hegemony and voluntary association. Domestically, democracy seems to provide such a successful synthesis, while security communities may be seen as examples of such a synthesis at the international level.

Any political system which largely relies on balancing power runs a number of risks. First, by excluding societal factors other than power (such as norms and shared values), and the possibility of concentrating power, it neglects important aspects of reality, for example, balance of power politics build on narrow power and utility calculations. These ignore other important motivations, consideration and societal influences on decision-makers. This may undermine its workings but also carries the risk of becoming self-fulfilling: a balance-of-power approach to reality may, in fact, create a balance-of-power world. Even if actors preferred qualitatively different foreign policy approaches, they may feel forced to conform. Balance-of-power politics thus may tend to homogenize international relations in dangerous ways.

A second risk of balance-of-power politics is ineffectiveness: there are many problems which require cooperation-operation between the parties for a positive resolution. The so-called cooperation-operation dilemma, which has been analyzed exhaustively by game theorists, often cannot easily be overcome if participants focus on relative gains, as they have to, if they operate under the assumptions of balance of power. Yet dilemmas of this kind are very real in a number of important international relations challenges, such as the maintenance of a sound global environment and the management of energy, water and food resources for a rapidly expanding world population.

Balance-of-power puts a premium on enhancing power *vis-à-vis* other players, and thus creates or exacerbates power and security dilemmas. It also enhances the risk of hegemony, as one of the players involved may succeed in amassing overwhelming power and use it - in the logic of balance-of-power behavior - to dominate the others. This also illustrates a further danger, namely, emphasis on balancing power subtly shapes attitudes towards politics in general, emphasizing differences and subjecting the scope and value of cooperation-operation to narrow utility calculations. This makes balance of power systems inherently unstable. As the actual distribution of power will constantly change in response to differential economic performance and technological innovation, adjustments are necessary but will be resisted. Thus, tests of power relations are highly likely and, indeed, necessary. Since balance-of-power systems will tend towards measuring power in military terms, this creates a constant risk of war.

Balance-of-power politics also are available only to Great Powers. Smaller powers will have to fall in line with the big players. Theoretically, they could also try to combine into a separate power bloc, but in reality this is unlikely to work: balance-of-power politics puts a premium on the ability to muster huge military resources, and smaller states are unlikely to concede national sovereignty over their own military forces sufficiently to form a power cluster. The assumption that medium and small powers could exercise a moderating influence over the Great Powers in a balance-of-power system (an assumption often made in security analyses of Asia Pacific) thus needs to be taken with a heavy dose of salt.

Lastly, balance of power politics may be inherently "stupid": they seem to lack the ability to "learn" and to transform themselves. At the very least, it is difficult to see which *inherent* mechanisms could lead to a modification of power politics to produce what variously has been called "mature anarchy", "moderate balance-of-power system" or "security cooperation-operation". Hopes that balance of power politics may be able to develop rules, norms and institutions to enhance prospects of stability and peace seem to rely mostly on external influences (such as the emergence of inter-national society, of shared norms and values, or the existence of a strong but benign hegemon).

Could economic self-interest be an inherent mechanism to moderate and constrain balance of power politics? Again, this notion enjoys considerable salience among analysts of East Asian security, notably those from the region itself.(13) Yet again, in the absence of other mitigating influences balance of power politics are unlikely to be modified by those considerations: within a hierarchy of objectives defined by their relevance to national power, military security will clearly enjoy priority, and economic interests will be defined in relation to national power. Balance of power politics thus seems much more likely to define and pursue economic interests in mercantilist terms than to subdue its concern with military power. Against the chance that economic interests might induce moderation in balance of power politics the risk of a reproduction of balance of power competition in the economic sphere must be weighed.

In short, to rely on balance of power politics as a framework for international governance seems risky. This conclusion, of course, is also what history teaches, but its lessons gain additional weight against the background of the destructive potential of modern technology.

Conditions for successful international governance

Successful international governance should thus rely on more than balance of power alone. It should build on assets of voluntary association provided by international society, such as a sense of community built on shared values and aspirations and transnational networks and social institutions. International society today already seems capable of providing some transnational problem-solving capacity. It also can underpin political efforts to do so through international regimes and institutions set up by governments. The latter in effect often represent incipient elements of hegemony or, put differently, a partial and voluntary transfer of national authority to resolve political issues through international mechanisms of cooperation-operation.

Some of this capacity for collective action would have to exist at regional levels. Regional security communities represent examples of successful international governance. There may be in reality very different forms of security communities, and different paths leading towards their establishment. The history of existing security communities seems to suggest, however, that the formation of such communities may be a non-linear process involving qualitative jumps, rather than step-by-step evolution. In any case, their establishment will always imply qualitative changes in patterns of state behavior which take it beyond the realm of power politics to make the security dilemma obsolete.

PART II: REGIONAL FACTORS AFFECTING INTERNATIONAL GOVERNANCE: A COMPARATIVE PERSPECTIVE

Successful international governance may depend essentially on the ability of regions to serve as building blocks of international order. Regions will thus have to be able to provide for a system of regional peace, stability and prosperity, while remaining open for cooperation-operation within wider, trans-regional and global frameworks. Their ability to do so will depend importantly a) on the characteristics of the region itself, and b) on key players. How amenable are regional settings in Europe and East Asia (which are defined here to include Western, Central and Eastern Europe - including Russia, the Ukraine and Belarus - for "Europe", and North and South East Asia for "East Asia") to effective cooperation-operation? Are there structural reasons which make the evolution of a security community (or security communities) in East Asia less likely than in Europe?

The Regional Settings: Commonalities

It is often argued that the two regions are fundamentally different - so different in fact that comparison is of little practical political value. I beg to differ. While there are obvious and important differences to be considered in drawing policy implications from cross-regional analysis, there are sufficient commonalities to warrant a comparative analysis, including analysis of policy implications.

1) Heterogeneity

The first commonality between our two regions is often seen as a major difference: heterogeneity. East Asia certainly is an extremely heterogeneous mix of cultures and conditions, which historically and culturally never formed a coherent region.(14) But so is Europe. After all, it is precisely Europe's heterogeneity which historians see as the prime cause for "the rise of the West",(15) and while culturally the heritage of the Roman Empire and Christianity has given "Europe" a certain cohesion, religious and political splits have produced conflict of enormous ferocity and persistence. Yet, as European history has shown, heterogeneity is not a factor shaping international relations in itself - it depends what you make of it. It can be used to justify dissociation (i.e. keeping one's distance from each other), but can also serve as the basis of economic exploitation or mutually beneficial division of labor; it can be a source of indifference, but also one of friction and war or of cooperation-operation and mutual learning. East Asia may be much more heterogeneous than Europe, but the differences seem to be shrinking. Whether they add up to a different quality seems dubious. Moreover, even if they do, it may not matter much.

2) Sub-regions

Both regions also share another characteristic: they are sub-divided to an extent which may make it difficult to conceive of them in any practical way as "regions". East Asia is divided into North East and South East Asia, the latter again sub-divided into Indochina and the maritime region. Europe is divided (by wealth and political stability) into East and West, but also (by religion and culture) into Scandinavia, "Western" Europe, the (Mediterranean) South, and the Balkans. Again, these divisions will not determine the degree of cooperation-operation or conflict within the region - though like the common feature of heterogeneity it will obviously make for patterns of cooperation-operation which are complex.

3) Great powers

Both regions also are marked by significant asymmetries in the distribution of national power; more specifically, both have one overwhelmingly large and (potentially) overwhelmingly powerful country within the region, which because of its size and importance cannot be integrated fully in the region alone, but stalks the global scene as a Great Power: in Europe, this is Russia, in East Asia, it is China.(16) To check their power, and to integrate them successfully into a system of international governance represents a challenge of global dimensions.(17) Neither of the two regions thus has much chance to remain self-contained, except under the thumb of the Great Power.

The existence of a Great Power which cannot be fully integrated in the region provides a common focus for others in the region: they will attempt to help balance this Great Power, to seek its tutelage through submission, or to integrate it within the framework of a regional system of governance combining voluntary association, checks and balances and hegemony. To achieve this, other countries in the region may seek external support - as both regions have done by relying on the United States to balance the Great Power but also to engage it in rudimentary forms of international governance (such as arms control, non-proliferation regimes, and informal regimes of crisis management), to reduce the risks of confrontation and development.

4) East Asia: A region - or an area?

No one would doubt that Europe is a region, not just an area, even i f its precise demarcation may be unclear. The notion of "Europe" has existed since the 15th century, and even then reflected a sense of community, of shared values and experiences. Today, a "European society" and a "European identity" clearly exists, though hardly as realities submerging or even eliminating national societies and identities, but as additional layers of social interaction and identity.

This is less obvious in the case of East Asia. Yet there are three good arguments for assuming that East Asia, too, is rapidly becoming a region. The first, of course, is the rise of intra-regional trade, technology and capital flows.(18) In 1990, about 42 percent of Asian merchandise exports went to other Asian countries; by 1994, this share had gone up to 48.5 percent. Intra-Asian trade during this period grew by 15 percent per annum on average; while export growth to North America averaged 8 percent, and exports to Western Europe only 5 percent per annum.(19) Intra-regional capital flows (mostly foreign direct investment by Japanese, but increasingly also by South Korean corporations and overseas Chinese enterprises) also exploded during the last decade: of the total amount of $ 146 bn which went to East Asia from 1986 to 1994, capital arriving from the NIEs and ASEAN together accounted for 51 percent, and Japan for a further 18 percent.(20)

The second reason for taking East Asia seriously as a region is the existence of several intra-regional social institutions and networks which bind countries of the region. Those include the Japanese *keiretsu* and *sogo shosha*, Chinese enterprises and family networks, and perhaps also Korean *chaebol*. They provide core organizational underpinnings for transnational activities and thus form important backbones of economic regionalization. (A related phenomenon, the emergence of what Robert Scalapino has called natural economic territories (NETs), is much more narrow in geographic scope but may contribute to economic regionalization by forming smaller building blocks for larger-scale economic integration.)

The third reason for assuming the East Asia indeed is becoming a region (i.e. is developing a meaningful regional society) is a sense of identity and common destiny which people in the region seem to share.(21) This sense of community is underpinned by economics, but also by rapidly expanding social and cultural exchanges and small but growing migratory movements of people. It is still a very young phenomenon, but its impulses arguably can already be felt in the political realm through the proliferation of official and "track two" multilateral dialogue activities about economic, social, political and security issues. Participation in those activities generally includes non-East Asians from Asia Pacific but this does not necessarily invalidate the existence of an East Asian sense of community. Although it rests, as Mahbubani argues, on a fusion of Western and East Asian experiences, it clearly is East Asian in character: APEC's Osaka summit in 1995 firmly set the patterns of decision-making and institutional development in an Asian mode, and the international political and security dialogue processes orchestrated by ASEAN (the ASEAN PMCs, the ARF and, most recently, ASEM) all bear a similar imprint. How deep and solid this sense of community is, and how much weight it will carry in terms of shaping regional developments, is another issue. Yet, with all its fragility, the very rapid evolution of a regional international society suggests real potential for future collective political action and community-building.

The Regional Setting: Differences

The two regions, however, do not only share some common features, they are obviously in many ways also very different. The following paragraphs highlight some of those differences and their implications for regional cooperation-operation.

1) Maritime vs. continental region

Europe basically is a continental region, while East Asia is predominantly a maritime theater. This difference may have implications for the characteristics and even the likelihood of warfare: a whole range of military action can be undertaken at limited costs and risk, and with hardly any collateral damage, if the objective is to gain control over maritime territory and/or maritime resources, or to strike at the sources of maritime power of an adversary.

2) Patterns of conflict

In both regions, the potential for war basically stems from four different sources: unfinished civil wars, which have acquired aspects of interstate conflict; conflicting claims to territory and natural resources; potential competition for hegemony; and unresolved security dilemmas. There are important differences, however, in terms of saliency and relative importance of those sources of conflict. In East Asia, the unresolved civil wars in Korea and China are the most serious and potentially the most violent international conflicts. In both cases, the parties in those civil wars have organized as states and have been at war with each other. Serious risks of international instability exist. Europe, too, has its unfinished civil wars, and those, too, have developed into interstate conflicts. Examples include the Northern Ireland problem and ex-Yugoslavia.

Yet those civil wars do not have the same potential for desta-bil-izing the whole region. One reason for this is the centrality of Korea and China to stability in the region; Europe's unfinished civil wars are at the periphery. Another reason is that in East Asia, those conflicts are directly linked to core interests of sover-eignty, national unity and regime security, which makes them particularly intractable.

Conflicting claims to (maritime) territories and the resources they contain come second in importance in East Asia. In Europe, territorial issues have largely been resolved. The most important differences, however, between East Asia and Europe concern the dynamic shifts in relative power and wealth which characterizes the East Asian region. They have no equivalent in Europe. In East Asia, there is at least the potential for competition for regional hegemony between China and Japan, as well as security dilemmas which - given prevailing definitions of interest and images of international relations - are much more pronounced than in Europe.

In total, apart from the potential for violence inherent in ethno-nationalist tendencies in Eastern Europe, which in the Bal-kans could easily ignite regional war, as well, the risks of violent conflict, let alone major war, in Europe seem to be low. A threat from a resurgent Russia remains a possibility in the longer term, but for years to come (and, in my view, for the foreseeable future) Russia militarily will simply not be powerful enough to exercise political hegemony over the rest of Europe. The potential for conflict seems much more serious in East Asia, posing more difficult challenges for conflict management.

4) Institutional density

There are also a number of important differences between the institutional settings in the two regions. They concern the number and the characteristics of institutions. European institutions are much more numerous, and the process of institution-building in Europe has basically been driven by security considerations. They are also rather "hard": there is extensive majority voting in the EU, and members can be taken to the Court. Even in the OSCE, there are ways through which a "consensus minus one or two" can be reached, and mechanisms which can be activated by a quorum of members. Institutions are also strongly geared towards rules, norms, principles and fixed procedures. If institution-building is a non-linear process, there is a good case for arguing that European institution-building has passed the threshold of "no return". European institutions, however, are often accused of being top-heavy, cumbersome and ineffective, and recently there seem to have been signs of institutional decay.(22)

In East Asia, by comparison, institutions are fewer, institution-building has been driven (with the partial but important exception of ASEAN) by economics, and they are "soft": consensus-orientation is very pronounced, and efforts to inject stronger elements of rules, norms, principles and structure have mostly floundered. If European institutions are top-heavy, their Asian counterparts may be "bottom-heavy", i.e. of very limited relevance in influencing foreign policy outcomes. If institution-building is about passing critical thresholds, those clearly have not yet been breached in East Asia.

5) Multilateralism vs. bilateralism

Closely related to differences in institutional density we also find differences in attitudes towards multilateralism. In Europe (with the partial exception of the UK and France), there is an almost reflexive inclination towards multilateralism.(23) In East Asia, multilateralism recently has been much touted, but its effectiveness remains open to question. Perhaps the most advanced example is APEC - but even APEC basically follows the principle of cooperation-ordinated unilateralist moves, rather than genuine multilateralism.(24) ASEAN, too, obviously is a multilateral exercise, as are the ASEAN-PMCs and the ARF. But here, too, the realities of cooperation-operation are mostly bilateral. Witness the telling recent example of the Australian-Indonesian defense agreement, which was announced in the margins of an ASEAN Summit Meeting.(25) By and large, East Asians so far seem to put faith more in bilateralism than in multilateralism.(26)

6) Implications

In sum, the differences between the two regions, while considerable, should not be exaggerated. For one thing, there are a number of common features, as well. Secondly, some differences may be more apparent than real if we allow for differences in time frames: East Asia may be in the process of approaching very rapidly (and on its own, different trajectory through history) a situation closely resembling that of Europe today; conversely, several observers have pointed to parallels between East Asia today and late 19th century

Europe. And lastly, the differences which do exist may or may not be critical for chances to build effective regional security regime. It does seem, however, that the challenges represented by the regional setting in East Asia today are greater than in Europe. Moreover, many of the potential sources of conflict stem from internal characteristics and developments of states in the region, and domestic factors, rather than structural characteristics of the region, will determine, I believe, the success or failure in efforts to build up effective regional governance in East Asia.

PART III: STATE/SOCIETY RELATIONS, FOREIGN POLICY CULTURES AND THEIR IMPLICATIONS FOR INTERNATIONAL GOVERNANCE

Much of recent analyses of security conditions in East Asia have classified countries according to their relative power and importance, with the assumption that systemic constraints would produce similar patterns of behavior for countries of similar power.(27) Yet this line of reasoning has never been entirely satisfactory in explaining international relations. In the past, for example, it failed to explain important differences in the "strategic cultures" of America and the Soviet Union during the Cold War(28) and also the very distinctive foreign policy cultures of Germany and Japan as "civilian powers".(29) Evidence as well as common sense suggest that particular national foreign policies will reflect both external constraints and opportunities and domestic influences ranging from historical experiences and cultural predispositions to characteristics of the political system. But if foreign policy conduct is seen as shaped by societal forces, rather than by systemic conditions, then it is plausible to assume that foreign policies will differ within and across regions not only with regard to specific policies, but also more fundamentally in their outlook of foreign policy: the way states look at the world and their own place in it, define their interests and objectives, and design their policy instruments and strategies. For this, I would like to use the term "foreign policy culture".(30) The analysis of foreign policy culture is an important but rather underdeveloped element in any assessment of prospects for international cooperation-operation, both at the regional and at the global level. National policy perspectives will largely determine the degree to which states will be willing and able to cooperation-operate, as well as the preferred forms of cooperation-operation.

Different foreign policy cultures do seem to exist both between and within East Asia and Europe. Examples of countries with particularly cooperation-operative foreign policy cultures include Japan and Germany (who were socialized into their "civilian power" foreign policy culture by America), as well as a number of smaller Western European countries and Canada and Australia. The ASEAN states have developed their own, distinctive approach, and have achieved considerable convergence in their respective foreign policy cultures. Through the ASEAN-PMC, the ARF and ASEM, ASEAN has also tried to project this foreign policy culture beyond its immediate realm. America has its own, very distinctive foreign policy culture, which combines a sense of mission with a liberal creed and the peculiarities of a democratic foreign policy. China may represent "a Great Power of a new type", as a German China watcher has argued(31) - or it may be about to revert to its traditional foreign policy culture shaped by China's hegemonic exercise of suzerainty and cultural dominance over much of East and South East Asia. More plausible, in my mind, however, is the assumption that today's China displays a foreign policy culture imbued with vintage 19th century European power politics.(32) This would be highly ironic if quite understandable, given the way European powers brutalized Chinese civilization from 1860 onward. China's foreign policy culture would in fact reflect its tragic encounter with European power politics.

What are the key features of those differences in foreign policy cultures? How can they be explained? And what are their implications for regional cooperation-operation? The following paragraphs try to sketch some answers to these questions.

1) Divergent forms of nationalism

An important distinction between foreign policy cultures relates to the stage of development of the respective nation-state. In this perspective, Europe is a region of (mostly) "old" or "defensive" nationalism. This seems to be true even for nationalism's youngest (and particularly vicious) variant, ethno-nationalism: ethno-nationalism, however aggressive in its consequences, basically is motivated by the desire to defend the identity and interests of an ethnic group under conditions of wrenching social change. Since ethnic groups as a rule simply do not have much of a chance to survive economically on their own, European ethno-nationalism is under strong pressure to find accommodation within existing states.

East Asia, by comparison, is a region characterized by a "young", assertive and potentially expansive nationalism: the tasks of nation-building (a profoundly "Western" notion) are far from complete, thus stimulating nationalism as an ideology mobilizing societies for social transformation. More specifically, nationalism in East Asia seems to represent a fusion of Western and Asian influences. The impact of the West on East Asia in the 19th century through its technological and military superiority unleashed efforts at "Westernization" or "modernization"(33) and produced anti-colonial movements (which in many ways reflected the European experience) where European colonialism had subjugated East Asian countries. Indigenous sources of nationalism in East Asia may be found in ethnocentric traditions in South East and East Asia. Asian ethnocentrism reflects cultural influences (such as the "mandala" principle of rule, religion, or Confucian concepts of the state).(34) Nationalism in Japan, however, seems to have changed as a result of Japan's experiences in the Pacific war into a rather European, "old" type of nationalism.(35) It is also interesting to note that processes of democratization in South Korea and Taiwan seem to have mellowed the strength of nationalist feelings. In Korea, prosperity and democratization seemed to produce a more sober attitude towards unification with the North, while in Taiwan, it has accentuated ethnic Taiwanese nationalism, a "defensive" form of nationalism.

2) Different attitudes to sovereignty

The prevailing forms of nationalism will inevitably shape attitudes towards national sovereignty and independence. In Europe, there is a general willingness to accept the sharing of sovereignty in formal or informal institutions. This reflects the defensive character of its nationalism. It is about defending vested interests, including that of the state, but normally willing and able to compromise for the sake of advancing those same interests through international cooperation-operation. In Eastern Europe, Western institutions (in particular, the European Union and NATO) powerfully attract most countries - they perceive association and eventual entry at the earliest possible date as the surest way to achieve security and prosperity. But even for those Eastern European countries for which this option seems remote (e.g., Ukraine), compromising national sovereignty in international institutions (in this case, the Commonwealth of Independent States or its more recent cousins) for economic and security reasons seems a more promising way to moderate Russian hegemony than insistence on full independence and autonomy. The only major exception in Europe, then, with regard to attitudes to sovereignty is Russia.

In East Asia, by comparison, sovereignty is fiercely guarded and treasured, and international cooperation-operation is conditioned on sustaining, even enhancing national sovereignty and autonomy. Again Japan seems to form an important exception to this rule, however. One of the key principles of post-war Japanese foreign policy has been reliance on US security guarantees in lieu of an autonomous national defense posture. By implication, this has produced a very symbiotic, highly complex and integrated relationship between America and Japan which is characterized by strong interdependencies and heavy "interference" in each other's domestic affairs.

3) Definitions of national interests, objectives and strategies, and images of international relations

A further category to differentiate foreign policy cultures focuses on images of international relations and the definition of national interests, foreign policy objectives, and strategies. Since actual decisions reflect those images and definitions, they are critical for overall foreign policy orientations. States will behave in accordance with how their leaders see the world and define their interests, yet their behavior may well turn into self-fulfilling prophesies: they may get the world which they imagine.(36)

In Western Europe, images of international relations and definitions of national interests are modified by the extrapolation of democratic norms and principles into the foreign policy arena and (for most countries) by a general willingness to share sovereignty. Domestic power sharing has enhanced a willingness to accept this notion in international contexts, as well (though this willingness obviously will vary with the specific international context), and the fact that European democracies (at least so far) have proved to be "strong states" has also broken the link between national security and regime security. Also, the perception of international relations within Europe has moved away from a traditional, "realist" view of international politics towards views associated with "complex interdependence":(37) thus, national interests no longer are strongly prioritized but fused; the traditional distinction between "high" and "low" politics no longer makes much sense in a context where practically all major political issue areas have acquired international dimensions and are addressed through European mechanisms. As Eastern Europe closes in on Western institutions (or tries to achieve a modus vivendi with Russia), similar views can be expected to prevail.

In East Asia, by comparison, national interests are shaped by concern about sovereignty and a desire to sustain domestic political stability and national unity. "Resilience" is a keyword in this context; it has assumed a central role in ASEAN foreign policy culture. While the distinction between "high" and "low" politics has become rather irrelevant within Europe, it is still strong in East Asia. Economic development, however, shares top priority with national security (or may be assigned even greater importance). While images of international relations reflect traditional "realist" assumptions about the centrality of power and balance-of-power politics, they also accord a high priority to economics, and thus also integrate strong awareness of economic interdependence. In thinking about security, the national security dimension remains central, in spite of efforts to promote international security thinking through cooperation-operative security measures and multilateral security dialogues. It also often remains closely linked to regime security.

4) Foreign policy style and the relevance of culture

A further difference in foreign policy cultures concerns patterns of diplomacy, the style of foreign policy conduct. This line of enquiry is epitomized most fully by Michael Haas' study on the "Asian Way" of international relations,(38) which argues that there indeed are fundamental differences between Asian and non-Asian foreign policy conduct. The Asian way to peace, according to Haas, operates at two levels - that of general beliefs and orientations, and that of practices and procedures - and incorporates six major principles: 1) Asian solutions to Asian problems, 2) equality of cultures, 3) consensus decision-making, 4) informal incrementalism, 5) primacy of politics over administration, and 6) pan-Asian spirit. This list bears considerable resemblance to summaries of the "ASEAN way", the "APEC way" or even the "Pacific way" of decision-making. ASEAN's formula of success is generally seen to consist of its insistence on informality and on non-interference in each other´s internal affairs, in consensus-building, voluntary and even unilateral but cooperation-ordinated decisions, in patient dialogue among political leaders, and tacit postponement of conflictual issues. The ASEAN approach relies on creating atmosphere, rather than binding rules and institutions; it prefers mediation to arbitration. APEC has evolved a similar pattern, which had emerged fully by the time of the Osaka Summit of 1995: its essence consists of voluntary and unilateral yet cooperation-ordinated trade liberalization measures.

This line of reasoning raises three questions. First, is there really a difference between European and Asian foreign policy cultures? Second, if there is, how meaningful is it? And third, if there are distinctive and meaningful features about Asian ways of conflict management, how successful are they? As to the first question, we have noted already that there are significant differences in foreign policy cultures between East Asia and Europe, but also within East Asia. The latter, in fact, are more pronounced than differences within Europe. The commonalities of style, which Haas identifies, may thus be more apparent than real - "tatemae", rather than "honne", in Japanese terms. Certainly, the gulf between the foreign policy cultures of China and Japan, for example, presently seems huge by any standard.

It is also clear that foreign policy cultures in East Asia today represent a fusion of Western and Asian elements, rather than exclusively Asian policies. This does not preclude, however, the evolution of novel yet effective forms of conflict management.(39) The ASEAN way is generally credited with considerable success in pacifying intra-ASEAN relations, and ASEAN has taken the lead in projecting this approach onto the wider Asia Pacific and even global scene through the multilateral dialogue processes of ASEAN-PMC, ARF and ASEM. Progress in those efforts has been slow, however, and there is considerable skepticism as to how effective existing multilateral security structures are.(40)

5) Political systems

Yet another line of reasoning classifies foreign policy cultures in accordance with their respective political systems. The most important example for this school of thought is, of course, the notion of "democratic peace" - democracies do not go to war with each other (though it is unclear to what extent this also holds for countries undergoing processes of democratic transition, and for countries with very young nation-states).

Countries in Europe are either democracies or polities in transition away from communism (the exception is Turkey, which, as a democratizing authoritarian system, in that respect resembles East Asia). In East Asia, countries are either authoritarian but undergoing more or less pronounced processes of democratization (a process which has largely been completed in South Korea and Taiwan), or Communist systems in transformation (I would include here China, Vietnam, Laos and North Korea). The major exception again is Japan, a fully developed democracy which was "socialized" as such by the American occupation. Conditions for "democratic peace" therefore do not yet exist, though the ASEAN notion of regional resilience built on national resilience, as well as the consensus about regional stability as an essential precondition for economic development (what might be called "capital peace") bear some resemblance to this.

6) Conclusions and implications

If we review the results of this very cursory survey of respective foreign policy cultures in Europe and East Asia, several conclusions emerge. First, there do seem to be important differences between foreign policy cultures in East Asia and Europe. In Europe, foreign policy cultures basically reflect mature, defensive nationalism which can be reconciled to a considerable degree (but not fully) with the advantages and exigencies of shared sovereignty. In East Asia, on the other hand, nationalism is still a young and an expansionist force, and plays an important role in enhancing political stability at home. Sovereignty is valued much more highly and guarded much more jealously, and national interests are defined accordingly. Calculations of balance of power and security dilemmas thus inevitably loom larger than in Europe.

Secondly, the outlook of Japan's foreign policy differs markedly from that of the other East Asian countries. Japan's nationalism seems more akin to that of Western Europe, and her attitudes towards sovereignty (though less perhaps its definitions of national interest) clearly distinguishes her from her neighbors. Japan also has a mature democratic political system with a rather different history from that of its neighbors, which finds its expression in Japan's very guarded attitude towards military power (the "Art. IX consensus"). Although it may be true that the foreign policy establishment looks at international relations from a thoroughly "realist" perspective,(41) this does not tell the whole story about Japan's foreign policy culture, which makes Japan the "odd man out" in East Asia.

Third, foreign policy cultures may create two kinds of complications for efforts to build effective international governance. First and obviously, a particular foreign policy culture will pose problems for effective international governance if it is reticent or even averse towards cooperation-operation. But second, and less obviously, problems may also arise out of incompatibilities between foreign policy cultures. Such incompatibilities exist both within and between the two regions. They may, of course, be reconciled through processes of convergence, or rendered harmless through recourse to outside support for arrangements of regional stability.

Both has been the case in the two regions: on the one hand, there have been processes of convergence - through institutions in the case of Europe, and through more informal approaches in East Asia. In Western Europe, foreign policy convergence has been driven by the processes of European integration and the Atlantic security community. It includes Germany, Italy and Spain, as well as most of the smaller member states of the European Union. France and the UK represent countries whose foreign policy culture represent an amalgam of their past as great powers with more recent constraints on their capabilities and the exigencies of European integration. Scandinavia represents a cooperation-operative foreign policy culture variant with its own, distinctive features, while those in Eastern Europe are still too unsettled to define. Russia's approach also has not yet crystallized; at present, it combines strong inclinations towards a traditional great power approach with adjustments reflecting new realities of Russian weakness and dependence on good relations with the West. In East Asia, ASEAN represent a clear example of converging foreign policy cultures. The ASEAN-PMC and the ARF are attempts to project this achievement onto the region as a whole, involving the North East Asian states (with the exception of Taiwan and North Korea) and the US, Canada, Australia and New Zealand. One way to perceive those processes of multilateral political and security dialogue is to see them as efforts to reconcile divergent foreign policy cultures within a common framework.

Processes of convergence in foreign policy culture need not always be benign. Examples for more worrying trends include convergence around "realist" assumptions and resulting efforts to enhance military security through building up national defense establishments in East Asia, and trends towards a re-nationalization of foreign policies in Europe. Although rising defense expenditures and military procurement in East Asia do not (yet) add up to a regional arms race, they accentuate security dilemmas and the risks of misunderstanding, misperception and miscalculation inherent in military balance-of-power politics.(42) And in Europe, re-nationalization threatens to corrode the effectiveness of institutions.

Yet, in spite of significant processes of convergence in foreign policy cultures, fundamental incompatibilities continue to exist within Europe (between France and the UK on the one hand and Germany and most of the other EU members on the other) and East Asia (most obviously, between China and Japan). In the past, they have largely been smothered by the presence of the United States, its close alliance with Japan and Germany, and by the Cold War overlay which subjugated much of international relations to power and influence from outside the two regions. But even after the end of the Cold War, those incompatibilities seem to require continued active US participation in sustaining regional stability.

The fourth at last conclusion concerns East Asia only. Foreign policy cultures there seem marked by considerable ambiguity and ambivalence - between maximizing national power and operating within the logic of economic interdependence, between state control over society and accommodation of societal influence, between building formal institutions and relying on informal networks, between multilateral dialogue and unilateral or bilateral security policies. This ambiguity can be explained rather cynically - governments may prefer to combine the rhetoric of harmony with hard-nosed but tacit pursuit of self-interest: "talk softly and carry a big stick", to quote Theodore Roosevelt. An alternative (and in my view, more convincing) explanation sees this ambiguity and ambivalence as expressions of complex and partly contradictory realities, hence as "cognitive dissonance". Both the logic of economic interdependence and that of power politics in that view are by now firmly implanted within the foreign policy cultures of East Asia, and dynamic economic and social change is rapidly enhancing the weight of the former. This cognitive dissonance encourages foreign policy learning and thus improves chances for creative new approaches to old problems, but it also carries risks of simplistic rejection of complex realities.

PART IV: IMPLICATIONS FOR ENHANCED COOPERATION-OPERATION IN INTERNATIONAL INSTITUTIONS

Let me briefly summarize the argument so far. Prospects for enhanced cooperation-operation and successful international governance will depend on interaction between state and society within, as well as between, countries. Regions will have a critical role to play in this. If they manage to keep their own house in order and keep channels open to cooperation with other regions and in global contexts, they could become important building blocks of successful international governance. Balance-of-power approaches alone, however, will not be sufficient to ensure successful international governance since they fail to address important societal dimensions of political reality and carry a number of inherent risks.

Our comparative assessment of chances for enhanced international cooperation-operation in the two regions East Asia and Europe has focused a) on commonalities and differences between the two regions with relevance to their capacity for collective action, and b) on patterns of interaction between state and society, in particular, on respective foreign policy cultures. I have tried to show that the potential for effective collective action exists in both regions. In East Asia, it is still rather rudimentary and pushed forward by transnational, societal forces, while it may be declining in Europe precisely as a result of societal constraints on governments and institutions. The challenges and obstacles to be overcome seem to be considerably more important in East Asia, however. The reasons are a greater potential for political instability, the nature of conflicts in East Asia, but most importantly, foreign policy cultures which are relatively more divergent and intrinsically more averse to the evolution of effective capacities for collective action.

Deficiencies of regional cooperation-operation
Western Europe has been successful in the transformation of inter-state relations and foreign policy cultures away from traditional balance of power politics, and it is beginning to draw Eastern Europe into this achievement, as well. Overall, challenges to regional governance may be less pronounced than in East Asia, although European stability may be threatened from the peripheries in the East and in the South. Europe's capacity for effective collective action in coping with future challenges still seems insufficient, however, and there are also worrying signs of institutional erosion and decay. The key problem is deficiencies in effectiveness. While Europe has highly developed and institutionalized forms of voluntary association built on shared values both at the transnational/ societal and at the intergovernmental level, and while it also has transformed the balance of power into effective checks and balances against hegemonic abuse of power, it suffers from a deficit in leadership which so far America has had to provide.

In East Asia, the approach to regional governance is bifurcated and highly ambivalent. While regional society is still weak, this may now be changing very rapidly under the impact of dynamic and highly flexible transnational networks of interdependence. A common identity also seems to be developing, and there already exists considerable capacity of international society to solve problems in the economic realm. Voluntary association also finds new expression in the proliferation of official and "track two" dialogue activities and "soft" institutions with peculiarly "Asian" approaches in both the economic (PECC, APEC) and the security realm (ASEAN PMC, ARF, CSCAP). Stability seems to be ensured, however, predominantly through the operation of rough balances of power and power politics both at the subregional level (Korean peninsula) and the regional level (China vs. America and the US-Japan security partnership); only in South East Asia are there signs of a transmutation of balance of power politics. East Asia thus has to move forward on two fronts simultaneously: towards a transformation of interstate relations and the development of capacities for effectivecollective regional action. Such capacities for collective action (which need not be military action, nor comprehensive in participation) will be needed to underpin the balance of power elements of a successful system of regional governance, which until now have been provided by the US presence and the US-Japan Security Treaty. Both will be needed in the future, as well, but need to be enhanced through supportive arrangements. Examples might be cooperation-operation between America, Japan and China in ensuring stability on the Korean peninsula(43) or ASEAN's common position *vis-à-vis* China on the Mischief Reef incident, which did seem to have some impact on Chinese attitudes.(44)

Capacity for collective action will also be needed, however, for the establishment of authoritative rules and arrangements in and for East Asia. While these exist, in principle, at the international level (primarily in the form of the WTO and the Bretton Woods institutions in the economic realm, and that of the United Nations for issues of international order), East Asia (and Asia Pacific) so far has relied mostly on America's presence and leadership, and residually on the "Asian way" of consensus-building and unilateral yet coordinated action. It is hard to see this approach survive, however, once the easy gains from cooperation have been realized. It also puts the onus of effective rule-making at the global level and thus potentially contributes to overload problems at this level. Asia Pacific's "open regionalism" and its novel way of organizing regional governance thus reflect a number of deficiences, as well as specific advantages and opportunities.

Towards enhanced cooperation in international institutions

At present, capacity for effective collective action thus seems limited in both regions, though it is further advanced in Europe. Yet even in Europe, it is ultimately the United States which ensures, through her presence and leadership, regional stability and peace, and the same is even more evident in East Asia. Does it matter? It may not. America may be willing and able to sustain its role of "benign hegemony" for the foreseeable future, as the rhetoric suggests. Yet it would be prudent for both Europe and East Asia not to start from this assumption for at least three good reasons. The first is the continuing decline in America's relative weight and power in international relations. This will inevitably weaken America's capacity to sustain its post-war role.(45) Secondly, even if it had the capacity to do so, there are growing uncertainties about America's willingness to continue in its role as benign hegemon. American society is changing, and tensions are mounting. This is beginning to show in its foreign policy culture. Thus, America's partners can no longer be sure whether America will want to continue as hegemon at all (for example, it declined to do so for years in former Yugoslavia), or whether it will not shift to policies which maximize American interests without any regard for systemic consequences (witness the Clinton Administration's emphasis on American economic interests as a key foreign policy concern).(46) Thirdly, even if America were willing and able to sustain its role as benign hegemony, Europe and East Asia would do well to enhance their respective capacities for collective action simply because this would, if done responsibly, in fact increase the probability of America doing her share: by being able to secure regional stability, if need be, without America. Europe and East Asia would actually help to keep America constructively engaged.

How could regional cooperation-operation be enhanced in East Asia and Europe? Europe has achieved a transformation of balance of power and the evolution of a dense and highly institutionalized international society. Objectively, the only remaining balancing problem outside an institutionalized context concerns Russia. Given Russia's still huge destructive arsenals, US guarantees will continue to be important and a residual presence will be desirable. But the challenge of Russia basically lies in its weakness and internal upheavals, not in its power. Balancing Russian power will thus probably be neither particularly relevant nor particularly difficult. To sustain effective international governance in Europe, Russia will have to be integrated in the system, and this can only be achieved through transnational and intergovernmental efforts at association.

Europe's main problem is to develop capacities for effective collective action. In the economic realm, this has already been achieved to a significant degree, but beyond that, Europe has

shown woeful deficiencies in organizing herself to achieve the
desired results. The impulse to overcome those deficiencies probably will have to come from European societies: the Maastricht
Treaty unfortunately demonstrated that courageous political leadership by governments has become prohibitively difficult. Yet, as
this episode has indicated, European societies presently appear to
constrain, rather than facilitate the development of effective
political capacities for collective action.

In East Asia, by comparison, mutilateral political processes ex-
tract dynamism from societal forces, above all from business. Yet as
the transformation of balance of power politics still has to be
achieved, those gains may be superficial. To achieve such a transformation will require a two-track effort of sustaining yet
transcending balance of power. This, in turn, will be possible only
with substantial changes in the foreign policy cultures of key
players. America will have to change its foreign policy culture
from "hegemonic multilateralism" to an acceptance of joint decision-making and mutual adjustment. China, as well as a number of
other East Asian countries, will have to accept constraints on their
national sovereignty. And Japan will have to increase its contributions to effective regional governance while retaining its "civilian
power" foreign policy culture. A good chance to sustain and enhance
processes of learning foreign policy in this sense may well lie in the
realm of international society - specifically, in a proliferation of
economic interdependence and transnational business activities, but
also in dialogue processes, exchanges and joint projects such as this.

*   Prof. Dr. Hanns W. Maull has a chair in International Relations
    and Foreign Policy at the University of Trier, Germany.

Notes

This paper has originally been prepared for the Conference on
"Europe in Asia Pacific", Bali, Indonesia, May 28 - 31, 1996.

1.   Among the "Cassandras" are: Richard K. Betts, "Wealth,
     Power, and Instability", in: *International Security*, Vol. 18 No.
     3, Winter 1993-94, pp. 34-65; Aaron L. Friedberg, "Ripe for Ri-
     valry", in: *International Security*, Vol. 18 No. 3, Winter 1993-
     94, pp. 5-33; Barry Buzan/Gerald Segal, "Rethinking East
     Asian Securities", in: *Survival*, Vol. 36 No. 2, Summer 1994,
     pp. 3-21 ("Should the US fail to help build a regional dialogue

on security and should East Asians fail to take up the challenge of multilateralism, the region may become the most important zone of conflict in the twenty-first century" (p.20)); Paul Dibb, "Towards a New Balance of Power in Asia", London: *IISS* 1995 (Adelphi Paper No. 295); Douglas T. Stuart/William T. Tow, "A US Strategy for the Asia-Pacific," London: IISS 1995 (Adelphi Paper No. 299), and Kay Möller, "How Much Insecurity in East Asia?", in: *The Pacific Review*, Vol. 9 No. 1/1996, pp. 114-124 (a review article of Dibb´s monograph which argues that Dibb's moderate optimism based on his policy recommendations for regional security cooperation represent in fact a leap of faith).

2. Michael Haas, *The Asian Way to Peace, A Story of Regional Cooperation*, New York: Praeger 1989.

3. Kishore Mahbubani, "The Pacific Way", in: *Foreign Affairs*, Vol. 74 No. 1,. Jan.-Feb. 1995, pp. 100-111.

4. Cf. the publications quoted in footnote 1.

5. Cf. Möller, op. cit., passim.

6. Cf. Hanns W. Maull, in: Jonathan Story (ed.), *The New Europe*, Oxford: OUP 1993, pp. 140-160.

7. It is obvious that the term "region" here implies entities of different size and quality, depending on the respective context (intra-/international). Both, however, serve as intermediate levels in the complex processes linking individuals with world politics.

8. For fascinating studies exploring the interaction between international society - in this case, represented by financial firms and international capital markets - and governments cf. Ethan P. Kapstein, *Governing the Global Economy*, Cambridge, Mass: Harvard UP 1994 and Eric Helleiner, *States and the Reemergence of Global Finance: from Bretton Woods to the 1990s*, Ithaca, NY and London: Cornell UP 1994.

9. Cf. Barry Buzan, *People, States, and Fear, The National Security Problem in International Relations*, Brighton: Harvester Press 1983, pp. 65ff

10. Kenneth Waltz, *Man, The State, and War*, New York: Columbia UP 1959.

11. Cf. Robert Z. Lawrence, "Emerging regional Arrangements: Building Blocks or Stumbling Blocks?" In: Richard O`Brien (ed.), *Finance and the International Economy*, Oxford: OUP 1991, pp. 24-36; Detlev Lorenz, "Regionalisation versus Re-

gionalism, Problems of Change in the World Economy", in: *Intereconomics*, Vol. 26 No. 1, Jan./Feb. 1991, pp. 3-10.

12. The argument in this section rests, of course, to a considerable degree on the analogy with economic regionalism. For the debate on economic regionalism cf. Lorenz, op. cit.

13. Mahbubani, op. cit.

14. Cf. Gerald Segal, *Rethinking the Pacific*, London: OUP 1990.

15. Cf. William H. McNeill *The Rise of the West*, Chicago: Chicago University Press 1963.

16. It is interesting that this pattern can actually also be applied to the past. In the late 19th century, the dominant European power which was too big to be handled by the region alone was Germany; in East Asia, whose integration into world politics took place only in the second half of the 19th century, Russia and then Japan arguably played this role before World War II, while the Soviet Union held this position during the Cold War.

17. Cf., for China, Yoichi Funabashi/Michel Oksenberg/Heinrich Weiss, "An Emerging China in a World of Interdependence", New York: The Trilateral Commission 1994 (A Report to the Trilateral Commission No. 45); James Shinn (ed.), *Weaving the Net, Conditional Engagement with China*, New York: Council on Foreign Relations Press 1996.

18. For a detailed discussion, cf. Sueo Sekiguchi/Makito Noda (eds.), *Economic Interactions and Interdependence in East Asia*, Tokyo: Ushiba Memorial Foundation 1994, particularly Ch. I.

19. World Trade Organization, *International Trade, Trends and Statistics*, Geneva: WTO 1995, p. 73.

20. Cf. *The Economist*, March 2nd, 1996, p. 52.

21. Cf. Yoichi Funabashi, "The Asianization of Asia", in: *Foreign Affairs*, Vol. 72 No. 5, Nov./Dec. 1993, pp. 75-85; Mahbubani, op. cit.; idem, The Pacific Impulse, in: *Survival*, Vol. 37 No. 1, Spring 1995, pp. 105-120.

22. Philip Zelikow, "The Masque of Institutions", in: *Survival*, Vol. 38 No. 1, Spring 1996, pp. 6-18.

23. This, incidentally, does not imply that bilateralism is neglected but only that certain forms of bilateralism - those developed as explicit alternatives, rather than as necessary preconditions, for multilateralism - generally are shunned. To illustrate: the Franco-German bilateral relationship has long been the engine of multilateral European integration.

24. Richard Higgott, "APEC: A Skeptical View", in: Andrew Mack/John Ravenhill (eds.), *Pacific Cooperation: Building Economic and Security Regimes in the Asia-Pacific Region*, Canberra: Allen and Unwin 1994, pp. 66-97.
25. Cf. *International Herald Tribune*, Dec. 15, 1995.
26. For an evaluation of multilateralism in Asia Pacific cf. Paul Evans, "Building Security: The Council for Security Cooperation in the Asia Pacific (CSCAP)", in: *The Pacific Review*, Vol. 7 No. 2/1994, pp. 125-140; Andrew Mack/Pauline Kerr, "The Evolving Security Dialogue in the Asia-Pacific", in: *Washington Quarterly*, Vol. 18 No. 1, Winter 1995, pp. 123-140; Dibb, op. cit., pp. 44ff.
27. Cf. footnote 1 for examples.
28. Cf. Alastair Ian Johnston, "Thinking about Strategic Culture", in: *International Security* Vol. 19 No. 4 (Spring 1995, pp. 32-64 (36f). Johnston offers a very good introduction to the concept of "strategic culture", which closely resembles the term "foreign policy culture" used here. For a discussion of strategic culture in East Asia, cf. Desmond Ball, "Strategic Culture in the Asia-Pacific Region", in: *Security Studies*, Vol. 3 No. 1, Autumn 1993, pp. 44-74.
29. Hanns W. Maull, "Germany and Japan - The New Civilian Powers", in: *Foreign Affairs*, Vol. No., Winter 1990/91, pp. 91-106.
30. Cf. fn 28.
31. Christoph Müller-Hofstede, "Reichtum und Macht. Wirtschaftliche Dynamik und politische Risiken in Ost- und Südostasien," in: Wichard Woyke/Paul Kevenhörster (eds.), *Internationale Politik nach dem Ost-West-Konflikt, Globale und regionale Herausforderungen*, Münster: Agenda Verlag 1995.
32. Cf. David Shambaugh, "Growing Strong: China's Challenge to Asian Security", in: *Survival*, Vol. 36 No. 2, Summer 1994, pp. 43-59.
33. The subtle difference between the two notions was fully recognized early on. Thus, in late 19th century Japan, there were two different schools about the best way to reform Japan - one trying to turn Japan into a Western country, the other relying on adaptation of Western techniques and methods while retaining the essence of Japan.
34. Cf. Jürgen Rüland, "Ethnozentrismus, Nationalismus und regionale Kooperation in Asien", in: Brunhild Staiger (ed.),

Nationalismus und regionale Kooperation in Asien, Hamburg: Institut für Asienkunde 1995, pp. 1-20.

35. An interesting illustration of differences between "old" and "young" nationalism in East Asia were the very different attitudes in South Korea and Japan in the recent Takeshima/ Tokdo Islands dispute. Cf. *Financial Times*, Feb. 12, 1996.

36. Alexander E. Wendt, "The Agent-Structure Problem in International Relations Theory", in: *International Organization*, Vol. 43 No. 1, Summer 1987, pp. 335-370.

37. Robert O. Keohane/Joseph S. Nye, jr., *Power and Interdependence*, Princeton: Princeton UP 1987 (2nd, rev. edition).

38. Michael Haas, *The Asian Way to Peace, A Story of Regional Co-operation*, New York: Praeger 1985. Cf. also Francois Godement (ed.), "Conflict Resolution in Asia: Exception or Example?" Theme paper presented at the European Union-Asia Cultural Forum, Venice, Jan. 1996.

39. This is the thrust of the argument of Mahbubani, *The Pacific Way*, op. cit.

40. Cf. "The Slow Progress Of Multilateralism in Asia", in: *Strategic Survey*, 1995/96, London: IISS 1996, pp. 189-196; Amitav Acharya, "A New Regional Order in South East Asia: ASEAN in the Post-Cold War World," London: IISS 1993 (Adelphi Paper No. 279), esp. pp. 57ff; Andrew Mack/Pauline Kerr, "The Evolving Security Discourse in Asia-Pacific", in: *Washington Quarterly*, Vol. 18 No. 1, Winter 1995, pp. 123-140.

41. Peter Katzenstein/Nobuo Okawara, *Japan's National Security*, Ithaca, NY: Cornell UP 1993.

42. Andrew Mack/Desmond Ball, "The Military Build-up in Asia-Pacific", in: *The Pacific Review*, Vol. 5 No. 3, 1992, pp. 197-207.

43. The recent initiative by the United States and South Korea about a multilateral security dialogue involving North Korea, China and Japan, as well as South Korea and the US, from this perspective seems a useful initiative.

44. Cf. *Strategic Survey* 1995/97, op. cit., p. 190.

45. Cf. Stuart/Tow, op. cit., pp. 6ff.

46. This view is sometimes contested in America but widely shared in East Asia. See, e.g., Ralph Cossa, "The Japan - U.S. Alliance and Security Regimes in East Asia", A Workshop Report, The Institute for International Policy Studies/The Center for Naval Analysis 1995, p. 10.

Chapter 2

K.W. Radtke: "East Asia on the Threshold to the Twenty-First Century"

The *Tiananmen* Incident and the collapse of the Soviet Union symbolize the beginning of an historical turning point whose long-term significance we are still unable to guess. In order to maintain global leadership, the United States has had to restructure its relationships with countries in Asia-Pacific. China's rise as an economic great power is still accompanied by question marks concerning internal stability, and uncertainties concerning the implications for comprehensive security in East Asia. Japan wishes to reaffirm its security insurance by strengthening its security treaty with the United States, yet is aware of the fact that within less than two decades Sino-Japanese trade may well be the dominating trade relation in global trade, by far surpassing the role of US trade. Taiwan wishes to increase its ability to manage its affairs independently, yet is struggling to reduce its economic dependence on mainland China. Both Taiwan and Japan wish to prevent serious tensions between the United States and China, but at the same time agree to cooperate in long-term missile defense projects directed not only against North Korea, but against perceived threats from China as well. South Korea and China exchange defense missions. Southeast Asia is perhaps less united internally than cooperation in ASEAN may suggest, but appears united in its policy of engagement with China without appeasement.

The implications of the rise of Indian influence in the region are as yet unknown. APEC set out as an institution for economic integration, but its role as a facilitator for political and defense dialogue becomes increasingly important. Together these developments are changing the parameters of the international system in Asia.

Current developments in Asia underline once more that the interrelation of economics, politics, and security undermine formerly seemingly clear-cut separate spheres, including the moral one (Asano, p. 29). The interaction of economics and politics, history and culture, and security requirements creates dynamic patterns different for each of the participants in the international system. The individual "personality" of states - which itself is not a permanent, fixed trait - may differ considerably. The personal background of leading politicians may also influence not only the style, but also the substance of policies, as may be the case in the replacement of Warren Christopher by Madeleine Albright, who has a strong European (Czech) background. The international system is a complex aggregate of qualitatively different entities; it is a system whose understanding requires a combination of analytical tools, a meta-discipline in which methods of economic, political, cultural and other approaches are valid only in so far as they enable us to produce useful statements and observations. The combination of these diverse tools itself relies more on intuition and experience than on pseudo-scientific correctness, and the resulting analysis ought to provide a sense of direction to decision-makers, without any pretense of prophetic futurology. This essay should therefore not be read as an effort in political science, rather as an attempt by an historian to come to grips with current changes and their historical implications.

Towards a global community of market democracies?

Western ideologies, such as communism and market democracy, aim to impose a fairly homogenous economic and political order on the globe, and both share a commitment towards internationalism and universal values. The present writer definitely does not deny the fundamental differences between both ideologies, but there are certain structural similarities which make them appear to be mutual mirror images. Perhaps slightly exaggerated, the former communist call for the international unity of workers has now been replaced by the call for the internationalization of markets and the establishment of a global business system, a development which one might expect to strengthen middle-class society, and the foundations of parliamentary democracy. In an ironic twist of history, economic restructuring is also leading to structural changes in the system of parliamentary democracies, including substantial changes in the political and moral values of the state. In his remarks to the Pacific Basin Economic Council on November 25, 1996, Mickey Kantor outlined his philosophical view about the relation of the state and enterprise:

> "In a modern interdependent globalized world, there is no way that governments can keep up with the private sector. You move money and technology and capital and people all around the earth, nearly at the blink of the eye, as well you should. ...We have seen our job over the past four years as attempting to understand how the world has changed...also to make sure we have become the blocking backs for the running backs of the American business community. We need to clear the tracks for the engine of growth. We're not in the engine and we're not even in the caboose...we need to make sure you can do your jobs. Sixty-two percent of the US exports go to APEC countries and economies, six percent more trade to our Asian partners and APEC than goes to the European Union. ...Now, we're in a post-Cold War, post-industrial, heavily communication-techno-logy-oriented country where most of the products we make today have some aspect of the protection of intellectual property. ...You have become - all of you - and your colleagues around the world, whether you're in small and medium-sized businesses, many of whom are represented here today, or in large businesses - the new ambassadors for America's foreign policy... Our new markets, being four percent of the world population, are the 96 percent who live out side our borders ...trade has become a larger part of our economy. In 1995, trade represented 31 percent of our economy...it's growing to 31 or 32 or 33 percent of our entire economy. Trade is growing faster than our GDP..." (*USIA*, 25 November 1996).

In his remarks, Mickey Kantor redefines in a very pragmatic way the "personality" of the post-1991 American nation-state. On a different occasion, he cited America's aging population, and zero population growth as a reason for the need to increase productivity and build (overseas) markets. The consequence is that "each worker produces more because of technology and capital investment and new markets."

The former US ambassador to Tokyo, Michael Armacost, also referred to the changing role of the state: "The liberalization of financial markets accelerated international capital flows and undermined the ability of governments to control the value of their own currencies".

If it is indeed true that governments are losing power to inter-national business, this raises fundamental questions concerning the continued exercise of democratic rights through the institutions of parliamentary democracy. During the past few years, there has been an important trend in major industrial democracies to reduce political control over Central Banks, and thus remove an essential element of economic policy-making from democratic decision-making. Japan, too, has plans in this direction, but there are even reports that the Central Bank has in fact dictated Japanese finan-cial policy through a committee working in secret since 1990 (*Asahi shimbun*, 4 December 1996). The spread of a system of internation-ally accepted legal rules in trade and other areas is by itself no guarantee for fair play. It may reinforce existing power relations by enshrining them in legal garment, but it may also at times be used to become a means of protecting the weak, thus showing the tradi-tional Janus face of any legal system.

Just as Japan's march towards modernization fundamentally changed the essence of the premodern Japanese polity it set out to defend, trends towards globalization may equally, and on a perma-nent basis, alter the basic parameters of democratic institutions, an essential pillar of market democracies. By the same token, these developments will alter the structure of civilizational values worldwide, despite the essentially romantic desire of some to maintain traditional images of cultures and civilizations. One may even discover that the paradigms for a typology of civilization will differ from region to region, within and outside of Asia. For East Asia, for instance, I would find Professor Huang Xinchuan's (Peking University) concept of a "cultural realm where Chinese script is used" (*hanzi wenhuaquan*) more interesting than superfi-cial assumptions of an Asian Confucianist realm (Qi Zheng, in *Shijie jingji yu zhe ngzhi*, December 1995), global references to "Asian values" (Okabe, p. 41), or Samuel Huntington's paradigm of civilizational clash.

We are now living at a historical junction where traditional civilizations, but also the essence of the European concept of a nation-state and market democracy (short for: parliamentary democracies with a market economy) are undergoing basic trans-formation, making an historian rather reticent to construct universalistic concepts for a future international system, to be used as a blueprint or guideline for politicians of great powers in the world after 1991. The dynamics of short, middle and long-term changes overlap, making it difficult to develop a simple picture of the new roles which actors in Southeast and East Asia will fulfill in the twenty-first century.

In the words of Nakanishi Terumasa (Kyoto University), East Asia is in a transition phase where it is still impossible to concep-tualize these new developments (*Nihon Keizai Shimbun*, 4 April 1996).

Metropolis USA

As Mickey Kantor pointed out, domestic needs determine a good deal of the dynamics of national activities beyond the borders of a state. Domestic social and economic patterns of development are a powerful element pushing towards the expansion of economic regions, forces that can become an important factor for political integration as well. Under the guidance of an imperial center, such developments work towards the creation of patterns of dependency on the metropolis. The metropolis itself is drawn into increasing global involvement requiring leadership in a wide area, weaving a pattern of multilateral relations under direct or indirect leader-ship. Such leadership rests partly on a symbiosis of economic and political actors, a symbiosis whose functioning is strongly influ-enced by cultural and historical patterns of behavior. They will inform political leaders in their struggle towards the develop-ments of new in international institutions geared to promote economic growth and security. These institutions must be flexible and dynamic at a time when rapid economic changes influence security equations, and military innovations - in particular after the Gulf War 1991 have forced governments all over the globe to rethink their military concepts. Since 1991, the United States, like many other countries, has engaged in serious efforts to come to grips with the new global situation, resulting in the production of numer-ous new strategies (onthe development of US security thinking, Shikata, and Guo, p. 22 and passim; see also Joseph S. Nye, "The Case for Deep Engagement" , in *Foreign Affairs*, July-August 1995, vol. 74, no. 4). The rethinking of global strategy has gone through various phases, but common to them is a thorough reappraisal of the role of China and Japan not only in Asia, but within the global system.

Dynamic stability

As Kantor's position indicates, the US is not so much bent on preserving the status quo, but on changing the parameters of global economics and politics. In this sense, historical paradigms may be insufficient to understand the future configuration of the international system in Asia-Pacific. The trend is towards a new modus of global great power management, and current politics are searching the appropriate framework. A serious derailment from this pattern could lead to dangerous confrontations; it is equally true to say, however, that existing conflicts also have the potential to derail the prospect for great power management. Governments may be in an assistant role in the field of economics, they are in the front seat where security is concerned. Security strategies include the construction of international (temporary) coalitions and more permanent alliances. Political and global economic actors such as transnational companies are engaged in activities that involve, as a matter of course, an essentially multilateral playing field. The *physical dynamics* of military actions - actual fighting as well as deterrence posturing - cause a pattern of linkages that tends to be bilateral, just like the structure of company networks is deeply influenced by the technology of their products. Even in the case of more complex alliances such as NATO, these tend to be dominated by only a few main actors, or even just one major leader. In addition to alliances, there are also "partnership relations" (*huoban*), a term preferred by China when she describes cooperation with countries that are fairly close, without entering into formal alliances. China has now used this terminology fairly consistently, and China's refusal to regard the US as a potential close partner should be seen in this context. The limits of US-China relations were indicated in interviews with Chinese specialists on international relations, such as Zhang Yebai of the US Research Institute of the Chinese Academy of Social Sciences, who does not see any prospect for an alliance or "strategic partnership" with the US, since the social systems and values of both societies are fundamentally different, also pointing to large differences in historical and cultural background (*Xinhua*, 22 November 1996). The Taiwan missile crisis of March 1996 led to significant changes in Chinese and US political strategies. As argued by Professor Jia Qingguo (Peking University), the US has changed her China policies from confrontation early in the presidency to one of "pragmatic policies" of cooperation most recently, including the issue of Taiwan. During the recent talks between Qian Qichen and Christopher it was apparently agreed that the US does not support Taiwan's independence, Taiwan's entry into the UN or any international organization consisting of sovereign states. (*Xinhuashe*, 20 November 1996). In fact, it would be more accurate to state that the US has moved to defer the choice between a strategy of engagement, constrainment (Segal) or even containment. Joseph Nye has expressed some of the reasoning lying behind the apparent decision to put off strategic choices for the time being. He wishes to avoid a situation where the US would have to choose between allies and foes in Asia, as in nineteenth-century Europe, when England was in opposition to the European mainland. Rather than opting for a policy necessitating a choice between friends (Japan) and foes (China, or vice versa?), the US should work towards new patterns for cooperation which obviate the need for such a choice. (This might give the US good opportunities to play off Japan and China against each other.) In a recent symposium organized by the Asahi Shimbun in November Joseph Nye argued that Taiwan should not declare independence, China should give Taiwan "more international space", favoring increased economic ties (*Zhongguo shibao* November 27, and *Asahi Shimbun*, November 26, 1996). In this context, Lee Tenghui's call for a reduction of Taiwanese economic dependence on mainland China, and the announcement of the establishment for diplomatic relations between South Africa and Beijing, point however in the opposite direction. Developments around Hong Kong, too, will be seen as a touchstone of Chinese intentions, and influence US perceptions and decision-making in the second half of 1997.

China and the US highly appreciate the "success" of the recent meetings and the apparent improvement in Sino-US relations, but one cannot at times avoid the feeling that both have a fundamentally different estimate of what they have gained during the meetings. Both countries tend to interpret current changes in the global system in different ways. China agrees to increasing multilateral economic links, including China's entry to the WTO. As far as security is concerned, China seems to favor the concept of a "multipolar" world as apparent from Li Peng's speech at the Asia Conference in Bangkok at the beginning of March. The establishment of an Asian Pacific security order encompassing China, as proposed by the Australian Foreign Minister in November, seems

highly unrealistic. (*Zhongguo shibao* November 7 1996). In addition to the traditional dislike for multilateral security systems
China fears that any such system be dominated by the US. This is
one of the reasons why China is now favoring a "separation of
politics and economics". The globalization of the economy has also
promoted the establishment of multilateral organs dealing with
security issues, but this process has not yet left the infant stage.
The most important public forum is the ASEAN Regional Forum
(ARF), operating since 1993. Many are convinced that the ARF is
not suited to solve security issues in Northeast Asia, especially as
far as the Korean peninsula is concerned. Winston Lord suggested in
an interview with Worldnet on 28 March that there exist, in fact,
less formal arrangements for security dialogues concerning Northeast Asia. He stressed that no country in Asia will achieve
hegemony on its own, and he foresaw the rise of multiple power
centers. At the same time he emphasized the significance of security relations with South Korea and the alliances with Australia,
Thailand and the Philippines (*USIA*, 29 May 1996). One may
expect that the ARF will change its character with the recent
expansion of its membership. According to the *Asahi Shimbun* of 5
April the opposition of the US, Japan and Australia prevented the
participation of India in the spring meeting of the ARF, although
ASEAN had originally favored India's participation in January.

Nevertheless, one should not underestimate the positive contribution of the ARF and ASEAN. ASEAN issued a joint statement
calling for the peaceful solution of disputes in March 1995, followed by a similar move by the United States concerning the
dispute over the Spratlys. It was during an ARF meeting in August
1995 that the Chinese Minister for foreign affairs, Qian Qichen
declared that China would look for a peaceful solution to the
problem on the basis of the principles of UNCLOS. (*USIA*, 30 May
1996).

Towards a new system of great power balance in Asia-Pacific?
The United States has made clear her intention to maintain global
leadership into the twenty-first century. The collapse of the
Soviet empire, and the new perception of China as a global economic power requires a fundamental review of America's security
and economy, including strategy towards Asia, all the more so since
China does not fit the traditional image of an emerging military
power setting out to challenge traditional powers. For several
decades, the US had pursued a global strategy which aimed to

incorporate Japan and Germany, the main aggressor nations of the Second World War skirting the Eurasian land mass, in a global alliance against the Communist World led by the continental superpowers Russia and China. Part of the strategy was to integrate some of the smaller anti-Communist entities such as South Korea and Taiwan (ROC) as members of the international community with full sovereign rights under international law. The collapse of the Soviet Union speeded up attempts to introduce Japan and Germany as permanent members of the Security Council, thus putting a formal stop to the post-war period. If successful, such a move would contribute considerably to the consolidation of a new global order under US leadership, an order which in many ways would be structured along "Western" lines. Japan and Germany have been trying for some years to obtain a permanent seat on the UN Security Council.

For Japan more is at stake than just increasing opportunities for exerting political influence. Becoming a permanent member of the Security Council would be interpreted as a final conclusion to the post war period, during which the UN regarded Japan as an "aggressor nation". It now seems likely that the accession of Japan and Germany to the Security Council can only take place within the framework of a more broadly implemented restructuring of the United Nations.

Despite the growing intensity of relations between China, the United States, Japan and Europe, strategic thinking is still influenced by perceptions shaped during the past one and a half centuries. In analogy to the prewar rise of Japan and Germany, China is often seen as a newly rising power, and the US trying to preserve the status quo. Some conflicts and dispute in Asia are still perceived as a heritage of the colonial age. In Asia the process of decolonization, the dismantling of European empires, is still continuing. The collapse of the Soviet Union is not only significant because of the end of communism in the Western part of Eurasia, but has also undermined the foundations of the traditional Russian Empire, quite likely on a permanent basis. The transition of power in Hong Kong further illustrates the final phase of this process in China. For China the issue of relations between Taiwan and Beijing, and the future of the Korean peninsula, is also part of a colonial past.

According to the American minister of the Navy, Dalton, the growth of US economic relations with Asia demands an appropriate growth of security efforts by strengthening multilateral security arrangements. These would be directed towards "flexible defense", based on alliances, consultations to increase mutual confidence, constructive engagement towards China, and a framework for dialogue with North Korea. This will not be "engagement at any price", according to Dalton (*USIA*, 13 May 1996). This is not the place to detail the military balance of power in Asia, but it seems useful to recall briefly basic ingredients of US security commitments in Asia.

America's continued presence in Asia may be described as follows: 1) Permanent presence of 100,000 American troops, mainly in Japan and Korea. 2) Bilateral links with allies such as Japan, Thailand and the Philippines, as well as bilateral consultations on security with China, Indonesia and others. 3) Actions to prevent the spread of weapons of mass destruction 4) Cooperation in the area of theater missile defense, where the United States possess undisputed technological leadership. There are doubts, however, which countries in Asia are prepared to accept political and financial long-term commitments required by the acquisition of such systems. 5) The further deepening of the formal security alliance with Japan.

The third point is not merely an attempt to make the globe "safer"; it is closely linked to the attempt by the US to prevent any erosion of its own deterrent capability. The negotiations on the Comprehensive Test Ban Treaty (CTBT) were concluded successfully, but questions remain about the ability of North Korea (and perhaps China) to undercut US attempts to maintain a permanent global control over weapons of mass destruction under US leadership. Such questions will undoubtedly have figured prominently during the recent visit of the Head of the American CIA to Beijing. There are few signs of an "appeasement" towards China and North Korea on this issue.

However, the idea that global security can be achieved through joint management of the new great power arrangement is a dangerous fallacy in a world, where the percentage of the global popula-tion enjoying a decent living standard is perhaps twenty percent, and further decreasing. It is doubtful whether further marketization can cope with such trends. Belief in "free trade" as preached by some governments resembles the shibboleths of former ideologies - there simply is no scientific "proof" that free trade will solve essential systemic problems such as much needed global stabilization of currencies and markets for raw materials. Nakanishi (pp. 9-10) lists some specific issues which are unlikely to be solved by any one economy, such as imbalances in the American financial system, consequences of the relocation of industries, aging populations, and expected rises in the price level of raw materials.

Abandoning the status quo, while striving towards dynamic stability

Except for North Korea, American security concerns in Asia focus on China. The US is prepared to put pressure on China, should engagement fail. In this context, shifting perceptions of a "China threat" require a particular significance in this transitional period. Shortly after the collapse of the Soviet Union hopes for a speedy construction of a stable democracy in Russia, and a concomitant peaceful transformation of China were running high, and it seemed only a matter of time before Asia would be peacefully included in a new post-communist world order under US leadership. Some observers argue that "China" constitutes the last serious "problem", an obstacle in the way of constructing such a well-ordered global system of market democracies. Despite often voiced apprehensions about a "China threat", more recently there has been a conscious effort in the US, Canada, Australia and elsewhere to tone down earlier perceptions of a China threat. The outside observer finds it difficult to arrive at sound judgments when some current information supplied by the interested parties from time to time turns out to have contained more than just a bit of misinformation. This applies both to security, when a specialist on Chinese military affairs such as Paul Godwin, US National Defense University now plays down the "China threat", but also to economics, where statistics have lost a good deal of reliability, and gained a reputation to be a convenient political weapon in trade disputes (see *The Economist*, 23 November 1996). This becomes an important issue when we remember that the revision of the US security strategy in Asia was directly linked to reports on a North Korean threat.

Due to the fact that China poses no great risk to US global interests for the medium term, the US has been trying to formulate a China policy which aims for China's peaceful integration into the "international community", but preserves the option of future containment policy. It is in this context that the US has been restructuring the pattern of bilateral relationships with her allies, in particular Japan. One of the immediate consequences of the current situation is that governments of countries allied with the US will find it harder to use the "China threat" to pressure the

US, as they used the "Soviet threat" to increase their leverage versus the US. Although issues of foreign policies have not played a major role in the run up to the American presidential elections it has not always been easy for the Clinton administration to formulate a balanced policy without exposing itself to accusations of appeasement. Yet Clinton's policies do not deviate from a basic assumption of continued American global leadership in security matters, but also on economic issues, as demonstrated by the tough line pursued inside the Asian Development Bank. (*International Herald Tribune*, 27 June 1996.) China has made great efforts to reduce tensions with all her neighbors, including India, assigning countries that are at least "friendly neutral" the status of "partner" (*huoban*). This includes Russia, with whom she agreed to establish a partnership relation (*huoban*) in 1994. The image of a "China threat" is very complex, and involves military factors, but also apprehensions about the future weight of China's economy and its global effects.

Many countries in Asia avoid assigning to China the role of "aggressive nation", at least in public, since there is a well-founded apprehension that such an approach would hamper, rather than foster, the solution of disputes. It is also not easy to convince even America's allies of the feasibility of the American-produced, extremely expensive missile defense system. Mainly intended to avert North Korean terrorist blackmail, the operationalization of such a system will unavoidable cause Chinese countermeasures. Some countries regard the weight of China's economy as a threat, while a Taiwanese newspaper pointed out that China's economic growth was beneficial to China's neighbors (*Zili zaobao*, 27 November 1995; also *Wenhuibao*, 2 December 1995, Hong Kong).

So far, there are no serious attempts at global market management to prevent an uncontrolled scramble for resources and raw materials, water and energy in the struggle for development among developing and industrialized countries on a scale far surpassing the struggle for markets and resources preceding the outbreak of World War II.

It is quite striking that in the face of such predictions China has been emphasizing that she will be able to feed her population and produce sufficient raw materials (energy), stressing that she will pose no threat to international markets or China's neighbors. This may be an argument to calm international concerns at a time, when it is still well remembered that Japan embarked on military adventures in order to secure resources. Chinese leaders may, however, also be trying to assuage domestic concerns, especially within the armed forces, who fear that Chinese projection of force into areas such as the South China Sea is unavoidable in order to secure the survival of China's growth economy. In the early phase of the Clinton administration "economy" seemed to have won the day. Between 1991 and 1993 it appeared, as if military deterrence and security politics would take a back seat, with "economics in command." During Clinton's visit to Japan in 1993 the future of the US-Japan security relationship appeared to have figured only in a minor role. This "oversight" was soon rectified when a crisis loomed over North Korea's nuclear policies, but most still perceived this crisis as one of the few anachronistic remnants of a past age, the period of the "Cold War" (cold for Europe, hot for Asia). Relations between North Korea and the world, which had been in a state of crisis especially since 1994, had temporarily been stabilized by the establishment of the KEDO agreements, when the visit of the Taiwanese leader Lee Tenghui to the United States caused another period of tension between Beijing, Taipei and Washington. This reminded Japan and other countries that "security" had not disappeared from the international agenda, casting a shadow over the initial euphoria about a post-communist world in which peaceful economic competition would replace the threat of military confrontation.

The possible acquisition of weapons of mass destruction by "rogue states", and its consequences for regional security do not fit the traditional image of a "balance of power" among the "great powers", substantially eroding the capability of the great powers to enforce order from above. Many politicians and specialists, in particular in China, Taiwan and Japan have doubts about the appropriateness of the term "balance of power" in the context of East Asia. The asymmetries between China, Japan, Korea, Taiwan and countries in Southeast Asia, and the way in which an external power (the United States) participates in regional power, have created a pattern that is completely different from nineteenth-century Europe. Relationships between the US, Japan and China have developed very rapidly during the past few years. This is not merely the result of the conspicuous increase of the economic, military and political influence of China but part of global shifts towards increasing economic interdependence, which itself is clearly driven by the most powerful economic actors of the great powers. Scarcity of resources, old and new sources of conflict will continue to give rise to serious disputes and tensions, requiring a careful conflict management by the great powers involved. In the absence of any effective multilateral regime the only promising approach lies in acknowledging that conflict management can only be exercised by resurrecting cooperation among the "great powers". New forms of deterrence, economic interdependence, unacceptable risks involved in any escalation of military clashes on even a minor scale force the participating great powers to devise a new pragmatic joint approach towards security, which I have dubbed "Directorate of Asian Pacific Powers". Differing from nineteenth-century balance-of-power politics in which shifting alliances could be used, only Japan and the United States are able to maintain an alliance of primary global importance.

Despite its significance, the US-South Korean alliance is a function of US global interests, rather than a primary alliance by itself. All countries agree that their own security cannot be maintained by military means alone, but can only be perceived in terms of comprehensive security, in order to control what is essentially an opaque situation on the Korean peninsula. More than anywhere else, Korea shows that a stable security regime can only be established by cooperation beyond formal alliances.

It has become clear by now that defense cooperation in Asia is no longer a coalition of anti-Communist governments bound by the common goal to prevent a "communist" threat under US leadership. By want of a better term I chose the term "directorate" to cover the "informal" cooperation between the US, China, Japan, later possibly once more joined by Russia, for the maintenance of stability in Asia. The members of this "directorate" are not equidistant from each other - *vide* the close cooperation between the US and Japan. Several factors are however likely to increase the room for independent maneuver for Japanese foreign policy, such as a rapid increase in the importance of the Sino-Japanese economic relationship. Should Russia, in one way or another, re-enter East Asian politics by improving its relations simultaneously with both Japan and with China, this would further increase the room for maneuver of Japanese foreign policy. The greatest impetus for cooperation comes from the commonly perceived need to control potential conflicts (such as Korea), or disputes over maritime boundaries and other territorial issues (Senkaku). The eruption of even minor military clashes could, if left untreated, easily escalate and cause major damage.

China: a threat in the long run?

Even during that past age of ideological confrontation Asia had not always perceived conflicts in the context of a principled struggle between "good" and "evil", between capitalism and communism. The danger remains that the rise of a powerful China would be conceptualized as a fundamental threat in the tradition of the post-W.W.II global division. There are attempts to prevent such a renewed split of Asia. The Clinton administration itself declared that it wished to avoid a new period of long-term confrontation between China and the United States. Winston Lord expressed his vision of the American government during a hearing of the Senate Finance Committee, where he pleaded for the continuation of China's most favored nation status:

"We are dealing with a complex, difficult and prickly partner whose power is growing, whose leadership is in transition, and whose government is turning increasingly to a nationalism that is conditioned by thousands of years of experience as the dominant "Middle Kingdom" and more than a century of humiliation by foreigners. It is a myth that America should respond to our differences with China by seeking to control or contain it. Such a policy would be misguided and, in the end, unsuccessful. It would constitute a self-fulfilling prophesy of turning China into an enemy. It would require a major shift in our economic, military and diplomatic resources" (*USIA*, 6 June 1996).

At this moment there is as yet no clear consensus between the US and her allies on long-term security policies. The main reason is uncertainty about the assessment of China's future policies. The "opening of China" (which should never be associated with the "Open Door Policy" at the turn of the century) to international trade and investment, application for membership in the WTO and the strengthening of economic links with the rest of the world are not necessarily an expression of "opening up" in terms of Western style "liberalization". Perhaps more than anything else they underline China's strategy to play a global role through the weight of her economy. Integration into the world economy by no means implies Chinese acceptance of American visions for global economic and political structures for the next century. China has been trying to improve its access to international markets by gaining entry into the WTO since the middle of the eighties. One of the many considerations was the attempt to decrease US leverage on

China, since the US was able, through threats to withhold MFN
status, or by pressuring US allies, to limit Chinese access to international markets. It seems generally accepted that China will
become a member in 1997, since the reversion of WTO member Hong
Kong to China would otherwise create a rather abnormal situation.
Opting for a multilateral approach in economics, and a "great
power" approach in security matters, China demands that it be
admitted to the WTO on the basis of purely economic criteria.
Although the United States has maintained that China's entry
will be judged on the basis of "commercially viable" criteria it
seems fairly clear that security and political elements, such as
Taiwan's membership of the WTO, exercise an important role.
China's international links will significantly depend on the manner in which economic integration can be formalized, through
Chinese membership in the WTO, and through China's operation
in other bodies, such as the APEC. Much will depend on China's
assessment of the usefulness of such institutions for China.

Doubts have been raised whether China's accession to the
WTO will make it lose interest in active participation in APEC,
relegating membership in APEC to the status of a stepping stone
towards the strategically more important membership of the
WTO. Long Yongtu, a high Chinese official, saw APEC paying
more attention to developing countries than the WTO, and hoped
that the WTO would learn from APEC (*Xinhua*, 26 November
1996). APEC became an important forum for accelerating economic
integration in Pacific Asia after the collapse of the Soviet Union,
when the United States decided to change its traditional opposition against multilateral economic networks other than ASEAN in
the region. American support for APEC seeks to assure optimal
access to markets in Asia. ASEAN, a grouping that is less cohesive
than the EU, receives particular attention, not in the least because
of the fact that by 2005 it is expected to form a market valued at
one trillion dollars, with ten member states and 500 million inhabi-
tants and a massive foreign trade, of which the US is expected to
obtain a share of 250 billion dollars.

The great number of member states of APEC, which includes
countries as different as China and the United States, makes it
very difficult to achieve binding formal agreements. Nevertheless,
it provides a framework to test the feasibility of a multilateral
approach in a region that seems to prefer bilateral security arrangements.

There is an ongoing debate in China on the long-term consequences for China's new economic thrust. There is praise for the benefits of having access to American and other markets. Others fear (or even hope) that economic integration will of itself lead to a fundamental adjustment of China's own economic and political order. This is one of the reasons for Beijing to attach significant importance to the continuing role of Hong Kong as a transit point between the global economy and China - complete integration into China would entail the loss of Hong Kong's special position, and its function as a buffer. The intention to speed up the convertibility of the Chinese currency has not influenced the decision to maintain, and support an independent and stable Hong Kong currency. In the same vein, Hong Kong's role as a financial center is not to be taken over by Shanghai. Eventually, the manner of China's integration into the global economy will be of more importance than the internal reforms, such as the scaling down of public ownership of means of production ("state enterprises"), especially if integration is accompanied by "cultural penetration", an accelerated foreign influence into all spheres of Chinese society. Russia is confronted with similar questions, but differing from China Russia still has to solve the question of how to restructure the colonial empire in Eurasia into a viable modern state. China is very serious about maintaining its national integrity and sovereignty, which includes Taiwan, Tibet and some other areas; while China is concerned about maintaining control, Russia has to engage in the creation of a structurally different new political entity at a time, when politicians in Moscow seem to worry more about the health of Yeltsin.

The United States: the arbiter of Asia?

The international system in Asia cannot simply be understood in terms of autonomous patterns of increasing economic interaction independent of security policies. The security role of the United States in (East) Asia has frequently been likened to that of a stabilizing power, a balancer or arbiter. It has been argued that even China prefers a continuing US military presence to the build up of a purely Asian military balance in which Japan, South Korea and other powers would play an important role as independent military powers in their own right. As long as the United States has the political and military potential to construct an effective containment or "constrainment" of China it seems self-evident that China's "acceptance" of the US security role is ·specifically conditioned upon US ability to prevent the rise of Japan as a major, independently acting military power in Asia. On the other hand, US economic involvement in Asia constitutes a brake for attempts to resurrect policies to contain China. According to a Taiwanese analysis (*Zhongguo shibao*, 26 November 1996) US policies are also driven by the realization that the US does not only need new markets, but also needs the cooperation of China to be able to act as balancer. The closer defense cooperation with South Korea and Japan, which will also include the setting up of a Theater Missile Defense system covering Taiwan as well, requires careful consultation with Peking in order to avoid the impression of China's encirclement. Without China's cooperation, the solution of vital questions such as the protection of the environment is doomed to failure. As I will set out in more detail below, both Japan and Taiwan are in favor of non-conflictual relations between China and the US, despite the active participation by Japan and others in collective defense efforts which clearly aim to constrain China.

Stability can also be undermined through shifts in economic developments. The United States realizes that a trade war with China would damage their strategic interests since such a conflict would destabilize Hong Kong and Taiwan, both economically and politically. Should American policies threaten to destabilize East Asia, this could fundamentally alter the attitude of Asian governments towards the United States.

Newly-developing patterns of integration and cooperation have not obviated the strategic use of global deterrence by the United States, and this is one of the basic reasons why China (and some other countries) are unlikely to accept the US as an arbiter for Asia in the long term, requiring a new form of management for comprehensive security. The major significance of international politics in Asia since the collapse of the Soviet Union is the emergence of a new pattern, in which the major military powers able and willing to demonstrate force - the US and China - arrive at a new structure of bilateral relations to manage their strategic and security relationship in Asia-Pacific. The increase of multilateralism in (South)east Asian politics in recent years seemed to herald a greater role for playing by rules acceptable to all countries, but China still prefers to deal directly with those military powers that matter, especially the United States. This preference also emerges in the way that relations with Russia are conducted through bilateral top-level meetings and summitry, similar to the pattern of meetings with US officials. China is apprehensive, lest the establishment of a multilateral security system under US leadership leads to a struggle for hegemony in Asia-Pacific, possibly resulting in a major confrontation, if not conflict between China and the US. In fact, there are few signs that the United States would be prepared to change its traditional reliance on general deterrence and specific alliances to be replaced by a genuine multilateral security organization.

Chinese foreign policy

By its own definition, China is still a communist country. For a considerable period, the ruling communist party has declared economic growth to be China's top strategic priority. It has been argued that the Chinese communist belief crisis - lack of belief in Communism as an heuristic and legitimizing doctrine - has pushed the leadership to use nationalism instead. It would be wrong to assume that the Communist Party would aim to replace a dysfunctional communist ideology by a nationalism that could seriously hamper the effectiveness of the CCP's strategy, by involving China in counterproductive confrontations with her neighbors. This is also at the root of recent official dissociation from the publication "China, too can say no". There are widely different views within Chinese politics concerning China's future long-term strategy, and also divergent assessments of the future role of the US and Japan in Asia. Many in the armed forces still remember the decades of political confrontation with the West, the Korean and the Vietnamese wars, and view the United States as basically opposed to the rise of China as a global power. The armed forces regard the maintenance of China's unity and integrity as their particular responsibility (*Jiefangjun bao*, 24 May 1996), and it is highly likely that such traditional views inspired the decision to set off the Taiwan missile crisis in March 1996. The intensification of the US-Japanese security relationship since 1994 has been interpreted by Chinese analysts as part of a "soft encirclement" of China, where foreign economic engagement in China and strategic encirclement are part of a two-pronged strategy to ensure the "peaceful transformation" (*heping yan bian*) of China (*Zhongguo shibao*, 22 April 1996). The US decision to send aircraft carriers patrolling in the vicinity of the Taiwan Straits was the main reason for the decision to alter the course away from military pressure, and use China's growing economic clout in the pursuit of basic strategic aims instead, also inspired by a genuine fear that the Taiwan crisis would trigger China's isolation, pitting it also against the ASEAN countries. Under Jiang Zemin's leadership some organizational reforms were carried out which streamline the planning and execution of foreign policy. The "Coordinating Committee for foreign policy" has been designed after the example of the US "National Security Council"; its first chairman was Liu Huaqiou, very active in negotiations with the US during the Taiwan crisis. There have also been repeated changes in the command structure of the Chinese forces.

Shortly after the crisis, Li Peng spoke of China's strategy of "global engagement" (*Xinhuashe*, 6 May 1996). China's concept of international engagement is based on the idea that this enables China to reduce as much as possible America's dominating role, in addition to promote China's own interests. If China's economic growth continues, it will in due course even increase Japan's economic interdependence with China, and thus weaken Japan's alliance with the United States. It has been guessed that in ten years from now, the Chinese economy will have replaced Japan as the economic "engine" in the region (*Lianhe zaobao*, 5 December 1996). China keeps emphasizing the importance of her economic growth as when she reports that her share of the US market is becoming increasingly more important compared to that of the "four tigers" (*Xinhua*, 21 November 1996). China's keenness to join the WTO is now also part of China's strategy of "engagement", but the Chinese government is increasingly exposed to calls for protectionism from its own industrial lobby, and a call which is not confined to state-owned industry. China has committed herself not to introduce new laws or policies that are inconsistent with WTO obligations. It would be wrong to assume that a non-communist China would automatically be less protectionist.

As indicated by Chen Youwei, China now intends to increase its leverage over Taiwan in the first instance by increasing Taiwanese economic dependence on the mainland; secondly, by applying pressure to reduce Taiwan's "international space", and thirdly, by focusing its military power southward. Another Chinese concern is fear of international isolation. The maintenance of good relations with Japan is essential for China. Next in priority are the countries of Southeast Asia. China has also unfolded new diplomatic initiatives in Central Asia, the Middle East (securing stable energy supplies) and in Africa. With Chinese support, North Korea may soon agree to hold four-party talks with South Korea, the US, and China (*FEER*, 12 September 1996).

China is trying to counter any attempt to isolate her by starting a number of foreign policy initiatives designed to prevent isolation from countries in Southeast Asia, and pushing them towards closer cooperation with Japan and the United States. During the fifties China attempted unsuccessfully to prevent Japan from increasing its influence in Southeast Asia. China's involvement in guerrilla movements, and its support for North Vietnam during the Vietnam War, its own conflict with Vietnam over Cambodia, and Chinese territorial claims in the South China Sea have all contributed to make countries in Southeast Asia wary of Chinese policy. Especially during recent months China has consciously endeavored to tone down her differences with ASEAN countries, including Vietnam, on issues such as the South China Sea. Recently China proposed the setting up of an "ASEAN Foundation" which found a positive echo among ASEAN members. ASEAN speeded up China's acquisition of the status of "dialogue partner" of ASEAN. ASEAN also decided to have the PRC participate in the Conference of Ministers of Foreign Affairs (*Asahi Shimbun*, 11 June 1996). China continues to provide military assistance to some Southeast Asian countries, such as Thailand. One should not overlook informal links of members of ASEAN armed forces with their Chinese counterparts.

On the basis of the history of Japan's prewar aggression against China this author holds that "war is the continuation of economic warfare by other means". China's use of her growing economic strength has even been linked to predictions that the economic share of developing countries twenty-thirty years from now will, for the first time in two hundred years, surpass the share of the rich Western countries (He Fang, in *Guowai shehui kexue qingkuang*, January 1996). Rather than using military tactics of globalized guerrilla warfare to weaken industrialized countries along the lines of Lin Biao's "People's War", China might now use the economic strength of the "underdeveloped" world to strategic ends. Then, the "strength" of China's alliance with third world countries lay in the revolutionary potential of the poor underdog. Still an underdog when comparing the per capita GNP of developing countries, the joint economic strength of the Third World might deliver strategic gains unattainable by previous strategies of guerrilla warfare.

Japanese foreign policy

Japan's position versus the United States is often described in terms of a junior partner, whose main foreign policy task is to anticipate changes in US foreign policy. Japan has traditionally attempted as far as possible avoiding decisions involving taking sides. Despite the traditionally cautious attitude of Japan, Japanese public opinion (like public opinion in Germany) has become quite critical on some aspects of Chinese foreign and domestic policies.

It would be incorrect to underestimate the leverage Japan has exercised towards the US from time to time in the past, when Japan could use the proximity of the Soviet Union (and China), and electoral behavior in Japan, to obtain US concessions in exchange for an "obedient" and reliable partner Japan. Japan has not only been a passive partner in the formulation of US-Japan security. A well-known case in point is the influence of Japan in US policy on the transfer of Soviet SS-20 from Europe to Asia. In 1992, only a few years ago, many wondered why Japan was not more forthcoming in adapting her defense planning in the spirit of "peace dividends", but this was a decision in the face of a security situation which left Asia with issues more difficult than those obtaining in Europe shortly after the collapse of the Soviet Union. Yet Japan's position and influence *vis-à-vis* the United States decreased as a result of the collapse of the Soviet Union. Japan was even worried that "Japanese concerns would be neglected as East-West tensions dissipated" (Armacost, p. 132). Tensions in Asia do not merely affect Japan's military security, but tend to exert a negative influence on Japan's economic security. A high Japanese official was quoted referring to Hashimoto's conversation with Clinton at Manila, where Hashimoto was opposed to the isolation of China, since "China is an important partner in our region. I am pleased that the situation (US-China relation) is developing towards a correct direction" *(Lianhe zaobao*, 25 November 1996) Both Taiwan and Japan are in favor of non-conflictual relations between China and the US (*Zhongguo shibao*, 26 November 1996). Japanese foreign policy has reacted fairly swiftly to the new situation. Previously, Japan's foreign policy was an array of linear, bilateral relations between Japan and the US, China, or the UN. Nowadays, the interrelation of actors has forced a rethinking of policy making. (Nakanishi, p. 12) Japan's new *Yearbook of Foreign Affairs* (*gaikoo seisho*) emphasizes that Japan has to search for a multilayered foreign policy able to cope with an increasingly complex situation. Non-Japanese observers may be surprised by the ease with which the traditional narrow interpretation of the peace constitution, in particular the unwillingness to engage in "collective defense" seems to have been thrown overboard. It remains to be seen whether the recent election results, and the ensuing difficulties in forming a stable coalition government with a sizable majority, will affect the formulation of security policy in the coming months.

The major milestone in the evolution of Japan's security policy is the adjustment of Japan's security relationship with the United States, a process that started in 1994, and was sealed during Clinton's visit to Tokyo in April 1996. The strengthening of the US-Japan security relationship, symbolized by the revision of the treaty in April 1996, was also due to Japanese initiatives who "helped nudge the United States in 1995 to revise its strategy in Asia Pacific" (Segal, p. 125), in particular since November 1995 (Perry's visit to Tokyo).

America herself is not yet accustomed to such a more independent Japanese role. Sakuma, who has been head of the joint Chief of Staff since 1991, emphasized that the establishment of a "Council on defense issues" (*bôei mondai kondankai*) was perceived by some in the United States as a first step to put a distance between Japan and the United States. Sakuma emphasized that among all important countries in Asia it was only China which carried out its security policies completely independent from other countries. According to him Japan's approach to security issues is still too passive, since it hardly considers independent Japanese actions without immediate assistance by the American forces. Sakuma pointed out that in this new age of communication networks and rockets old style thinking fixed on "fronts", as during the Second World War, has become anachronistic. Discussions indulging in theoretical speculations about the "constitutionality" of collective defense often lead to absurd conclusions (*Asahi Shimbun*, 24 May 1996).

China's actions versus Taiwan have contributed to this significant change in Japan's foreign policy, preceded by perceived threats from North Korea since 1993. In the past, Japanese practical strategic thinking focused on issues such as the security of sea lanes, but recently Japan's strategic concerns have widened. Japan increased her security relationships with countries in Central Asia which became members of NATO's partnership for peace, as well as Mongolia which established a security dialogue with the US in 1996 (Ma Yinchu, p. 23).

The discussions concerning the revision of the "Guidelines" of 1978 started in May, and the details are still being worked out. Most important should be the extension of the area considered vital for Japan's security. An extended interpretation would comprise the Middle East, the Korean peninsula and Taiwan. A military conflict over the Nansha Islands would likewise be regarded as affecting Japan's security. The result of these deliberations will be presented to the Japanese-American Consultative Commission on Security before the end of 1996. It is particularly the expansion of the area covered by the US-Japan security agreement which has encountered strong Chinese opposition, as in Qian Qichen's comment having met the Japanese prime minister Hashimoto on April 22: "I said that if this treaty is to be extended to cover the region, then it would give rise to big problems." When US security relations were strengthened during Clinton's visit to Tokyo in April, Li Peng expressed his fear in a conversation with the Japanese opposition politician Ozawa Ichiro on May 6 that if America is set on governing the world on its own, instability would result. By exerting pressure on Japan China hopes to coax Japan into adopting a more independent position versus the US. The South Korean Defense Minister welcomed the new Japan-US security relationship as a contribution toward stability. President Ramos of the Philippines concurred, but expressed his hope that Japan would also foster security dialogue in Asia. Not quite unexpectedly, the Malaysian prime minister Mahathir gave air to his apprehension that this could contribute to an arms race in Asia, an opinion he repeated during his visit to Japan in May. Indonesia's Foreign Minister Alatas has pleaded for restraint (*Jiefangjun bao*, 20 May 1996). It is also realized that there is as yet only limited Asian support for a strong Japanese role in Asian security, as stressed by the former Japanese Ambassador in Washington, Kuriyama Makoto (*Asahi Shimbun*, 23 May 1996). The situation in Asia can however not be adequately described in terms of a strategic triangle without taking into consideration the strategic importance of the Taiwan issue in these equations. Japan does not intend to change her "One China policy" (a top official of Japan's Ministry of Foreign Affairs, quoted in *Asahi Shimbun*, 21 May 1996), or put pressure on China by threatening to upgrade relations with Taiwan, but it seems equally true that an outright Chinese military attack on Taiwan might easily result in fundamental policy adjustments of Japan's China policy (*Asahi Shimbun*, 19 and 21 May 1996). Japan's pro-Taiwan policy has been given renewed emphasis through the appointment of Sato Shinji as Minister for MITI. Sato is well known for his pro-Taiwan sympathies. The Taiwan crisis was followed soon by another controversy involving China and Japan, the dispute over the Senkaku islands. Japan and China have started discussing the island issue. In China there remains a suspicion that tensions between China and Japan, the Senkaku issue in particular, if not instigated by the US, could nevertheless be used by the US to meddle directly or indirectly in Asian affairs, creating hot spots around China, especially in the South China Sea, in order to build an anti-China alliance (Guo Guan, p. 25).

This is an issue that affects the United States as well. A United States Defense Department official reaffirmed that the US-Japan security treaty applies to the Senkaku, since it is a "territory under the administration of Japan", taking care to avoid calling the Senkaku a "territory of Japan." It was against this general background of increasing tensions with China that Chinese nuclear tests at the beginning of June caused strong Japanese diplomatic protests. There were public discussions on exerting pressure on China, for example, by cutting Japan's low-interest loans to China. The Japanese government argued that these loans were the most important, active instrument of Japan's China policy, not to be used easily as a means of pressure. On the face of it Japanese protests against Chinese nuclear tests seemed very much an emotional reaction. The government decided to reduce grants to the People's Republic, without effect on the much more important huge low-interest rent loans. During recent weeks, when US-relations with China seemed to be improving, at least temporarily, China and Japan also moved to indicate a warming in their relation, when Prime Minister Hashimoto invited Jiang Zemin to visit Japan next spring.

Outlook

Towards the middle of November the brief summit between President Jiang Zemin and President Clinton was preceded by, among others, the meeting of the US-China Joint Economic Committee and the meeting of Warren Christopher with his counterpart Qian Qichen, implementing a general understanding between the US and China in May to increase high-level contacts. The leaders of both countries are under severe pressure to combine the need to cooperate economically, with equally severe pressures from their respective domestic political constituents and opponents. The Chinese leadership must demonstrate that its policies prevent Taiwan from increasing its *de facto* independence and undermine the economic position versus strong foreign competitors on the Chinese market, while Clinton must not be seen as giving in too much on issues such as Taiwan, market access, proliferation, and Chinese policies which are construed by some as "Chinese expansionism".

Partly as a result of this situation, the new approach towards managing US-China relations displays a two-tier feature, in which manageable economic issues, including China's accession to the WTO, are conducted fairly independently from those strategic long-term issues such as the position of Taiwan, China's territorial claims (in the South China Sea), the strengthening of US alliances with partners in Asia (Japan, Thailand, the Philippines) and the Pacific (Australia), the establishment of a theater missile defense system under US leadership, or even the issue of human rights.

In the current climate of "globalization" a remark on the role of Europe seems in order. Europe has a role to play in particular in Southeast Asia but will for the time being be unable to rival US influence. Despite Europe's economic links with Asia, including formal links between the EU and Asian countries, the EU has endeavored only during the past two or three years to emphasize a genuine wish to become a significant player in the region. The ASEM meeting in Bangkok in March 1996 was one of the highlights in this development. Despite the limited political influence of Europe in Asia some countries, including China, have welcomed a European presence since it may lower the threat of an increasing polarization between China and the United States, or at least increase Chinese ability to play off the United States and Europe.

Despite the current "pragmatic" mood this mix of issues affords only an uneasy balance, in which issues such as "Taiwan" or the positive trade balance in China's trade with the US may disrupt attempts to manage relations securely, quite apart from the situation on the Korean peninsula which remains unpredictable. Although China continues to oppose Taiwan's *de facto* independence, the current Chinese leadership seems confident that it can use the economic weapon to increase Taiwan's dependence on Beijing. Disagreement on the effectiveness of this fundamental strategy could lead to moves to dislodge the current Chinese leadership from power, with possibly severe consequences on the international system in Asia-Pacific. The future cannot yet be managed with certainty.

*   Prof. Dr. Kurt W. Radtke is professor of Modern Japanese History at Leiden University, The Netherlands.

Notes and references

(Except for the *Xingdao ribao*, the titles of Chinese newspapers and *Xinhua* refer to the electronic editions. *USIA* refers to texts on the website of the United States Information Agency.)

Armacost, Michael H. *Friends or Rivals? The Insider's account of U.S.-Japan Relations*, Columbia UP, 1996.
Asano in: *Gaikoo jihoo*, November/December 1995.
Guo Guan in: *Shije jingji yanjiu*, 1995, no. 4.
He Fang in: Zhonggwo shehkeyuann ryhbeenshuoo yanjiouyuan (ed) *Guowai shehui kexue qingkuang* (Nanjing) 1996.1.1-4 p. 4 - 43.
Ma Yinchu in: *Guofang daxue xuebao* (Jing), November 1995, pp. 71-73.
Nakanishi Hiroshi in: *Gaikoo fooramu*, January 1996.
Okabe Tatsumi in: *Gaikoo fooramu*, January 1996.
Segal, Gerald in: *International Security* 20:4.
Soejima in: *Seiron*, August 1996.
Tanaka, Akihiko in: *Gaikoo fooramu*, 1996, No. 4.

Chapter 3

In 1933 the independent republic of East Turkestan was proclaimed in what is now better known as the Xinjiang region in the People's Republic of China (PRC). That event at the time was a spillover from the civil war in Russia and the expansion of Soviet power thereafter. Not a few divisions belonging to the white side after the 1917 revolution took refuge to Chinese Turkestan, another name for Xinjiang, with all the chances of political destabilization in the region as a consequence. Their promises, agitation and ideological fervor enabled the Soviets to undermine the position of China's central government. Murder plots and armed local rivalries did the rest to make the region an inhospitable place for the rest of the thirties. The *News from Tartary* collected in 1935 by the brother of James Bond's spiritual father and special *Times* correspondent, Peter Fleming, is testimony to that. The unruly surroundings brought expeditions like Sven Hedin's to explore the feasibility of a highway from Peking to the region's capital, Urumqi, to a premature standstill. The Berlin-Peking line via Urumqi by the German aerospace company with its geopolitical correct name "Eurasia" had to suspend activities. It was still very much in the tradition of the "Great Game" played between Russians and Britons from the latter part of the 19th century onward. (1)

It was not only in Iran and Afghanistan that those contests between big powers took place. Central Asia also belonged to the geopolitical sphere of interest: whoever was in charge of the heart of the continent could wield control in many respects. Especially after the Russian tsars had established their foothold there and became interested in Chinese regions, Britain reacted by sending scientists and the true predecessors of 007. And so it went on until well into the interbellum, when Fleming tried to find out about Bolshevik doings.

The reports of April 1996 about Uighur separatists acting on behalf of an East Turkestan who had turned Islamist were followed last June by a declaration of Chinese authorities in Tibet, announcing to the Daila Lama "a struggle for life and death". Tibet was the former center stage in the "Great Game". Other minorities in China's western provinces show separatist leanings as well. The newly independent states of Central Asia, in spite of Iranian and Turkish inroads still favorably disposed toward Moscow as longtime beneficiaries of the Soviet system, have to cope with religiously inspired unrest and minority problems. Apparently, they harbour some movements opposed to Chinese rule. Significantly, Beijing adopted a far more proactive strategy against Islamic groupings only after the conclusion of a "milestone agreement" last April in Shanghai between the presidents of the PRC, Russia and the three Central Asian Republics bordering on China: Kazakhstan, Tajikistan and Kirgizistan. Party newspapers in Xinjiang reported its purpose as the struggle against separatists and containing the Islamic upsurge. (2)

Judging by recent press commentaries and studies, the "Great Game" label is *en vogue* again. It conveys a sense of what the future agendas of major powers are about. The contours and broad outlines of those, combined with down-to-earth interests on a country-by-country basis, allow for a host of policy options and coalitions. Especially when all of the involved states are attuned to the available political means of power, a full and detailed examination is required of their security policies, defense doctrines and strategic options, technological ability and military capabilities. Elements thereof are of course indispensable in trying to discern some broad courses which events might take. But to what detail, knowing that all kinds of devils and dragons hide in there? Descriptions of emerging strategic patterns are as much a question of perspective as of condensed facts and figures. What, for instance, does it mean that defense spending in Asia as a percentage of GNP is not or hardly on the increase, given the phenomenal GNP-growth in some of the countries concerned? Not to speak of the apparent difficulties in establishing the exact outlays for military expenditure in various Asian countries. Assuming conditionality and ranges of interpretation is a prerequisite when we touch upon a number of scores, with China as focal point each time.

New "great games" in Central Asia? Connections with maritime security

Truly modern "great game" traits spring to mind if a revived Silk Road is related to the search for and transport of energy. East Asia's economic growth rates imply an increasing dependency on oil imports from South-West Asia and the Middle East. By 2010 between 90 and 95 percent of the oil needed will have to come from there. Since 1993 China has been an importer of oil and Indonesia could become one in ten years' time, barring a massive increase in new oil fields and production. Now South Korea, Taiwan and Japan join the states most dependent on oil imports now. From these extrapolations several main factors and developments, both in the heart of Asia and more to its coastal areas, can be seen as an ensemble. Application to each of the major nation-states involved provides a clue to what they are after in "grand strategic terms". It also explains why things Central Asian and in the Chinese hinterland bordering on Pakistan, India and Russia, are connected to the present day maritime security issues primarily in South-East Asia.

When Iran's President Rafsanjani inaugurated on 13 May, 1996, a new cross-border link between Iran en Turkmenistan in the Silk Road Railway, he lauded the achievement: "...(it) shortens the long distance between Chinese ports to the Persian Gulf, is the bridge for the region and the world". Shortly afterwards the PRC called for an even more grandiose scheme, the construction of a "Pan-Asia Continental Oil Bridge". It is meant to be a solution to East Asia's future energy needs by linking oil and gas pipelines on China's coast with those in the Xinjiang Uighur Autonomous Region, Central Asian Republics, Russia and Middle East countries. The continental oil bridge will extend from China to Japan, through what is designated as 'China's Taiwan' and to the Republic of Korea (ROK). Xinjiang with its developing oil and gas infrastructure and other parts of China's western regions are thus projected as major transit areas.(3) It would an exaggeration to see an anti-Western "Trans-Asian Axis" between an Iran-led bloc and the PRC easily at work here. At closer scrutiny this proposition is hardly tenable if, for example, the differences between Iran and Turkey are examined. In addition, Iran's northern Central Asian neighbors are tied somehow to Western security structures via OSCE, the North Atlantic Co-operation Council and NATO's Partnership for Peace, not to speak of Islamic instigated turmoil in China and Beijing urging Pakistan to stop supporting radical fundamentalists in Afghanistan. Suppression of Islamism will hardly be conducive to warm feelings between the PRC and Teheran. Or can they step over these problems, for the sake of an overarching anti-Western strategic alliance providing regional hegemony, if not more? Are they aiming to push back Russia's still preponderant position and whatever small latitude the West has in these remote areas? Are the alleged strategic supplies from Beijing to Iran in missile and nuclear technologies a building block in this grand scheme or simply the product of day-to-day politico-diplomatic considerations? If the former is true, how realistic is it for the PRC to then become the referee of the energy needs of East Asia's industrial economies? It is difficult to imagine that the odd ones out such as India, and the US and Japan would acquiesce.

The Economist usually gives detached views on current matters or empirically based forecasts. On occasion the time-honored weekly uses projections of present-day trends or worries into the far distant future. Its purpose is meant as a stimulant to more proactive formation of ideas, policies and strategies for the future. This is what its 1992 end-of-year issue sketched in a looking-back-from-2992 narrative "on the disastrous 21st century": it saw the pluralist alliances of the USA, Western Europe and Japan succumb to hyper-nationalism, shortly after the collapse of communism at the end of the 20th century. So narrow-mindedness finally carried the day instead of the combination multiparty-party democracy and free-market capitalism, in which a handful of authoritarians - most of them in Muslim South-west Asia and in Beijing - had never believed anyway. Two new powers took advantage of the confusion. The first was China. China's nuclear blackmail of Japan by detonating a nuclear warhead in 2009 over the sea off Yokohama made Japan to China what Switzerland had earlier been to its big European neighbors. The second new main force was the New Caliphate. China and the New Caliphate formed a new alliance that, after having dealt with the "decaying corpse of Russia", was to dominate the 22nd and 23rd centuries.

For such a scenario to take place, control of the strategic sea routes and highways along which energy flows to Pacific Asia would be vital. First and foremost is the passage from the Persian Gulf around India to the Straits of Malacca. Enter the pentagonal relationship Iran-Pakistan-India-Burma-China, three of them having or believing to be in the process of getting nuclear weapon facilities. Four of them are busily acquiring and testing medium range missiles. In the context of the oil routes between the Middle East and East Asia the strategic competition between India and China is of interest, with Burma in rather a prominent position. The military regime there has the PRC as its most important supplier of arms and military advisers. Moreover, port projects and naval facilities have caused a host of reports, rumors and speculations. China and her People's Liberation Army (PLA) would stand to benefit massively. The southern Silk Route from Yunnan to Burma, an old dream of successive regimes in Beijing, would become a reality. It is reported that the PRC is building some kind of reconnaissance installation on the Burmese Coco Island, about 30 miles north of India's Andaman Group to monitor Indian missile tests, naval and air force movements, and international shipping. That New Delhi's suspicions abound is shown by some highly speculative stories of more facilities on behalf of the Chinese for air operations or a ground forces formation, the equivalent of an army corps.(4) Most reports refer to Burma as a Chinese client state. Others see considerably more freedom of maneuver for Burma, even under the present regime. Burma's recent accession to the Association of South East Asian Nations (ASEAN) gives that leverage, as well as ASEAN's on Rangoon. If only partly reliable, the reports on Chinese-Indian naval rivalry in the Gulf of Bengal do have a relation with questions of maritime security east of the Straits of Malacca.

Center-stage but not always: The PRC and the South China Sea
Energy is of paramount importance in the evolving differences over islands in the South China Sea and adjacent waters, though by far not the only factor accounting for the incidents in an area accustomed to maritime disputes. That conflicts during the past few years have acquired sharper edges, is now generally ascribed to PRC positions and actions. This is not without grounds, but it is questionable whether the sole responsibility for a deteriorating situation should be laid at Beijing's door. The strong interest in things maritime in the countries belonging to the Association of South-East Asian nations (ASEAN) is only too obvious. High economic growth rates, often in double digits, and rapid population

growth, increasing from 182 to 487 million between 1950 and 1993 (5), make exploring and exploiting every possible oil and natural gas field and fishing ground imperative. The thirst for energy will inevitably lead to a situation in which a large share of (South)east Asia's need for oil must be supplied from the Gulf. The transit passage from the Gulf to the whole of East Asia is not served by maritime disputes. The shipping lanes increasingly suffer from another peril, piracy. Fishing faces intensified competition. Against the backdrop of Asia's huge populations, food production is perhaps not for long a question of Malthusian proportions. China's problems in agricultural production and the presumed shortage of arable land lends an additional sense of urgency to fishing rights and shrinking fishing stocks.

The maritime problems and territorial disputes in the South China Sea and the neighboring straits and waters can be divided into about eight zones of potential conflict. Some of these involve (prospective) members of ASEAN only. Disputes in the Gulf of Thailand between the coastal states there, in the Andaman Sea between Burma and Thailand, and in the Straits of Malacca between Malaysia and Indonesia give rise to series of incidents. Whether these are minor and controllable irritants is open to debate. Increases in defense expenditures occur in all ASEAN-states with the exception of Vietnam. Some observers point to the defense strategies of Singapore which aim at deterring Malaysia and Indonesia or to the characteristics of military hardware, which show that ASEAN-countries "...are just as worried about each other's motives as of China".(6) Those inclined to see intra-ASEAN problems over real estate as minor disagreements nevertheless point to a rather sensitive implication: there is not necessarily a Southeast Asian we-feeling *vis à vis* the PRC. The times that most Pacific Rim nations speak of China as a remote threat only have passed.

It is by far the biggest of the powers now heavily involved in disputed island groups and islet chains, such as the Paracels and the Spratlys. Furthermore, the situation whereby Beijing is at odds with Vietnam over questions of jurisdiction and concessions of oil prospecting in the Gulf of Tonkin and along its continental shelf, has given rise to some naval confrontations and blockades already. A potential conflict with Indonesia concerning primarily gas exploration activities in the waters around the Indonesian island of Natuna looms although China has explicitly stated that she has no claim to it. To this end, however, China made public a Chinese map showing Natuna as part of an exclusive Chinese economic zone.(7)

In fact, many of these disputes concern the UN Convention on the Law of the Sea (UNCLOS), which enables nations to declare those 200 nautical mile exclusive economic zones around their coasts and to subsequently resort to the exploitation of the deposits and resources within and beneath them. Differences in maritime delineation and overlap are not the issue here. The question of recognized sovereignty over pieces of land and islands precedes stipulations and interpretations of maritime law. Territorial waters and economic zones, in other words, follow from ownership, once established. It boils down to the quality of "historical" claims to areas, and it is here where the PRC contributes to the disputes and tension in the South China Sea.(8) As early as in 1974 China forcefully took possession of the Paracel Islands until then held by South Vietnam. Since then the People's Liberation Army Air Force (PLAAF) has laid a modest airstrip there. Recently, China went a step further by declaring a 200-mile zone around the Paracels. This was in contravention of UNCLOS, which does not allow continental countries to draw those zones around their islands, let alone entire archipelagos or to own the entire sea area between such islands and the mainland coast. Since 1992 China has stepped up her campaign to regard the sea as national territory. In that year an alleged law was passed declaring ownership (again) over the Spratlys and Paracels in the South China Sea, and Taiwan and the Diaoyutais (better known by their Japanese name, Senkaku Islands, claimed by Japan as well) further north. China's assertion of sovereignty did not go beyond territorial waters of the islands at that time. This is no longer true. The point of departure is a map of 1947 inherited from the Nationalist Chinese government. It allegedly shows nine dotted lines indicating ownership therein over all waters, islands and resources. In May 1995 the Chinese took recourse to it, thus augmenting China's jurisdiction over sea areas by about factor eight to more than 3 million square kilometers. It is a small consolation for others that Mao Zedong in his younger days even went farther out so as to include the Japanese Ryukyu Islands and the Pescadores. The entire South China Sea belongs to Beijing according to the map of 1947.(9) It includes the Spratlys, already the most contested chain to which Vietnam, the Philippines, Taiwan, Malaysia and Brunei also lay claims. Although historical evidence pertaining to the PRC Nansha Islands (the Chinese name for the Spratlys) claim is doubtful at best, it has not kept China from militarily underwriting its claims and has led to well-reported clashes with the Philippines. The naval encounter in 1995 over Mischief Reef - rocks turned into "islands" with structures built by the PLAN, the Chinese Navy, so that sovereignty and territorial waters could be declared - brought Manila to appeal to the Mutual Defense Treaty with the US. Although only applicable to the metropolitan territory of the Philippines, the treaty can be re-sorted to for consultations. After a naval encounter in January 1996, protests from Manila were all but forceful. Every now and then, however, China makes concessions, apparently when bigger powers like Japan and Indonesia hand in protestations.

Politico-military consequences and options

China's attitude is now a vexed question. Beijing let ASEAN know during its August 1995 conference in Brunei that she was seeking peaceful solutions. Equally, China does not want to interfere with the rights of free passage through the South China Sea. But the PRC recently announced she would come with more maritime base-lines specifically delineating claims to the Spratlys and else-where. Reverberations of unilateralism were clearly felt through-out Pacific Asia. Influenced by these ripples Indonesia and Australia signed in December 1995 a security treaty which gave Jakarta a backcover and the Australians a forward ally. Canberra is also intensifying military cooperation-operation with the US, amongst others through common exercises. In Vietnam the Russian Pacific Fleet was permitted anew a naval presence in Cam Ranh Bay, limited but telling all the same. Hanoi is now also courting C.-in-C.s of the US Pacific Command from time to time!

In the framework of the Five Power defense agreement linking Singapore and Malaysia to New Zealand, Australia and the UK, a substantial British naval force will sail South East Asian waters next year. That also is a sign of continued commitment to that arrangement after the UK has ceded sovereignty over Hong Kong to the PRC on 1 July 1997. Various ASEAN countries urge upon the US to become more active, politically and via the 7th Fleet. Even if being selective, it shows at least some receding of mutual appre-hension among ASEAN members. It conveys an ambivalent attitude towards the US as well, oscillating between relying on American power and driving home a message to the West of a deep mental-cultural divide on the grounds of Asianism. Efforts to keep Wash-ington away from East Asian get-togethers like the economic caucus express that. Likewise, European and American proposals to talk about human rights fall on rocky grounds both for intrinsic reasons and the risk of weakening ASEAN-unity given its highly diverse regimes. Stances like these may have helped to convince Beijing to accept multilateral talks with ASEAN members after July 1995 meeting of the association.

Not surprisingly, China's military options and capabilities offshore are also open to a widely divergent debate. In theory the facilities and the airstrip in the Paracels, China's southernmost mainland air base, 345 kilometers from Yulin and 920 kilometers from Spratly Island are enough to support all Chinese combat aircraft.(10) There is, however, hardly any room for sheltering aircraft, maintenance, storage of fuel, munitions and other logistical supplies. In effect that means that the PLAAF have a range problem which goes back to Mao Zedong's strategic war principle of luring the enemy in, thus placing the main emphasis on the strength and assets deep inland. The PLA Navy (PLAN) still have too many shortcomings, despite considerable modernization programs, for sustaining operations well away in the South China Sea. They are faced by a number of highly modern air forces of some of the ASEAN countries, of which advanced American F/A-18D and F-16C/D combat aircraft and Russian MiG-29s in the case of Malaysia, amongst others, are a part. Their navies and missile weaponry are updated, modernized and extended steadily, making the region one of not being very far away from an acceleration in their arms build-up. Whether the PLA would prevail in a confrontation on some scale is highly uncertain. It is dependent on the way the PLA's mass and quantitative advantages and deception are used and whether the opposing side holds together. Here doubts set in, and China could classically try to take a coalition apart. Scenarios are not at all certain as to the outcome of a clash in the South China Sea.(11) That cannot be said of those who at present deny that the PLA will shortly be a fighting force to be reckoned with in offshore operations. Especially the PLAN is far from being good enough for that,(12) an assessment to be called into question, the pace of Chinese naval modernization programs is considered. Progress in the fields of air defense and anti-submarine warfare has been substantial in a relatively short period. Modernization here just fares better than comparable PLAAF programs.(13) What the precise situation is, is as much open to discussion as the question what exactly does China want to achieve via the "Spratly question".

Beijing and Taiwan

Linking this question to the Taiwan issue possibly gives a better key to understanding Beijing's motivations and intentions in conjunction with Chinese strategic thinking. That also enables the positioning of other relevant military capabilities and options in a broader context. The present situation concerning Taiwan is the fruit of various interacting basic developments stemming from the end of the Cold War and from socio-political developments in the PRC and Taiwan. The disintegration of the former USSR diminished the need between PRC and USA for a mutual strategic understanding aimed at creating a counter-balance to Moscow's military power. The suppression of the student movement on Tiananmen in June 1989 washed away the underpinnings of the strategic relationship. General post-Cold War improvements after 1989 in Asia about, for example, the solution of the Cambodian problem, the improvement in the South-Korean relationship with the PRC and contacts over trade issues were no substitute for the erstwhile Sino-American strategic partnership. At the same time Chinese political assertiveness with military means has reaffirmed America's security obligations toward Taipei. These were toned down somewhat for the sake of Beijing, following normalization of US-PRC relations in 1978. The obligation is again firmly circumscribed in the Taiwan Relations Act of 1979: America sees any effort to determine the future of Taiwan by other than peaceful means, including boycotts or embargoes as a threat to the peace and security of the western Pacific area and of grave concern to the US. Later clarifications or reaffirmations of standpoints to Beijing, like selling only "defensive" weapons to Taiwan, did not fundamentally change this. There is now greater American leeway in the approach of the PRC, and a Taiwan with a far greater *de facto* rejection of Beijing's "one China, two systems" is prepared to join but a democratic, non-communist one China. Fundamental democratization processes flowing from societal developments are bringing about a Taiwanese version of industrial democracy and signaling that traditional socio-ethnic cleavages of the Kuomintang heritage are coming to an end. These trends, which seemingly form an unstoppable process on the island,(14) in the eyes of the leadership of the Communist Party of China, aroused revulsion in Taiwan after Tiananmen 1989 anyway. Both elements characterizing this situation - potential greater American room for maneuver and the Taiwanese "ideological" threat on both the account of the "one

China" tenet and the liberal democracy issue - apparently brought the Beijing leadership to act.

When, why and by whom in Beijing the decision was taken to start intimidating Taiwan, at the turn of 1995 is still subject to speculation. True, between 1991 and 1994 Beijing and Taipei enjoyed good relations by the mechanism of private foundations. That process was interrupted by politically exaggerated incidents such as the private visit of the president of Taiwan Lee Teng-hui to the US in 1995. Apparently that sparked off discord in the Beijing leadership. PLA top figures were said to have had an interest in holding missile tests near Taiwan in the summer of 1995, to divert the attention from an anti-corruption campaign planned by President Jiang Zemin. It was directed against corruption in connection with the PLA business empire. Moreover, Jiang was at the time in favor of improving relations with Taiwan, when suddenly the US permitted Lee Teng-hui to visit his former university in the US. Other factions in the PRC further exploited Jiang's setback to carry through their supposedly diversionary Taiwan-maneuver.(15)

From a structural point of view, however, PRC's intimidation campaigns since the summer of 1995 in the Strait of Taiwan can be seen as a component of China's redefinition of national and security interests. This reappraisal is dominated by a strong pre-occupation with national sovereignty and undoing what is still felt as the period of humiliation and shame brought upon China by the Western powers, Russia and Japan. Hong Kong reverted under Chinese sovereignty in 1997, to be soon followed by Macao. Taiwan should in fact be added to the sequence. The dilemma for Beijing then is either to have some kind of cultural unity restored by peaceful and liberalized economic exchanges between dispersed Chinese who fall under various independent political centers and regimes, or to let unity reign supreme. The elimination of independent or autonomous regimes in places which always have been judged as Chinese and bringing them under Beijing's control again is implied. If unity is not maintained, China's control over minorities seeking self-determination will be lost. The Uighurs, Tibetans, and Mongols mentioned earlier, live in spacious territories vital to China's defense. Although this may appear defensive, the claims on various sea areas clearly have offensive overtones which are figured in still uglier fashion in Chinese press reports as need for "living space". Energy shortages, food possibly in short supply in due course, population pressures and competition for other scarce resources, whether or not from oceanic environments perhaps partly account for that. The circle seems complete once China's growing self-image as the next world power is brought in, and her growing aspirations to have a preponderant position acknowledged regionally.

If the PRC then adopts some sort of satisfying or even maximizing behavior, what obstacles may it expect? Classical balance-of-power policies by its neighbors and other Pacific states would obviously be an answer. In addition, there is China's difficult security situation since she is surrounded by political entities not permanently friendly disposed to Beijing. China directly faces on or near its borders eight of the most numerous or formidable armed forces in the world: those of the USA, Russia, India, Vietnam, Japan, the two Koreas and Taiwan.(16) If Beijing strategic think tanks really are charmed by geopolitical ways of thinking including the more dubious offspring, they are probably inclined to see the US dominating large parts of the Gegenküste, the Pacific Rim coasts facing mainland China. This present state of affairs is perceived as a result of both the Second World War and the Cold War, and pure imperialist power politics. In this line of reasoning the US is not a stabilizing force, and the area of the Gegenküste of the main strategic adversary begins with South Korea, Japan, Guam, Taiwan, running further south rather than with Hawaii and California. Taken together they secure a glacis, an advance area. In this context Taiwan has an absolute blocking position and stands in the way of Chinese strategic deployment. Hence, the Taipei government continuing as a *de facto* sovereign entity is inadmissible. Further down the path of forceful policies toward Taiwan, lies the immediate question of how the Chinese leadership will continue with China's economic policy. Is this policy subordinate to Beijing's grand strategy? Or is it seen as the very foundation for a strategic grand design, certainly in the long run, to catch up in advanced investments, production techniques, technological power equations until well into the 21st century? The PRC will have to ask itself what leverage will Japan, ASEAN members, the US and the EU derive from this catching up. Before taking this argument to a conclusion, the point is whether Beijing's perceptions wholly conform to the above tenets of Realpolitik. What if Beijing is overly confident or fearful of influences arising from questions of leadership, the memory of Tiananmen, secessions or other specific Chinese predilections not induced to cool power-political observations? The absolute necessity to keep the fiction of Chinese unity intact may lead to some very emotional reactions, little related to

Realpolitik if damaging effects are not foreseen. Things and feelings Chinese apparently can trump rational, economic calculations.
Another element undermining the vision of China consistently
manifesting itself as a superpower in its own right is the ambivalence, if not outright distrust, towards Japan. This attitude has its
origins in a mix of widely varying perceptions. Only part of them
are based on rational projections what the Japanese economic and
technological base could achieve and change in the East Asian
military balance. Historical memories together with actual analysis still lead many in Beijing to view the US presence in East Asia
as useful and stabilizing and one which makes Japan feel secure.(17)

Can Taiwan deter the PLA?

The answer to this question is no if the intensity of emotions and
national feelings become hurt by a sudden, Taiwanese declaration
of independence or if Beijing feels strong enough to accelerate her
strategy of coercion and expects the US to be displeased with continued Taiwanese diplomatic activism. The answer is yes if
Taiwan, in a psychological situation of calming down, refrains from
too many autonomy enhancing initiatives, whereby an unprovoked
attack by Beijing would be wholly unacceptable to the US. But it is
here where the pain at present lies. Taiwan cannot efface herself
and remains attractive as a role model to those Chinese coastal
regions facing her, provided her economy and society are not driven
out of their present course. Taiwan feels increasingly cornered by
the PRC, especially after the Hong Kong connection for "indirect"
trade and investment with the mainland is blocked in 1997. Beijing
will not miss the opportunity to present dealings with Taiwan as
100 percent direct and internally Chinese thereafter. If there is no
sign of Taiwan giving in somewhat, the PRC may again resort to
intimidation tactics.

Whether it was sensible in mid-February 1996 for the Chairman of the Joint Chiefs of Staff in Washington, General John
Shalikashvili, to openly doubt PLA capabilities to carry out a
full-scale invasion of Taiwan, is open to question. The PRC does not
possess enough power projection and amphibious capabilities for
that. In a technical sense that is true, despite the considerable
progress that the PLA has made towards exactly that capability
during the last few years. Initial amphibious landing capacity of
naval infantry, airborne units and elements of dedicated land forces
divisions, however, is not adequate. This assessment is not funda-

mentally challenged if rapid follow-on actions by one or two Group Armies fit for offshore operations are taken into account.(18) The total capacity may be relevant for offshore actions against some smaller islands, but further away from the mainland problems of air cover and sustained sea control arise. General Shalikashvili's remarks, however, may direct Beijing's military thinking towards employing operational level variants of "human wave tactics". Aiming at quantitatively suppressing Taiwanese firepower and air defenses and overwhelming the islands by some ten-to-one ratios of mostly older PLAAF aircraft, naval craft and ground forces divisions must secure a swift victory to avoid repercussions otherwise. Such a course is unlikely to be in the cards. The PLA erecting new command centers, logistic and missile facilities in Fuzhou in the province of Fujian, falling under the Military Region opposite Taiwan, Nanjing, points to the enormous coordination and communication problems involved. A mass invasion would require the participation of far more units and material than the numbers involved during the psychological intimidation campaign that was backed up by five PLA divisions with 65,000 troops, around 200 aircraft and 120 warships.(19) Taiwan has repeatedly said that she can repel a PLA attack involving 20 divisions, 2,000 fighter planes and 200 warships. Given Taiwan's size, of these units only a maximum of 300 aircraft and 5 divisions could be engaged at any one time. The Chief of Taiwan's General Staff thought in 1989 that Beijing might need as many as 50 divisions to invade, the first wave consisting of 15.(20) Taiwan is indeed able to put up a formidable defense. Her defense expenditure joins the ranks of that of European big powers when undisclosed amounts are added to the official budget. Funds of $35 to $40 billion buy Taiwan a force qualitatively superior to the PLA in many fields. One notable exception presumably concerns submarine warfare. Here the PLAN has made significant progress, as indeed it is perceived to have made throughout South East Asia. Many nations there want to bolster their submarine fleets and anti-submarine warfare capabilities. The difficulty to detect submarines even in shallow zones of the East China Sea around Taiwan was revealed by the unnoticed intrusion of the North-Korean submarine in South Korean waters before it crashed last September.

A most disquieting aspect still to be mentioned is the PLA's missile tests during the period between July 1995 and March 1996. Last March, China's tests made M-9 missiles land within 50 miles of the Taiwanese ports of Keelung in the North and Kaohsiung in the South. This exercise demonstrated that with enhanced accuracy by the Global Positioning System and improved guidance through target updates from PLAN-ships, the PRC can potentially impede maritime commerce, debilitate critical communications and logistical centers and undermine trust in the entire Taiwanese economy.(21) Do these tests show an inclination to a high degree of risk-taking once emotive issues connected to sacrosanct Chinese unity are involved, without consideration of well-known American obligations to Taiwan? The answer could well be in the affirmative if the concomitant threats by Chinese generals of nuclear strikes against Los Angeles - following the sending of American naval forces near Taiwan - are considered. This offensively sounding verbal bluff to seal off China's defensive position is a far cry from the days of Mao Zedong. The difference this time is that China now has a real capability to think in categories like these. Another possibility is that the missile tests near Taiwan were deliberately chosen to test the resolve of Washington and to get an indication when Taipei might give in. A bounded rationality perspective would have made Beijing realize that intimidation can bring about fruitful bilateral negotiations on the joint exploitation of disputed resources in the South China Sea, but that very perspective would probably also counsel that such an approach will bring about highly undesirable effects to Beijing in the end. Many South and South East Asian countries may have stronger leanings towards the US and American encouragement for wider Japanese security obligations, including some form of theater missile defense, which would devaluate China's ballistic missile potential.

Of Chinese missilery and strategy

Discussions on security in Asia and beyond have indicated that the modernization of China's nuclear arsenal is lacking. Generally, most of the attention is given to the Chinese acquisition of conventional arms and weapon technology from Russia, Ukraine and Israel. That changed as well in 1996. In May the US urged Russia and the Ukraine not to deliver SS-18 missile technology to the PRC. The MIRV-ed SS-18 missile carrying 10 nuclear warheads was a major bone of contention during the SALT and START talks of the seventies and eighties. The Start Treaty allows the SS-18 booster to be used for commercial purposes. Chinese launching capabilities in that domain could indeed use a boost to lift heavier loads. But SS-18 capacities could also improve Beijing's global nuclear reach in the short term. There is now a minimum, nevertheless credible, nuclear deterrent force. The deterrent character of China's nuclear doctrine poses problems of interpretation, however. Beijing's declaratory policy with a no-first-use guarantee, which was renewed in 1995 in connection with the Review and Extension Conference of the Non-Proliferation Treaty (NPT), is still to be seen as having a strategic countervalue orientation; that is to say, for the time being it is aimed at retaliation against population centers, owing to a lack of technique necessary to target counterforce military objects. Below strategic ranges, for which practically only the 13,000 km range CSS-4 missile is available the picture is different. Only the distance to US territory is relevant here. Here a range of systems for distances between 600 and 5,000 km are available.(22) With those weapons most places in neighboring countries and places further away in Russia and India can be reached. Mostly medium range ballistic missiles have been exported to Saudi Arabia, Syria, Iran and Pakistan. Bombers and short range tactical nuclear weapons have also been further developed and have sometimes been integrated in PLA exercises. Little is known about PLA doctrine and employment concepts which seem to contain some disturbing tendencies of their dubious military utility.(23) In any case, in spite of the 1995 NPT and current Comprehensive Test Ban Treaty (CTBT) efforts to which the PRC adheres, its nuclear programs can still have a substantial impact. The possibility that the recently adopted CTBT might not come into force definitively, owing to opposition from India towards nuclear disarmament by the five nuclear weapon states, revealed that regional disputes and mistrust in large parts of Asia can continue to frustrate arms control efforts. This applies to the Missile Technology Control Regime (MTCR) as well. Continued interest in missile developments in many Asian countries fits this picture. In addition, there was a debate about a supposedly effective nuclear deterrence in 1990 between Pakistan and India, then going through another of their periodic crises. The difference this time seems to have been a message by Pakistan, disclosing her nuclear capability to the government in New Delhi.(24)

The integration of the nuclear factor in Chinese doctrinal and military strategic thinking did not get much attention until recently, whereas the concept of "People's War" was well received since its inception. Mao's ideas on revolutionary warfare were of paramount importance although not exclusively so. There were also Chinese traditions of designing defensive strategies directed towards first evading, then yielding and giving way to one's adversary before turning the tables on him at a time of one's own choosing. The verbal flare-ups of political forward elements especially during the Cultural revolution - Mao declared nuclear weapons irrelevant, Lin Biao spoke about the global struggle between the cities of the rich and the countryside of the poor, third world - had to hide major vulnerabilities. China was insufficiently industrialized to make the transition to the second basic tenet of the Chinese strategic tradition, namely, that of a forward defense strategy, seeking decisive engagement well forward.(25) Mao's "People's War" heritage was extremely difficult to change. Since the Korean War, however, necessary modifications and adjustments in the strategic and operative concepts within the "People's War" doctrine have been made. The core concept here is "active defense". The way to conduct it, given formidable technological weapon sophistication in modern war conditions, became the pretext for some structural changes in the PLA. The recognition of "People's War under modern conditions" far from solved all the conceptual problems, however, as the border war against Vietnam demonstrated in 1979. For Deng Xiaoping that event provided the arguments to start a gradual modernization program also in this field, both conceptually and in the domains of technology and hardware. In the 1980s the program resulted in major reductions of militia and PLA personnel strength, and in organizational-conceptual changes such as the introduction of combined arms operations. In this context Beijing's transition to an offshore power-projection capability was announced in 1988. Developments like these are not to be seen as the definitive overhaul of China's established defense doctrine but as one giving Beijing an operational level forward capacity. A "strategic offensive posture" would require far more extensive nuclear, naval and joint forces build-ups in order to materialize. The PRC's defense budget has undoubtedly risen sharply during the last few years. Much of R&D and hardware expenditures is possibly not accounted for by the budget. Compared with the experience of the USSR where the defense effort was allowed to eat the civil economic basis, the PRC leadership on the whole has steered a more careful course. That prudence is in conformity with ancient Chinese military teachings is exemplified by those of Sun Tzu and Cao Cao that "master of mobility" and, one might add, logistics. Cao Cao, who lived from 155 - 220, counseled against military adventures if one's own military technological and material base could not match the comparison with the main competitors. It is a good rule to go by, and one which Mao Zedong preached but did not live up to altogether.(26) Deng put into practice again in the eighties: only with faster economic growth can there be greater progress in defense construction. Since defense received the lowest priority in Deng's modernization program throughout the 1980s, spending on defense stagnated. The question is whether China will continue to cling to the careful prescription. There are signs that the topic of Chinese defense expenditures, which will equal Soviet outlays of fifteen years ago, has become a Politikum in strategic discussions.

Strategic baselines in North-East Asia and the PRC
Behind the well advertised and lesser known maritime disputes in the North-East Asian quadrangle Russia-China-ROK-Japan, hides a host of "big league" economic and geostrategic interests. If the USA is drawn into the equation, it becomes possible to place mutual distrust in an equalizing or balancing perspective and strongly differing mental maps in a broader one. The distrust is not caused by Washington, of course. On the contrary, the stability in the area hinges to a large degree on the US alliances and security arrangements. A determining factor for big power agenda-setting, however, is the fact that here nations with a distinct sense of self-image and historic mission in the world meet. It is from this domain that gross misunderstandings and apprehensions could arise once more, despite the Cold War being over or just because of it.

The nuclear dimension is not abetted as long as speculation about North Korea's military potential in this field continues. North Korea has in her arsenal at least one tested nuclear-capable missile with a range of about 600 miles. In addition, the Taepo Dong II missile brings much of Asia but also places like Hawaii and Alaska within range.(27) Missile technology is offered in Pyongyang's military export package. Pyongyang could still trigger similar and nuclear programs in neighboring countries, should IAEA safeguard inspections in Pyongyang's installations and waste sites not be continuously allowed or provide dissatisfying results. Prospects improved on 11 July 1996, with the signing of the protocols between the US and North Korea for the delivery of two light-water reactors to replace the old ones capable of producing weapon grade plutonium. If the issue lingers on, a reunited Korea could even find itself back with a nuclear weapon potential. That industrial powerhouse with more than 70 million people could wield considerable influence. Surely, Beijing would not like such a state on her border if it continued to be allied with the US. For the time being the North Korean problem remains an issue from which considerable difficulties and tensions could arise. Isolation and famine could cause a dying dragon to spit once again. Defectors from the North report about war preparations and plans to "conquer the South in a week", but they also speak about famine and other dramatic situations.(28)

Of importance is the treaty of friendship, cooperation-operation and mutual assistance of 11 July 1961, signed by Zhou Enlai and Kim Il Sung. The relation Beijing-Pyongyang lost much of its value to the PRC after the Cold War changed and relations with the US took on a global strategic character. As to the Korean peninsula, Beijing also assumed role of "honest broker". That necessitated it to qualify the clauses on assistance in the friendship treaty, applicable only in the event of an unprovoked attack on North Korea.(29) Relations between the two further cooled down after the post Cold War recognition by the PRC of the ROK. Recently, however, China seems interested in improving relations with Pyongyang. To that end the 35th anniversary of the friendship treaty was elevated to an important event by both sides. It was reminiscent of the days when ideological commonalities and fervor between the old comrades in arms were deemed more important than economic interests. Nevertheless, Beijing is probably worried about the situation in the North of the Korean peninsula and from its position it is best placed to help keeping the lid on.

Were the "agreed framework", in which the North Korean nuclear program is to be converted, to collapse, South Korean and Japanese nuclear programs would possibly be instigated. Especially the latter would starkly enhance Chinese apprehensions of Tokyo's ultimate intentions. It could induce Beijing to even modify her deployment of nuclear forces and targeting strategy.(30) Japan would then have an argument to build some kind of TMD-defense. Although Japan's attitude leaves room for ambiguity about her nuclear options(31) which are remote owing to constitutionalist and moral codes deeply ingrained in her population, the Chinese hammering on this issue has borne some fruit. There is some irony in the worth of this for China, who openly toys with the idea of targeting Los Angeles, launches missiles around Taiwan, holds the Japanese lifeline, an oil route from the Persian Gulf, as potential hostage in the South China Sea. Disputes about the uninhabited Senkaku Islands northeast of Taiwan could cause tension between both countries to escalate because of fishing rights and the possibility of new oilfields there. On the other hand, Japan, like South Korea, still falls under the security guarantees of a big, nuclear ally.

It would be the absence of such reliable military alliances "...that goes a long way toward explaining the impetus toward proliferation by certain countries".(32) The question is, will that American guarantor retract still more of its capabilities in Pacific Asia? If so, Japan will become ever more tempted to increase at least some naval and air power capabilities. Diplomatically, the project is very sensitive to manage, also in view of Korean and ASEAN feelings. The degree of sensitivity is reflected by decisions made at the beginning of 1996 in Tokyo and Seoul to announce the establishment of overlapping 200 mile economic zones. These decisions have renewed the attention to the unresolved issue to whom the Bambus Islet belong. The question of the Bambus Islet, called Tok-to by the Koreans and Takeshima by the Japanese, is a very emotional one for South Korea. The possession of Tok-to concerns more than fish or oil or territorial gain. So much symbolic meaning is attached to this dispute that Seoul immediately staged a naval exercise near Tok-to. It was accompanied by outbursts of the sort that "a war against Japan is not possible, alas", in even the highest political circles.(33)

Despite all the talk of rearmament, Tokyo is actually in the process of streamlining its Self-Defense Forces: from 180,000 to 160,000 ground forces personnel, from 60 to 50 destroyers and 350 to 300 fighter aircraft.(34) The politicized famous 1 percent of GNP spent on defense does, however, not include Japan's space program and some other defense related expenses. Even that round digit amounts to more than $50 billion. Japan buys itself considerable striking power, but with many strings and extremely restrictive rules of engagement attached. Should the accession of Japan as a permanent member of the UN Security Council be hindered or promoted given the associated obligations in military fields other than humanitarian or peace-keeping operations? Behind the figures some major concerns and questions loom. The aforementioned figure of manpower is just as much a result of efficiency measures as a reflection of decreased enlistment. The lack of keenness to enlist is consistent with public apathy toward defense questions and a constitutionally enshrined pacifism. Many still share this attitude. As recently as 1994 Japan's Socialist Party reversed its position and declared the SDF to be constitutional.(35) Next, the figures on a leaner defense indicate that Japan continues to rely on the American shield, which apparently still reliably guards against some potential threats. The 1995 Defense White Paper contains matters of concern: China's armed forces enlargement, Beijing's claims to sea areas vital to Japan's flow of oil from the Persian Gulf, the tension between the Koreas, and, somewhat surprisingly, the "still formidable Russian force in the Far East". The meaning of the US-Japan Mutual Security Treaty as an anchor both for Japan's predictability in the eyes of her neighbors and in view of destabilizing factors and undercurrents in much of Asia, still seems widely recognized. New baselines emerge, however: the eternal trade disputes, wars over chips and cars with Washington could set in motion a chain of intensifying misunderstandings. They serve as expressions of deeper underlying differences in world outlook. In that sense Ishihara's book, *The Japan that can say "No"*" and Friedman and Lebard's heavily criticized book on "the coming war with Japan", prominent at the beginning of this decade, were forerunners. The latter study in 1991 was about natural resources and market access - presented as the causes of Japan's military ventures between the 1920s and 1945 - as sources of renewed conflict. It reflected the deep bewilderment about Japanese mercantilism in the US and witnessed anew bellicose developments. Predictions of this kind mostly overlook the fact that it would take Japan at least ten years to build a military force 60 percent of that of the US, despite her impressive industrial base.(36) If this does not dispel the myth of a swift Japanese rearmament even if Tokyo wanted to, then technology does.

Surprising as this may sound, Japan's technological organization is probably not geared to the forward edges of defense technologies as it is to industrial-commercial fields. The American defense-industrial and technological base is far ahead, especially in systems engineering in the domains of airpower, missile-defense and space systems.(37) Ten years ago at the height of the FSX-aircraft drama, which soured US-Japanese relations, US feared Japan would take over the market for aircraft as well. As a densely populated country and highly vulnerable to attack, Japan would be in need of exactly those systems and bar theoretical nuclear developments at her own accord.

Maritime security issues are an important factor in the Russo-Japanese relation. The Kuril Islands to which Japan lays claim overshadowed that relationship during the Cold War. Recently improved relations have led to cooperation in defense.

The relationship between China and Russia could grow once again into a strategic alliance for which both sides argue for medium-term considerations. They give Moscow time to consolidate and recapture lost strength, and buy a quiet border in the Far East. It provides Beijing with much needed military-technological infusions in naval and airpower fields amongst others. Russian military aircraft still receives a favorable press at international exhibitions. For the time being the Russians are possibly the only ones still able to reach advanced levels of systems engineering, not lagging far behind the US. As a capability inherited from the Soviet past, one can only wonder how long this branch can escape the fate of the dismal state that other sectors of the Russian economy are in. With Israel, Russia is ostensibly a country willing and able to provide the PLA with aircraft technology. How far the PLA must travel before it runs up against Russian interests, is a strategic subject of debate in Moscow. Furthermore, there is a host of very direct interests and considerations regarding Central Asia, not necessarily in line with those of Beijing. The Chinese have not forgotten the treaties of the 19th century with Russia, which relinquished hundreds of thousands of square kilometers of Siberian and Far Eastern territories.

Some final remarks
In view of the vast potential for conflict and the tensions building up in the region, it is to be hoped that the much advertised and talked about multilateral frameworks in Asia take off seriously. Integrating the PRC will be a cumbersome and difficult process, involving various regional and Asia-Pacific groupings as well as bilateral Japanese, American and European Union efforts of the type shown in the Asia-Europe meeting earlier this year. A replica of the CSCE for Asia was an old idea of the Soviet party leader Brezhnev. The motivations for holding that meeting have since differed entirely. Given Asia's size, subregional arrangements of the type of the ASEAN Regional Forum (ARF) could find a place under an OSCE-type roof. Military security and confidence building measures and other means to make military relationships more transparent could find a place there. In ARF Japan and Indonesia have taken initiatives to this end already. A major point in question, however, would be how to nudge China further away from a free-riding approach to multilateral arms control issues. This entails avoiding as much as possible obligations which might impede Beijing's defense policy, while profiting from the benefits

of arms control agreements of others; like START, scaling down American and Russian inventories, *ipso facto*, upgrading its own and those of other nuclear powers.(38) Yet, that the PRC has been gradually drawn in is exemplified by her attitude towards the CTBT and the halting of nuclear testing this year in connection with that. A related sign is China's attitude towards the UN peacekeeping, gradually becoming more supportive. There is evidence of military transparency in the form of publishing defense budgets and defense white papers by a number of ARF participants, China included. Still, the task of making the composition visible, purchasing power and structure of defence budgets is a major enterprise in itself, and a cumbersome one at that, given the questions of how to discount inflation, exchange rates, military pensions, the computation of R&D and material expenditures and so on. The PRC's official budget in 1994 and 1995 amounted to about $7 to 7.5 billion; Western estimates are frequently four times higher. Some analysts, however, arrive at expenditures of only some 63 billion yuan as against the official figure of 52.3 billion yuan for 1993.(39) Taiwan and Japan's budgets of $40 to 50 billion lie in or slightly above the ranges of the big European NATO powers. India, important in the overall Asian power political context, planned, by contrast, the 1996-1997 defense budget of $7.93 billion for an armed force with a personnel strength of around 1 million.

China will undoubtedly keep her center stage position in the interplay of forces in Pacific Asia; that is, if her present economic development is not affected by leadership struggles and the like. If attempts at constructive engagement or confidence building in the politico-strategic field do not succeed, the need for containment of the PRC draws nearer, provided other Asian countries are willing. This development would create unmanageable tension and instability in the region where internal problems of countries wash back and forth across borders and are easily exploited for nationalist or diversionary purposes. Everything else remaining equal, Washington would have to carry the main load. Whereas an integration scenario would require a subtle military approach and military back up, under the hypothetical circumstances of a confrontation the US Pacific Fleet would face exacting demands. Indeed the question then arises, to what degree and in which strategic directions would its forward deployed Seventh Fleet have to enact assertive strategies? In addition, how to convince the region of the friendly but self-conscious perceptions of American resolve without taking too much risk in countering unfriendly influences, while at the same time stifling potential adversaries in the conviction that it will take them a very long time before they have solved their defense problems? In view of these conflicting demands, how credible is it to constantly convey the message that offensive power projection will be accompanied with prohibitive costs? A strategy of this kind would be costly and at variance with present discussions in the US to further reduce the number of aircraft carriers. Allowing the growing enmity in Pacific Asia to run its course or making adaptations by choosing Beijing's side in a classical way of paying tribute to achieve appeasement, is all thinkable. In due course, however, when China's power becomes more feasible, a choice among the options will proximate.

* Boris Timmer, Military Academy, Breda, The Netherlands.

Notes

1. P. Fleming, *News from Tartary* (London 1936). The German translation of Fleming's book,*Tataren-Nachrichten* (Frankfurt 1995), was reviewed in NZZ 7/3/1996.
2. Y. Bodansky, "An Islamist Resurgence in Xinjiang Poses a Threat to PRC Leadership", *Defense and Foreign Affairs Strategic Policy* (June-July 1996), pp. 6 and 7.
3. Yossef Bodansky, "Asia Prepares for Energy Crisis", *Defense and Foreign Affairs Strategic Policy* (June-July 1996) pp. 1 and 8; see also his article on Islamist resurgence, op. cit., p. 7.
4. Andrew Selth, "Burma and the Strategic Competition between China and India", *The Journal of Strategic Studies* 19/2 (June 1996), pp. 213-230.
5. Damon Bristow, "Between the Devil and the Deep Blue Sea: maritime disputes between ASEAN member states", *RUSI Journal* (August 1996), pp. 31-38.
6. ibid., p. 32-33.
7. June Teufel Dreyer, *China's Strategic View: the Role of the People's Liberation Army*, Strategic Studies Institute of the U.S. Army War College (Carlisle B, April 25, 1996), p. 14.
8. Henry J. Kenny, "The South China Sea - a Dangerous Ground", *Naval War College Review* vol. XLIX no. 3 (Summer 1996), pp. 99 and 100.
9. "Seas of trouble", *The Economist* (May 25th 1996), pp. 66-67; see also Kenny, op. cit., pp. 100-103. Further background to be

found in Mark J. Valencia, *China and the South China Sea Disputes,* Adelphi Paper 298 (IISS London, October 1995).

10. Felix H. Chang, "Beijing's Reach in the South China Sea", *ORBIS* (Summer 1996), p. 361.

11. ibid., p. 372.

12. Point made by Bristow, op. cit., p. 37; see his footnote 22 especially on: Eric Grove, "The Myth of Chinese Sea Power", *Parliamentary Brief* (London 1996).

13. Larry M. Wortzel, "China Pursues Traditional Great Power Status", *ORBIS* (Spring 1994), pp. 163-181.

14. Tse-Min Lin, Yun-Han Chu and Melvin J. Hinich, "Conflict Displacement and Regime Transition in Taiwan - a Spatial Analysis", *World Politics* 48 (July 1996), pp. 453-481.

15. W. van Kemenade, "Crisis rond Taiwan is vooral afleidingsmanoeuvre", *NRC-Handelsblad* (11 maart 1996).

16. Andrew J. Nathan, "China's Goal in the Taiwan Strait", *The China Journal* 36 (July 1996), pp. 87-94.

17. Thomas J. Christensen, "Chinese Realpolitik", *Foreign Affairs* 75/5 (September 1996), pp. 37-53.

18. Based on various Taiwanese sources, some IISS Military Balance publications of the past few years, Larry Wortzel, op. cit.; see also David Shambaugh, "Growing Strong: China's Challenge to Asian Security", *Survival* 36:2 (Summer 1994), p. 53. A Chinese PLA Group Army is about the equivalent of an army corps plus various divisions joined eventually by elements of other services.

19. "PLA Missiles Diminish Value of Taiwan's Islands", *Defense News* , Washington (August 26, 1996), p. 8.

20. Peter Kien-hong Yu, "Taipei's Perception of its Deterrence Situation(s) from April to July, 1989", in Richard H. Yang (chief ed.), *China's Military: the PLA in 1990/1991* (Kaohsiung, Taiwan 1991), pp. 68-69.

21. Article in *Defense News* (August 26, 1996), op. cit. Also contains information on Taiwan's hidden defense budget and military outlays.

22. Col. John Caldwell and Alexander T. Lennon, "China's Nuclear Modernization Program", *Strategic Review* (Fall 1995), pp. 27-38.

23. Alistair Iain Johnson, "China's New 'Old Thinking' - the Concept of Limited Deterrence", *International Security* , 20:3 (Winter 1995/96), pp. 5-42.

24. Devin T. Hagerty, "Nuclear Deterrence in South Asia: The 1990 Indo-Pakistani Crisis", *International Security*, 20:3 (Winter 1995/96), pp. 79 -114.
25. S.E. Henning, "China's Defense Strategy: a Historical Approach", *Military Review* (May 1979), pp. 60-67.
26. John Wilson Lewis and Xue Litai, *China's Strategic Sea Power* (Stanford 1994); pp. 211-219 provide a discussion on this aspect, although not necessarily complete on every score.
27. Alvin Z. Rubinstein, "North Korea's Nuclear Challenge", *Korea and World Affairs* (Spring 1994), p. 24. See also Angelo M. Codevilla, "Defenseless America", *Commentary* (September 1996), p. 51.
28. Reported by North Korean MiG-19 pilot, who defected in May 1996 to the South; see *NRC-Handelsblad* (28 mei 1996).
29. Alvin Z. Rubinstein, op. cit., pp. 31-32.
30. John Caldwell and A.T. Lennon, op. cit., pp. 32-33 annex footnote 40.
31. Various sources allude to this; see A.Z. Rubinstein, op. cit., p. 39 annex footnote 33. Recent analysis by Thomas Bernauer deem Japan as prospective nuclear power highly unlikely, during Autumn Session of the International Studies Association, held in Japan.
32. Alvin Z. Rubinstein, op. cit., p. 39.
33. "Een oorlog tegen Japan zou het mooiste zijn", *NRC-Handelsblad* (17 februari 1996); see also *NZZ* (21. February 1996).
34. Sadaaki Numata, "Japan: toward a more active political and security role?", *RUSI-Journal* (June 1996), p. 12.
35. Richard Halloran, "Japan's Military Force: Return of the Samurai?", *Parameters* (Winter 1995-96), pp. 28-41.
36. ibid., footnote 8, p. 40.
37. Michael J. Green, *Arming Japan - Defense Production, Alliance Politics and the Postwar Search for Autonomy*, Columbia University Press (New York 1995), p. 4.
38. Alistair Iain Johnson, op. cit., p. 38.
39. Gudrun Wacker, *Die chinesische Bedrohung: Wahn oder Wirklichkeit*, Berichte des Bundesinstituts für ostwissenschaftliche und internationale Studien Nr. 51-1995 (Koeln, September 1995), p. 9. For doubts about the higher estimates see: Shaoguang Wang, "Estimating China's Defense Expenditure: Some Evidence From Chinese Sources - Research Note", *The China Quarterly* number 147 (September 1996), pp. 889-912.

Chapter 4

Klaus Fritsche: "Russia: Looking for New Allies in East Asia"

The events of April 1996 strongly symbolize the changes that Russian foreign policy has undergone since 1992. While Russia began by proclaiming a "strategic partnership" with the USA, already by last November her defense minister, Grachev, told the West that in response to NATO's planned eastward enlargement, Moscow might see herself forced to seek new allies in the East. In March 1996 the new Russian foreign minister, Evgenii Primakov, declared the "strategic partnership" with the West to be "dead",(1) and only a few weeks later, at the end of April, President Yeltsin declared as Russia's aim to form a "strategic partnership" with China.

In my paper I would like to outline the developments that led to this policy change and the reasons underlying it. I shall then go on to show how it is reflected in Russia's bilateral relations with China. In conclusion I shall attempt to show the possible paths that Russian "Ostpolitik" may follow. In this discussion it should be noted that in this context "east" and "west" should not be understood in their purely geographical sense. "East" or "vostok" denotes the orient, whereas "west" is used as a synonym for the "developed countries", and also includes Japan.(2)

The dynamics of the break-up of the USSR and the idea of a "strategic partnership" with the West

Let us recall, the main driving force behind the break-up of the Soviet empire came from those political quarters for whom Russia's future was closely bound by its integration in the Western "community of civilized nations". These forces carried the flag of democracy, a state of law and a market economy and hoped via this route to overcome the country's increasingly evident economic and social problems. Pinned to this vision was not only the expectation of extensive economic aid from the West but the idea - the significance of which was in many cases entirely missed - that through "strategic relations" with the USA Russia could secure for herself a role as a "global player" on the world stage.

Asia scarcely figured at all in these calculations. On the contrary, in Moscow there was a widespread feeling that the trouble with Russia was that she was too Asian.(3) In this respect the declarations of sovereignty by the Central Asian and Caucasian Soviet republics were regarded as liberation not only by the people of these regions. Also, for many Russian people these regions as well as Russia's links with the countries of the Third World constituted an economic burden rather than an asset.

This attitude also had an impact on Russia's relations with Asia. The Russian Foreign Ministry's "foreign policy concept" published in October 1992, for example, envisaged the "strategic partnership" between Russia and the West extending to Asia as well.(4) In the Asia-Pacific region too, capital inflow was expected from the West and security was to be secured through Russian-American cooperation. In addition, the OECD-member Japan was ascribed a special significance of her own for economic reasons. The same about-face took place in miniature on the Korean peninsula where Moscow shifted her allegiance from North to South Korea. And China, who had regarded the *putsch* of August 1991 in a favorable light, slid way down Moscow's list of priorities.

The impact of these developments on Moscow's foreign relations were not without controversy, however. Moscow's orientation towards the West was challenged above all by the "Eurasian" school of thought, which saw Russia as belonging to both Europe and Asia but at the same time as a "unique" entity that was distinct from both continents. But a homogenous "Eurasian ideology" has not developed. The more radical followers of this line have been propagating isolation from the West, while moderates have advocated Russia's role as a bridge between East and West.

This political debate was not without consequence for the Russian foreign policy. Also within the Russian leadership the view that both the Asian part of Russia and the Asian-Pacific region were of increasing importance for the development of Russia gained prevalence. So Yeltsin was quick to latch on to this idea and declared during a visit to Seoul in November 1992 that "Russian diplomacy ...must follow the spirit of the old Russian emblem on which a two-headed eagle is depicted looking both westwards and eastwards".(5) For a while, however, these sentiments remained at a rhetorical level. The antipathy between "Westernizers" and "Eurasians" of various stripes was to dominate the foreign policy debate until 1993 or 1994.(6)

Thus, while the communist and nationalist opposition was able to exert a certain amount of pressure, it was the increasingly widespread disappointment about the results of cooperation with the West that had the more decisive impact on the direction of foreign policy and resulted in the geopolitical perspective gaining the upper hand over the more idealistic outlook of "new thinking", even among the "Westerners". The concept of a "nation state" or "national interests" that was to be realized by firm adherence to a policy based on "balance-of-power"concepts came to the fore. The well-known saying that a state does not have permanent friends or allies prompted a proposal of pragmatism in foreign policy. Gorbachev's idea of securing worldwide peace through a managed multi-polar world system (for example, via the United Nations) is now seen as an illusion. External threat perceptions began to assume renewed importance *vis-à-vis* internal factors - as did the military factor as a means of averting such risks. It was now considered a myth that under the current circumstances the "power factor" and the role of the armed forces have lost former importance.(7) Moreover, in the new defense doctrine of 1993 the importance of the nuclear deterrent was once again writ large.(8) The reasoning behind this is simply that a country that aspires to the status of a "global player" but whose economic base is weak must resort to military might. And if conventional forces are in a state of decay, then she must fall back on her nuclear arsenal.(9)

In this reorientation of Russian foreign policy, which now gave priority to the post-Soviet area i.e., the CIS states, Asia gained in relative importance. There was also an unmistakable change of emphasis. Thus, China returned to the first place on Russia's scale of priorities in Asia, however, not just as a regional partner but as a global factor in the Russian-American-Chinese triangle.

Moscow openly began to play the "Chinese card" against the West. "Relations between China and Russia", Mikhail Titarenko wrote, for example, "ensure the requisite balance in relations with the West and in relations between East and West as a whole".(10)

What the relationship between Moscow's western and eastern orientations was to be and what shape it was to assume in practice was not clearly defined either by the Kremlin or by the Russian Foreign Ministry, however. Kozyrev's official statements on this point alternated between emphasizing the strategic partnership with the West and underlining the equal status of Moscow's relations with both East and West. At other times, though, he spoke of giving priority to Moscow's "eastern orientation".

A counterbalance to "Western hegemony"

Internal political developments in Russia and her growing differences with the West, particularly concerning NATO's planned expansion eastwards, shifted the parameters of the debate. Today, the discussion is no longer defined in terms of "Westernizers" versus "Eurasians", for the voices of the "Westernizers" have grown muted. The dividing line in foreign policy now runs between those political forces who, for a variety of reasons, would like to see a policy of maintaining balanced, pragmatic relations based on Russian national interests with all countries of the world, whether East or West, and those who advocate a "strategic alliance" with the East against the West.(11)

Some communists, in particular, adhere to the latter viewpoint. While officially the Communist Party of Russia reserves judgment on this question, it is known that Gennadii Zyuganov believes it is necessary to have "partners, if not indeed allies, along our borders".(12) Communist intellectuals express their views more openly. They see the American economic and military hegemony as a threat to the social and political future of the world. The China expert and member of the Far East Institute in Moscow Aleksandr Yakovlev, for example, whose views coincide with those of many others, states that only an alliance between Russia, China and India can prevent the "corrupting influence of Western absolutism".(13)

The nationalists on the political right have not taken a clearly defined stance on this question. They, too, advocate a revival of ties with old allies, North Korea being a particular favorite. Their attitude to China is contradictory. While some of them warn of the "Chinese threat", calls can also be heard from these quarters for a "strategic alliance" with China. How confused the position of, for example, the LDPD on this question is was demonstrated recently when Aleksei Mitrofanov, an LDPD member and chairman of the Geopolitical Committee of the Duma, not only paid a visit to Taipei in the wake of the latest Taiwan crisis but, following his return, called simultaneously for a "strategic alliance" with China and "the development of military ties" with Taiwan.(14)

The idea of an alliance with the East finds favor both among the military and the Russian government. In November 1995 Defense Minister Grachev warned that in response to NATO's planned eastward enlargement Russia would seek new allies in the East. An article by Pavel Felgengauer, who is considered to have close connections with the General Staff, is revealing on this point.(15) He believes the strengthening of China will lead to the formation of a new balance of power in Asia that could be advantageous to Russia. He calls for a strategic partnership not only with China but also with India and Iran. One of the goals of such an alliance would be to prevent the West gaining a foothold in Central Asia and the Caucasus. He believes that deliveries of military and nuclear technology would not be too high a price to pay for the achievement of these goals. Moreover, he concludes pragmatically, "if the ambitious plan to create a new continental strategic partnership in Asia is for various reasons not completely fulfilled, Russia will in any event be able to earn several billion dollars and at the same time send a clear signal to the West - that Moscow is not as isolated and weak as it seems".(16)

The appointment of a new Russian foreign minister also cleared up the situation. In an interview with *Izvestia* Evgenii Primakov declared the "strategic partnership" with the West to be "dead". While acknowledging that the world was moving towards multipolarity, he stated nonetheless that Russia should assume the role of a counterweight to the country that was attempting to resist this tendency and to dominate international relations. For "diplomatic reasons" he avoided actually mentioning the USA.(17) In a speech marking the seventy-fifth anniversary of the foundation of the Russian foreign intelligence in December 1995(18) he stated, moreover, that "in today's world Russia is one of the most important counterweights" to forces striving for hegemony and that China for this, among other reasons, had "a greater interest than ever before in developing relations with the Russian Federation". Primakov, too, ascribes particular importance to a possible Russian-Indian-

Chinese triangle, both in international politics and for the purpose of countering Islamic fundamentalism in Central Asia.(19) At the same time, however, he proposes - and this distinguishes him from the hard-liners on the Left and Right - establishing good relations with former adversaries, albeit relations that respect Russian interests. Here it is interesting that Primakov draws a distinction between the USA as the only country striving for world hegemony on the one hand and Europe and Japan with interests in multipolarity on the other and with regard to Asia repeatedly emphasizes the importance of good relations with Tokyo. This state of affairs was underlined by the visit of the head of the Japanese defense agency, who, while in Moscow signed a military cooperation agreement with Grachev.(20) Yet, Russian relations with Japan are strained due to the existing territorial problems of the Kuril Islands and the unsecured economic developments in Russia. Although the foreign trade, especially Russian exports, have been growing steadily during the last years (Table 1), Japanese investments have met with great difficulties.

Table 1   Japanese-Russian Foreign Trade (Million US $)

	Export	Import	Total
1992	1,076	2,402	3,478
1993	1,501	2,769	4,280
1994	1,167	3,490	4,657
1995	1,151	4,733	5,884
1996	1,043	4,015	5,058

Source: *Japan. An International Comparison* 1993, 1994 and 1995; for 1994: *The summary of trade in Japan.* Japan Tariff Association, Tokyo 1995, No. 3., 1996.

Moscow-Beijing: increasing cooperation and rapprochement

The "search for new allies in the East" is thus not limited to China, or even to Asia for that matter. It has become evident in recent years that Moscow is increasingly attempting, if with little success, to reactivate her ties with former Soviet allies. Examples of this policy are steps towards renewed engagements with Iraq, Libya and

North Korea.(21) For geographical as well as geopolitical reasons, however, China has a key role to play.

Border agreements
And indeed, since 1992 there has been a continuous improvement in relations between Moscow and Beijing, supported by a constant stream of high-ranking delegations. They are now less conflict-ridden than ever before in their history. A major dispute was settled in 1991, while Gorbachev was still in power, with the signing of an agreement concerning Russia's more than 4,000-kilometer-long eastern border with China. The demarcation process, which began on the basis of this agreement in 1992, is now almost complete. Yet to be regulated is the dispute over ownership of three islands,(22) and there are still problems over the demarcation of several kilometers in the Maritime province. In addition, agreement was reached in September 1994 on the fifty-six-kilometer-long western part of the Russian-Chinese border. The defusing of the border conflict was also reflected in an agreement signed on 26 April in Shanghai by the presidents of China, Russia, Kazakhstan, Kyrgyzstan and Tajikistan on confidence-building measures on their common borders.

Economic cooperation
The most dynamic development in bilateral relations in the past few years has been in the sphere of economic cooperation. In 1993 China moved for awhile into second place behind Germany as Russia's most important foreign trading partner. That year's record trading level of 7.68 billion US dollars(23) has not been equaled since then, however. In 1994 foreign trade turnover fell by almost 50 percent to 5.1 billion dollars, but in 1995 rose again by around 7 percent to 5.46 billion dollars with a Russian trade surplus of 1.9 billion dollars.(24) The decline can be attributed mainly to a drop in border trade for which stricter border controls and Russian dissatisfaction with the quality of Chinese goods are chiefly responsible. While China's share of Russian foreign trade is still small (4 per cent) due to structural composition, its significance is actually greater than this figure would suggest. The proportion of non-raw-material goods in Russian exports to China is well over the average - in 1995 it comprised 35.4 percent while this category of goods comprises only 1 percent of exports to Japan.(25) And both sides are hoping to further expand economic relations in foreign trade and mutual investment. The catalogue of possibilities for

cooperation presented by Yeltsin during his recent visit to China is an important indicator of the expectations of the two countries: the modernizing of industrial capacities formerly built with Soviet aid, Russian participation in the build-up of the Chinese nuclear energy complex and the "The Three Gorges Reservoir Project on the Yangtze River". Both sides declared their hope that mutual trade will be expanded to 20 billion US $.

Table 2   Chinese-Russian Trade (Million US $)

1992			1993		
Import	Export	Total	Import	Export	Total
3,526.1	2,336.3	5,862,4	4,987,4	2,691.8	7,679.3

1994			1995		
Import	Export	Total	Import	Export	Total
3,495.8	1,581.1	5,076.9	3,798.6	1,664.7	5,463.3

Source: For 1992 and 1993: DIW Data files *China's Customs Statistics*, Beijing and Hong Kong 1991-1994. For 1994 and 1995: Haiguan Tongji/*China Monthly Exports and Imports*, Nr. 12 (1994), p. 5 and Nr. 12 (1995), p. 3.

Security cooperation
Security cooperation, too, has also become considerably more intensive in recent years and a series of confidence-building measures have been agreed upon. In September 1994 during a visit to Moscow by Jiang Zemin the two sides agreed to cancel the target programming of nuclear missiles. They also undertook to refrain from first use of nuclear weapons against each other. In addition, on 12 May 1994 the two countries' foreign ministers signed an agreement on "preventing military incidents". The Shanghai Agreement of 26 April 1996 concerning confidence-building measures on China's borders with the post-Soviet states should also be mentioned here. This agreement was described by the Russians as a "non-aggression pact". It concerns a 100-kilometer-wide strip of land on both sides of the border and commits its signatories, albeit only with regard to the troops stationed in this area, to mutually refrain from aggression, to limit military maneuvers and to inform the other signatories about large-scale military activities. In addition, it

foresees an increase in friendly contacts between the border troops and border guards of the states concerned.(26)

Although the Shanghai treaty was described as an "historic" agreement, the fact should not be overlooked that there are as yet irreconcilable differences with regard to the 1993 agreement regulating the withdrawal of troops from this 200-kilometer zone. For geographical reasons Moscow regards the deployment of troops outside the 100-kilometer-zone as impossible. "The withdrawal of troops...is rather complicated for us", Defense Minister Grachev declared, "since in many areas this zone goes beyond the railway, practically into districts where there is neither housing nor the possibility of building them".(27) It is unlikely that the problem will be resolved in the near future, since even now both the military and politicians in the Russian Far East regard the present border protection arrangements as inadequate. But it seems that a compromise has been worked out because a binding treaty should be signed during Jiang Zemin's visit in spring 1997.

Cooperation in the armaments sector has become an important factor in bilateral relations. Figures on the extent of such cooperation differ since the Russian side has become more reserved about providing information on such matters. China is supposedly planning purchases to the tune of 5 billion US dollars for the near future. So far Russian sales have included "SU-27" fighter planes, the latest class of T-80 tanks and several kilo-class submarines, not to mention extensive deliveries of munitions and other items of military equipment. In addition, according to some reports Russia is to train a large number of Chinese pilots, and an unknown number of Russian scientists, up to 1,000 according to some Western estimates, and is working on the modernization of weapons systems in China. In this case these scientists may have been recruited directly by the Chinese without reference to Moscow. In addition, there are discussions about the license production of the most modern Russian weapons systems, in particular the "SU-27". According to the commander of the Air Force, General Deneikin, Moscow no longer hesitated and signed an agreement in December 1995 with Beijing on this matter. His statement was, however, followed by an immediate denial from unnamed representatives of the Defense Ministry who claimed that negotiations were still in progress.(28) Moscow is said to have made the sale of at least fifty "SU-27s" a precondition for her agreement to license production. Here too, reports about whether this number of orders has already been received are contradictory. Recent reports, however, have confirmed that a contract was finally signed at the end of 1997.(29)

United against hegemony and interference from abroad
The increased cooperation during the past three years has been accompanied by a reconciliation of opinions regarding various aspects of domestic and foreign policy. In the economic sphere it is now no longer South Korea or Taiwan that provides the model for Russia but China. The preservation of the unity of a multi-ethnic state is a key problem for both countries. Russian support for Beijing's "one-China policy" is reciprocated by Chinese understanding for Moscow's actions in Chechnya. Both Moscow and Beijing regard "Islamic fundamentalism" as a threat not only to their own internal stability but also to the stability of Central Asia.

Moreover, the two sides are unanimous in their rejection of Western interference and aspirations to hegemony and view themselves as a necessary counterweight to the West in the international arena. It was with this in mind that Russian Prime Minister Viktor Chernomyrdin and his Chinese counterpart Li Peng vehemently rejected interference of any kind at a press conference in Moscow in June 1995.(30) And it was Moscow's vote that in the same year prevented the condemnation of China by the UN human rights conference. During Yeltsin's visit to China the two sides went one step further. Yeltsin and the Chinese president, Jiang Zemin declared for the first time understanding and support for Moscow's stance on NATO's planned eastward expansion.(31) In addition, both sides stated in the "joint declaration" their resolve to develop further their already existing "constructive partnership" to form a "strategic partnership".(32) They observed that "hegemonism, power politics and the repeated imposition of pressure on other countries have continued to occur. Bloc politics has taken on new manifestations". For this reason "the two countries wish to join the rest of the world in a concerted effort to win lasting and stable peace".(33)

China: A "unique partner" or a "unique danger"?
In reality, however, the development of relations between Moscow and Beijing is more problematic than their statements might lead one to believe. The scope of these problems do not simply concern isolated issues of economic, political and military cooperation but encompasses Russia's fear of the "Chinese threat", a view that China is more of a new adversary than a new ally.(34)

Although in the past Russia was able to compensate for feelings of inferiority *vis-à-vis* the West with feelings of superiority *vis-à-vis* the East, she is now facing a different situation altogether.

The demise of the USSR and the rise of China have led to a "change in status".(35) Russia's superiority has disappeared. "For the first time in 400 years",•Deputy Prime Minister Sergei Shakhrai, complained, "China has overtaken Russia in the pace of economic development".(36) The China expert Vladimir Myasnikov even predicted a situation in which a "poor Russia" would be facing a "rich China". He continued, "Few people in Russia fully realize how serious this new Chinese challenge is. Here we have in embryo a potential historical rivalry between the two countries for the right to have a decisive say in world and regional affairs". And he concluded, "there are many arguments that China has better chances in this rivalry".(37) There are differing conclusions from this analysis, however.

The ultra-communist forces see no problems for Russia with this state of affairs. They conclude that China, as the last bastion of socialism, must play the leading role in the anti-Western alliance and Russia that of a "younger brother".(38) It is perhaps an irony of history that this position is today adhered to by the very forces who, during the Soviet era, were the most passionate in warning of the "Chinese threat".

The advocates of a policy that envisions a special role for the relations between Moscow and Beijing in the American-Chinese-Russian triangle likewise deny, at least in their official statements, that China constitutes a threat. "The national and state interests of Russia and China do not run counter to one another. This is underlined by historic ties stretching back almost four hundred years".(39) This terse statement was made by the very same Vladimir Myasnikov who two years earlier had warned of a "historic rivalry" between the two countries. However, in view of deteriorating relations with the West, fear of China is obviously giving way to what Myasnikov calls a "Russian-Chinese duet".(40)

By contrast, there are those for whom China constitutes a danger to the traditional rivalry between the two powers resulting from the geopolitical situation and from deeply ingrained historical and psychological currents. At the same time, they perceive the threat to Russia's security and territorial integrity as coming not only, and in some cases not even primarily, from the West (or in Asia from Japan and the USA). In their view China, even today, has yet not reconciled herself to the "unjust territorial treaties" of the past and is seeking revenge. As a result of the "change in status" in favor of China and the accompanying decline of the Russian Far East and Siberia, China is seen as having for the first time the opportunity to achieve these goals. Although some Russian analysts attest to a cautious and restrained attitude on the part of the Chinese leadership, others already speak of the existence of an active policy aimed at achieving a geopolitical expansion. In the view of the latter, China, while forgoing the use of military means, is resorting to peaceful methods of expansion (trade, investment, immigration). Such a strategy carries less risk but could ultimately produce the same effect as a military expansion.(41) The great fear here is that China's growing economic potential could lead to Russia's coming under increasing pressure and that the Russian Far East could become a Chinese raw materials colony. Some authors do not rule out the future loss of Siberia and the Far East.(42)

Today the main focus of anxiety, however, is the problem of illegal Chinese immigration to Russia, which is perceived as the beginning of a "peaceful conquest". According to various reports in the Russian media, more than 2 million Chinese - the reformist politician Yavlinsky even gives a figure of 5 million - have infiltrated into Russia, settled there and are occupying Russian territory. Whereas some sources see this as a spontaneous process, other "well-informed sources" in the Russian Far East believe that this immigration is part of a deliberate campaign by Beijing to "resettle surplus population from the Chinese Northeast to the Russian Far East".(43)

How much truth there is in such reports is difficult to say.(44) Certainly, there is, objectively speaking, a "demographic problem," since the densely populated north-eastern region of China borders on the very sparsely populated Russian Far East. It may also be assumed to be true that an unknown number of Chinese are illegally staying in Russia. Their motives differ, however. Some of them are involved in trading activities, others want to use Russia as a stepping-stone to the West. Others still want to settle permanently in Russia. No-one knows what the exact numbers are, but everything would indicate that the figures quoted are highly exaggerated. Following the opening of the borders after 1992, a large number of traders apparently slipped through onto the Russian side of the border. However, the situation changed with the introduction of new visa regulations at the beginning of 1994.

Whatever the case, the fact remains that historic fears of Chinese immigration lend themselves particularly well to mobilization for internal political purposes.

Chinese immigration has provoked a particularly sharp response in the Russian Far East. The governor of the Maritime province, Evgenii Nazdratenko, who, in 1992 as a member of the Supreme Soviet voted in favor of the ratification of this treaty, has been resisting the implementation of the provision of the Russian-Chinese border treaty of 1991 and has done everything possible to undermine attempts to hand over 1,500 hectares of unpopulated territory to China. Nor is Nazdratenko the only one to criticize Moscow's policy. Only a few weeks ago the governments of all the Russian regions bordering on China declared jointly that the territorial integrity of Russia was threatened by China and called for a strengthening of the defensive capability of army units.(45)

But how should the question of a Chinese threat be handled? While the (Atlanticists) response to the situation is to give priority to cooperation with the West, a faction of the advocates of a geopolitical approach call for maintaining an equilibrium in relations with both West and East. They would welcome the integration of China into international security structures in order to defuse the "Chinese threat". And they see Russia as engaging in a balancing act between the USA and China, but not as a "counterweight" to the USA. When it comes to concrete political issues, it is not always possible to distinguish clearly this position from that of those who advocate giving priority to relations with China. In general, however, a more critical attitude towards Beijing and particularly towards Russian-Chinese military cooperation are to be expected.

Is there a threat of a Russian-Chinese alliance against the West?

For the moment, however, owing to persistent contractions about NATO-expansion advocates of a "strategic partnership" if not an "alliance" with China and other countries of the East are gaining ground, although their proposals have proven to be poorly formulated. Their proposal for a Chinese-Indian-Russian alliance, for example, is unrealistic since New Delhi will not be prepared to join forces with Moscow against the USA, let alone do so in an alliance with China. These two "Asian giants" (as Primakov called them) with their conflicting great power aspirations are simply too much at odds with one another for this to happen.

It will even prove difficult to normalize relations with the one-time Soviet ally North Korea. Pyongyang currently regards an improvement in the relations with the USA as her only chance of survival. Russia is neither politically nor economically in a position to offer a viable alternative. Thus, the only new alliance in the East worthy of serious consideration is that with China.

Although Kissinger has predicted a new Russian-Chinese alliance for the beginning of the next century and assessed the "non-aggression pact" of Shanghai as "a deliberate effort by both China and Russia to reduce America's options in Asia",(46) such a development seems improbable despite the current rapprochement between Beijing and Moscow. For good reasons Russian observers, too, have their doubts about the usefulness of such an alliance.(47) It would, after all, not only damage relations with the West but also those with other countries in the Asian-Pacific region. Russia would thus be cut off from urgently needed sources of capital and technology with negative consequences for her further economic and social development.

An alliance with China would also be in contradiction to Russian aspirations to expand cooperation with India. The losses thus incurred could not be compensated for, despite growing cooperation with China. Moreover, China herself at present rejects on principle any thought of a military-political alliance with Russia, since it is greatly dependent on economic contacts with the West for the implementation of its modernization program. And Russia does not present a real alternative to these.

Other points of conflict may be added as well. Despite all declarations to the contrary, China at present has no interest in restoring Russia's status of a competitor in the Asian-Pacific region. Besides, there are the contradicting claims to influence in Central Asia and differing positions on banning nuclear testing. And even the problems on the Russian-Chinese border, particularly that of Chinese immigration to Russia, cannot be regarded as solved. The present low level of conflict between the two countries, as Robert Scalapino put it, has its roots not in the disappearance of conflict but in the fact that both countries are primarily concerned with their internal problems.(48)

Nevertheless, an intensification of the Sino-American conflict and a further deterioration in Russia's relations with the West, for example, in the course of NATO's planned eastward enlargement, could result in a further rapprochement between Moscow and Beijing at a level below that of a formal alliance. And even under conditions of a new rapprochement with the West, the Asian dimension in general and China in particular will remain a long-term priority for Russia. But whether elements of cooperation or confrontation will dominate depends largely on the outcome of Russia's internal developments. The consequences will not only felt in Asia but in the West too.

* Dr. Klaus Fritsche is senior resercher on Russia's relations with Asia, Bochum, Germany.

Notes

1. *Izvestiya*, 6.3.1996, p. 3.
2. See more extensively Klaus Fritsche: "Rußlands Außenpolitik: Die asiatisch-pazifische Dimension", in: *Berichte des BIOst*, Nr. 40 (1995).
3. See Evgenyj Bazhanov: "Russia and Taiwan", in: *Berichte des BIOst*, Köln, 1996, forthcoming.
4. MID Rossiiskoi Federacii: "Kontsepciya vneshnej politiki Rossiiskoj Federacii" (The Russian Federation's foreign policy concept), in: *Diplomaticheskii vestnik*, Special Issue, January 1993, p. 16.
5. ITAR-TASS, 18.11.1992, in: *DW Monitor-Dienst*, 19.11.1992, p. 1.
6. While a part of the "Eurasianists" underline Russia's role as a bridge linking Europe and Asia, others draw the conclusion that the restoration of the USSR is necessary.
7. See Andrej Kortunov/Sergej Kortunov: From "moralism" to "pragmatics": New dimensions of Russian foreign policy, in: *Comparative Strategy*, 1994, No. 3, S. 275. This reorientation could be observed in Western political thinking too. Nearly the same arguments were put forward by Wallace J. Thies: Rethinking the new world order, in: Orbis, Fall 1994, S. 621-634.
8. See the discussion about the Russian military doctrine in Mary E. Glantz: The origins and development of Soviet and Russian military doctrine, in: *The Journal of Slavic Military Studies*, Vol. 7; No. 3 (September 1994), S. 443-480.
9. See "Russia may boost atomic deterrent", in: *The Japan Times*, 14.3.1996, p. 4. "An organization affiliated with Russia's Defense Ministry in late February came up with a report calling for a stronger nuclear deterrent against Japan and North Atlantic Treaty Organization members".

10. Titarenko: "Severo-vostochnaya Aziya posle 'kholodnoj voiny' i interesy Rossii" (Northeast Asia after the "cold war" and Russian interests), in: *Problemy Dal'nego Vostoka*, 5/1994, p. 21.

11. See the description of the different lines of thinking among others in: Aleksei Voskresenskii: "Rossiya-Kitaj: al'ternativy razvitii otnoshenii net" (Russia-China: There is no alternative for developing relations), in: *Segodnya*, 12.4.1996, p. 9; Vladimir Shlapentokh: "Russia, China, and the Far East: Old geopolitics or a new peaceful cooperation?", in: *Communist and Post-Communist Studies*, Jg. 28 Nr. 3 (1995), pp. 307-318; and Klaus Fritsche: "Rußlands Außenpolitik: Die asiatisch-pazifische Dimension", in: *Berichte des BIOst*, Nr. 40 (1995), pp. 20-24.

12. "Russian communists favor cooperation with China", in: *Interfax*, 7.6.1995, as quoted in SWB SU/2325 B/7, 9.6.1995.

13. Alexander Yakovlev: "Strategicheskie problemy vneshnej politiki Rossii, Kitaya i Indii v kontekste tendencii sovremennogo mirovogo razvitiya" (Strategic problems of the foreign policy of Russia, China and India in the context of contemporary world development), in: *Kommunist*, Nr. 1 (1996), p. 110.

14. See ITAR-TASS, 27.3.1996, as quoted in SWB SU/2573 B/9-10, 29.3.1996.

15. Pavel Fel'gengauer: "Rossiya i konflikt v Taivans'kom prolive. Moskva-Pekin - novoe strategicheskoe partnerstvo" (Russia and the conflict around the Gulf of Taiwan. Moscow - Beijing: new strategic partnership), in: *Segodnya*, 13.3.1996, p. 5.

16. In this context it is of special interest, that on February 29, 1996, "China, Russia, India and Iran decided to establish a foundation for nuclear study' (Napsnet Daily Report, 8.3.1996).

17. *Izvestiya*, 6.3.1996, p. 3.

18. Evgenii Primakov: "75 let vneshnej razvedki Rossii' (75 years of Russia's foreign intelligence), December 1995, Manuscript, p. 10.

19. This idea was already formulated by Boris Jeltsin during his visit to New Delhi in the beginning of 1993. See also Vladimiar Abarinov: "Moskva nadeetsja naladit' 'treugol'noe sotrudnichestvo' s Deli i Pekinom" (Moscow hopes to develop "triangular cooperation" with Delhi and Beijing), in: *Segodnja*, 5.4.1996, p. 5. The idea is not very realistic, due to the competition between India and China.

20. Cf. "Japan and Russia agree to strengthen security dialogue", in: *Kyodo News Service*, 29.4.1996, as quoted in SWB FE/2599 E/1, 30.4.1996.

21. Cf. Klaus Fritsche: "Neue Annäherung Moskaus an Pjöngjang? Rußland und die koreanische Halbinsel", in: *Berichte des BIOst*, Nr. 13 (1996); Klaus Fritsche (Hrsg.): "Rußland und die Dritte Welt", Baden-Baden, 1996.

22. Contested have been three islands in the Argun River and in the Ussuri/Heilongjiang (Amur) near Khabarovsk, which are seen by Moscow as strategically important.

23. Based on Chinese figures.

24. *Xinhua*, 25.2.1996, as quoted in DW Monitor-Dienst Osteuropa, 28.2.1996, p. 3.

25. Calculation based on "Vneshnaya Torgovlya Rossiiskoj Federatsii" (Foreign Trade of the Russian Federation), Moskau 1993.

26. "Five-Nation Border Agreement signed in Shanghai", in: *Xinhua*, 26.4.1996, as quoted in SWB FE/2597 G/1, 27.4.1996.

27. "Russian defense minister wants compromise with China over border troops", in: RIA News Agency, 23.4.1996, as quoted in SWB SU/2595 B/16, 25.4.1996.

28. Vladimir Abarinov: "Kitaj poluchil rossiiskie istrebiteli" (China received Russian fighters), in: *Segodnya*, 14.2.1996, p. 3.

29. See Interfax, 17.12.96, zit.n. SWB SU/2799 (19.12.96), S1/5.

30. Source

31. Xinhua "reported Jiang Zemin as saying China understood and supported Russia's stand on opposing NATO's eastward expansion". ("Chinese and Russian president hold talks in Beijing", in: *Xinhua*, 25.4.1996, as quoted in SWB FE/2596 G/2, 26.4.1996).

32. "The two sides hereby announce their resolve to develop a strategic partnership of equality, mutual confidence and mutual coordination towards the 21st century". (Full text of the communiqué in: *Xinhua*, 25.4.1996, as quoted in SWB SU/2596 B/1-3, 26.4.1996).

33. ibid.

34. This question was asked by Aleksei Voskresenskii: "Kitaj: soyuznik ili novyj protivnik?" (China: Ally or new adversary?), in: *Segodnya*, 30.9.1995, p. 6.

35. Cf. Aleksei Voskresenskii: "Smena statusa" (Change of status), in: *Nezavisimaya gazeta*, 27.5.1994, p. 5.

36. Serge Shachrai: "Neobchodima strategiya otnoshenii s Ki-taem" (Developing a strategy for relations with China is necessary), in: *Izvestiya*, 20.5.1994, p. 4.
37. Vladimir S. Miasnikov (1994): The new historical competition between Russia and China. Paper presented to the E.A.C.S. Conference, 28 August-1 September 1994. Prague, 1994, p. 7, p. 28.
38. Alexander Yakovlev: "Rossiya i Kitaj: Sostoyanie i perspek-tivy otnoshenii" (Russia and China: State and perspectives of relations), in: Institut Dal'nego Vostoka (Hrsg.): "Kitaj v mi-rovoj i regional'noi politike" (China in world and regional politics), Moskau 1995, p. 47.
39. Vladimir Myasnikov: "Vtoroe 'khozhdenie' presidenta v Kitai" (Second visit of the president to China), in: *Segodnya*, 18.4.1996, p. 5.
40. ibid.
41. Sorokin: "Rossiya i igra geopoliticheskich interesov v areale velikogo okeana" (Russia and the game of geopolitical inter-ests in the Pacific region), in: *Polis*. Moskau. (1994)4, p. 20f.
42. ibid., p. 23.
43. Viktor Larin: "Yellow peril again? The Chinese and the Russian Far East", in: Stephen Kotkin/David Wolff: *Redis-covering Russia in Asia*. Armonk, NY, 1995, p. 290-301 (p. 298).
44. See Klaus Fritsche: "Das Gespenst der chineischen Kolonisa-tion des russischen Fernen Osten", in: Aktuelle Analysen des BIOst, Nr. 37(1995).
45. Oleg Kryuchek: "Yurii Baturin isuchaet sostoyanie del na rossiisko-kitaiskoj granitse" (Yurij Baturin studied the situa-tion at the Russian-Chinese border), in: *Segodnya*, 30.1.1996, p. 3.
46. Henry Kissinger: "Foreign policy is more than social engineer-ing", in: *International Herald Tribune*, 13.5.1996, p. 9.
47. Vladimir Abarinov: "Vygody soyuza s Kitaem somnitel'ny" (Benefits of an alliance with China are doubtful) , in: *Segod-nya*, 13.3.1996, p. 5.
48. Scalapino, as quoted in R. Legvold: "Russia and the strategic quadrangle", in: M. Mandelbaum (Ed.):*The strategic quadran-gle. Russia, China, Japan and the United States in East Asia*, New York 1995, p. 51.

Chapter 5

Manfred Pohl: "Korea: The Case for a Gradual Unification"

Everyone knows that as a state as well as a former model of self-reliant development North Korea is already doomed. Any direct confrontation with South Korean economic and political challenges would inevitably result in a sudden collapse and demise of both North Korea's political and social systems - the economy obviously already is in agony, the people are starving.(1) The latter facts can be seen by those who have visited the country. The author had the opportunity to visit North Korea in 1989 as a member of a German business delegation, and even then the general impression of daily life was rather depressing although the food situation was much better than today. Also, the author had various opportunities to talk to North Korean functionaries since the Democratic People's Republic of Korea (DPRK) has kept open her former embassy in the now defunct GDR, East Berlin. It has been transformed into the Bureau for the Protection of the Interests of the DPRK under the umbrella of the embassy of the People's Republic of China, while Germany has a representative in Pyongyang operating under the protective power of the embassy of Sweden. Members of the North Korean bureau visit rather regularly the Hamburg Institute of Asian Affairs which is loosely connected with the German Foreign Ministry (and of which the author is a fellow) to have informal talks, mostly on economic relations; the last high-ranking visitor in March 1997 has been the deputy foreign minister of the DPRK.

The North Korean leadership, at least Kim Ilsong and his clan seem to be living in a pipe dream. Ordinary people are mostly cut off from outside information, even if they do own a radio or a TV set. Party cadres, the military and party technocrats, and the elite are well informed about what is going on in the world; they have access to Japanese broadcasts, German magazines and American papers although sometimes the elite seemingly is unable to put the information into proper perspective. Those of the North Korean elite, who do have contacts with the outside world, appear to be quite polished. The author has spoken to North Korean diplomats and economists on a regular basis since Germany "inherited" the former North Korean embassy after the unification. While representatives of the North Korean government pay lip service (and quite convincingly so) to the "great and beloved leader, comrade Kim Ilsong" or the "dear leader, comrade Kim Jongil" and their "juche" utopia, they openly admit to the many difficulties the DPRK is facing right now.

After the collapse of the East European form of socialism, in particular the Soviet type, and the open-door policy of the Chinese neighbor, North Korea was left out in the cold. Suddenly, the heavily protected North Korean economy was partly exposed to the rules of international trade, such as hard currency transfers and demands for a minimum of quality standards. Representatives of German companies operating in the DPRK testify that North Korean partners are quite willing to adjust and produce, for example, fairly high-quality textiles. Encouraged by these very limited successes and obviously impressed by extremely good results of the Chinese "Special Economic Zones (SEZ)" North Korea now aims at establishing a SEZ of her own in the delta of the Tumen River near the borders to Russia and China at Rajin and Sonbong. The plan has received very favorable responses internationally. In September 1996 investment deals with North Korea in the planned SEZ reached 282 million US $. Among the deals were a five-star hotel, a motorcycle plant, prefabricated housing, improvement of telecommunication systems and the like. Investors came from Hong Kong, China, Thailand, and there were various overseas Korean groups.(2)

Irrational nuclear adventurism and starving people? Pressure will not work

How then was it possible that the DPRK leadership triggered off an international upheaval concerning its alleged nuclear armament program? North Koreans in Germany have a ready explanation: It was the Americans who used photographs taken from spy satellites to (falsely) accuse North Korea of producing plutonium and launching a military program to build a bomb. In talks with the author the North Koreans used four highly contradictory arguments:

- The DPRK never had the intention to build a bomb, but then the South Koreans are already working on a military nuclear program and have done so since the mid-seventies.
- Japan has "all parts" for a bomb. In this argument they used British information, which has been disclosed by, among others, the *South China Morning Post* of Hong Kong.(3)
- The IAEO is merely a willing tool of the US; the DPRK would never bow to the demands for special inspections of its nuclear research facilities, since those demands "originated in Washington and not in Vienna".

In the past the nuclear question has been made far too much a focal point by South Korea, the US on the one hand and Japan on the other. Even if North Korea had been hoarding plutonium with the intention to use it for the construction of nuclear weapons, it remains highly doubtful that North Korea would have been technically able to miniaturize the plutonium load to put it in a nuclear warhead, which then could be installed on top of the (in)famous "Rodong 1" rocket, a well sold item in Middle Eastern states. After having lived right on top of a vast nuclear arsenal (and still living next door to French and British nukes), the author has always argued that instead of clobbering the North Korean leadership and thereby confirming its aggressive xenophobia a softer approach would be more appropriate. North Korea´s leadership is intensely nationalistic, which translates into anti-Americanism although the DPRK leadership has worked eagerly to gain diplomatic recognition from Washington. In an interview with the North Korean deputy foreign minister in March 1997, the diplomat stressed four points:

1. The people of the DPRK are very proud and would never give in to outside pressure.

2. President Kim Young Sam of South Korea has "insulted" the DPRK, because he did not send a message of condolence after the death of Kim Ilsong. He is therefore not a welcome dialogue partner.
3. Before any talks between South and North Korea can start, the South has to abolish the security laws.
4. With regard to the role of the US in the Northeast Pacific he said that Washington is not really interested in assisting the Koreas to unify, but would rather keep the peninsula divided and maintain troops in South Korea as a lever against China and Japan.(4)

The present food crisis has created a situation in which North Korean leaders are probably more willing than ever to seek dialogue with their arch-enemies, the US, Japan and South Korea. China will have to play the role of mediator, for the Chinese leadership holds the key for any cautious openness on the North Korean side. The South Korean government thinks that China will never allow North Korea to collapse, but would rather send substantial help if the DPRK reaches a critical point.(5) To involve China makes it easier for the North Korean leadership to sit down at the negotiation table and overcome its anxious attitude of autistic rejection of any proposal for talks. North Korean representatives, who have talked with German counterparts, have always stressed that they would never bow to outside pressure, so any offer of food aid to the North Koreans must be free from any conditions to allow the DPRK leadership to save face. It is in the best interest of South Korea to help and thereby maintain the North for the time being because a sudden collapse of the Northern system would put an enormous strain on both the social and economic structure of South Korea.(6)

South Korean president Kim Young Sam has only limited options in his approach to the North Koreans. On the one hand Pyongyang has hitherto refused to talk to her Southern neighbor on the other hand the USA has taken the initiative to a degree which sometimes gave the impression that South Korea was pointedly left out of the dialogue with the North, especially during the Geneva talks. To breathe life into and to intensify intra-Korean dialogue would mean that South Korea gets the chance to act more independently; this however would imply that South Korea has some "carrots" to dangle before the North Koreans, and that Kim Jongil and his power elite is actually prepared to enter direct talks with the South. Any offer of substantial help to the North and more flexibility of the South Korean leadership to allow South Korean companies to freely enter business relations with North Korean partners would lead to a more relaxed attitude on the North Korean side. However, South Korea's president has shown a hard-line attitude towards economic relations with the North. Recently, South Korean companies were blocked from attending a seminar on direct investment in the North Korean SEZ at the Tumen River. South Korean students who have advocated more contacts with North Korea are still treated as criminals.(7)

In the "carrot-and-stick" approach the US provides some carrots. For instance, a diplomatic face-lift in the form of a permanent representative office of the US in Pyongyang would be very attractive to the DPRK. South Korea could offer more than food aid. Economic aid could be camouflaged as "trade under preferential conditions" since it could be very risky for the North Korean leadership to admit to its people that economic aid is necessary. For the time being a policy of boycott *vis-à-vis* North Korea will not work for two reasons. To begin with, a country like the DPRK, whose people are already used to starving and whose economy has run on continuously shrinking capacity and rapidly declining efficiency, cannot be effectively hit by economic sanctions. Secondly, many other boycott measures in recent history (for example in the former Yugoslavia), have never work effectively. In the case of North Korea China would certainly sabotage boycott measures for "old times sake".

German unification: not a model, but still a few lessons to learn

The first and foremost lesson Koreans can learn from the German unification is how not to do it. Unification in Germany has not been a planned and orchestrated process, but a historic development which was marked from the beginning by a dynamism of its own. A corrupt power elite in the GDR, totally isolated from both the people and economic reality, presided over a state which was already bankrupt long before the actual collapse in 1989/90. This system was finally toppled by a mass movement which quickly moved from the slogan "we are the people!" to the slogan "we are one people!" demanding national unification. It has been said many times that German unification was the result of a sudden collapse "in heap" of the German Democratic Republic (GDR). However, this is a misleading perception. The demise of the GDR only placed a period to a very long sentence which started with the

"Ostpolitik" of Chancellor Willy Brandt. On various levels of various political, social and economic organizations of West Germany contacts with GDR mass organizations and individual politicians in the East were established. The GDR leadership undoubtedly was convinced that it was merely "using useful idiots" to further its cause, but the fact was that the GDR was embraced - and then smothered by this embrace.

Thus the events of 1989/90 only marked the peak of a development which had begun with the West German "Ostpolitik", a concept nowadays echoed by South Korea's "Nordpolitik". The patient West German approach to intensify relations with the GDR is probably the only lesson which could be learned by the South Korean leadership. Former West Germany paid a high political price for improved contacts with the East: The GDR was recognized as an independent state (the so-called "Hallstein doctrine" was abandoned), and the GDR was allowed to gain an international reputation as a democratic socialist state. To many observers (for example in Japan) the GDR even appeared to be the "better Germany". West Germany, however, stuck to one important principle and insisted *vis-à-vis* the EU that intra-German trade was not international trade but domestic trade.

A gradual process of Korean unification therefore is highly desirable. In fact, it is the only way to unification on the Korean peninsula, yet the author is not at all sure that it can be easily achieved. The German example has clearly shown that events may gain a dynamism of their own, propelling the actors forward without them being able to control the process. There are strong indicators, however, that both the North Korean leadership (at least the so-called "technocrats") and the South Korean top decision makers are working hard for a "gradual solution". The question remains whether the North Korean leadership is still able to act freely. The recent defection of chief ideological thinker and member of the Central Committee of the Korean Worker's Party, Hwang Jang-yop, has been regarded in China as a sign that an intense power struggle is going on in North Korea. The uncomfortable relation between the military and the civilian technocrats could be concluded from the fact that the generals and civilian leaders paid their last respects separately to the late Kim Ilsong on 15 August 1996.(8)

In addition to the international organizations and individual neighboring states the US and European countries (especially Germany) have supported these efforts. Apart from the totally erratic and irresponsible attitude of North Korea regarding the nuclear question at the beginning, there are indications that North Korea is indeed trying to follow the "gradual model" of unification as she has insisted she would for a long time:

- After long, tedious efforts communication channels between the governments in South and North Korea have been set up. The present desperate food situation in the North certainly has helped in this respect although North Korea is still quite un-willing to talk. Thus the "talks" between the two Koreas are far from the intensity of interactions between the two Germanies long before unification. However, it is a beginning.
- Talks between high-ranking American and North Korean offi-cials have been held in Beijing as well as in Pyongyang and the US. According to unconfirmed reports the US government might be prepared to open diplomatic relations with North Korea if the government in Pyongyang agrees to fully cooperate in the nu-clear question and takes a more flexible attitude *vis-à-vis* the South. Any move in the direction of diplomatic ties must of course have Seoul's blessing.
- As was the case in Germany, the core of a gradual unification process is always business activities. Business men obviously find it easier to talk profits rather than politics and thereby foster channels of communication and relaxation of tensions.

The German unification model might be called an "absorption model" based on unique (and never to be repeated) historical cir-cumstances. Also it should be remembered that the former GDR never has been a sovereign state, the Soviet Union had the last word on political decisions. It was only after Moscow had decided not to interfere with the move towards unification that the GDR regime broke down - and unification happened. In the case of North Korea there is no such "big brother", not even China is in a position to influence Pyongyang. In the German case one part of a divided nation, the richer and more successful one, absorbed the other part; in effect German unification was paid for solely by West Germany, and the financial burden of unification costs will weigh heavily on the country for many years to come and will certainly have a major impact on Germany's ability to comply with the "Maastricht conditions" of the European monetary union.

Korea could very well avoid such pressures by using the strong elements of common North and South cultural, historical and ethnic heritage; here the Korean nation has a much better starting point than the Germans: While Germany only became a nation state in the late 19th century by unifying rather reluctant feudal states under Prussian predominance, Korea has been a national entity for many centuries. There are two very different scenarios concerning a very rapid, uncontrolled unification through a collapse of the North: Critical observers predict that there will be millions of people on the move towards the South once the Northern regime has broken down. Others say that the South Korean government will manage to control mass migration and disorder. But how? A chilling answer: By sending in the army and seal the border between North and South. Now this would certainly endanger all achievements of democratic developments during both the Roh Tae Woo and the Kim Young Sam presidency - is it really worth the price? There is no practical alternative to gradual unification in Korea.

Laying the groundwork for unification - prerequisites in the South
After President Kim Young Sam took office in 1993, he faced a few very tough problems; the successful solution of all or most of these problems is a precondition for managing any imaginable form of unification process. The fact that South Korea has not yet fully overcome its basically authoritarian structure might turn out to be a blessing in disguise since it would facilitate bringing the Northern and Southern systems together. Any form of unification process will have to pass through a transitory period of strong authoritarian centralism. The South Korean government, namely, the president will have to work on these problems to lay the groundwork for unification:

1. Inching closer to the totally incalculable North Korea to woo the hostile neighbor to closer cooperation, without loudly clamoring for an early unification (under South Korean conditions), although this remains the top priority on South Korea's political agenda. Recent aggressive acts by the North (for example, the intrusion of a spy-submarine into the South's territorial waters) have made the South Korean government more cautious but has not changed the agenda.
2. A continuous drive for domestic political reforms, above all relentless efforts to wipe out the rampant corruption both in the civil service and in the military; the recent·arrest of president Kim's son for alleged corruption has been a depressing set-back,

but also underlined that the president is prepared to act against a member of his own family, which is a major signal in a predominant Confucian society.

3. Reorganization of the traditional power structure in order to fight vested interests. Creation of a sound organizational base for himself will enable President Kim to lay the groundwork for his successor, who he will certainly select himself to ensure that he will be elected by the people. One of the most important measures Kim will have to take is to transform the ruling New Korea Party into a smoothly operating political organization by overcoming the latent factionalism.

4. Coming to terms with the "coup-like beginnings" of the recent historical development, an heirloom which President Kim Young Sam had to accept, however reluctantly, from his predecessor Roh Tae Woo. Kim however managed to successfully distance himself from his two predecessors by allowing them to be prosecuted for high treason and bribery. The trials against Roh and Chun were certainly revolutionary events.

5. Overcome unfair income distribution, particularly through revitalizing the huge, small and medium enterprise sector and slimming the mammoth "*chaebol*" groups. President Kim does not have a choice but to gradually open up the domestic markets, since the country has now become a member in the illustrious club of OECD. That protectionist politics are still very much at work is probably the single most disadvantageous or even disastrous "fallout" of following the Japanese model of development strategies. Finally, there is the vast sector of the underground economy of an estimated 35 trillion Won, which must be cleared up.

6. Finally, one of the most difficult problems of Korean political culture as a whole is regionalism as a basis for the distribution of power within the institutional framework of the (South) Korean administration. A rapid unification would enormously add to the still lingering resentment between, for example, South Westerners (Cholla province) and North Easterners (Kyongsang province). For the last thirty years South Korea has been ruled by military men and/or politicians hailing mostly from the North or Northeast of South Korea, and a unified peninsula would greatly increase the weight of the Northern regions (which have also in earlier centuries always dominated the rest of the country).

Riding a wave of generally favorable public opinion, President Kim Young Sam was able to challenge even the most formidable adversary, the military. Critics have accused Kim of making too much use of his popular drive against corruption and that his political reforms as a whole lacked a sound "philosophy" and therefore an operational system. The strong traditional forces which used to block any efforts for democratization, like the military cliques, the bureaucrats and the huge conglomerates (*chaebol*), are still very much represented in the political and administrative setup of Kim Young Sam.(9)

Korean unification: only a gradual process will bring success
The Korean unification process had to suffer some serious set-backs during 1993 and 1994. Only after the food situation in North Korea had become desperate, talks resumed, albeit under unfavorable conditions. The North is still rigid and inflexible when it comes to political moves to ease relations with South Korea both politically and economically. The obvious reason for this inflexibility is that the North Korean leadership has also learned its lesson from the German unification process - if a socialist regime moves too close to a successful capitalist one, the result may well be destruction through absorption. However, one forecast may well allowed: Both Koreas will find themselves in some sort of unified national "body" well within a ten year period, after all set-backs have been overcome:

- Kim Ilsong's nuclear poker play, which his son has been continuing for some time, has paid well for the North: The DPRK will get two light-water reactors, paid for by the KEDO (Korea Energy Development Organization). Meanwhile, the West will deliver 500.000 tons of crude oil per year to bridge the energy gap until both reactors start operations.
- Through negotiations with the US North Korea has been upgraded internationally although the DPRK remains a sort of paria state. This makes the DPRK even more inflexible *vis-à-vis* South Korea.
- North Korea skillfully makes use of the dormancy of South Korea's foreign policy decision-making sovereignty since the US has monopolized negotiations with North Korea during the past five to eight years.

Undoubtedly, these advantages for North Korea have been out-weighed by the recent disastrous developments of food shortage. The North is presently in a disadvantageous position and has to move away from ideologically fixed principles, for example, the ideology of "juche" or the idea of "self-propelled development". In retrospect, North Korea in 1993 and 1994 has made considerable points:

- As a result of the Geneva agreement the Kim Jongil regime has been greatly stabilized since the desperate shortage of electric power has led to a nearly complete breakdown of production. However, the stopgap measures to provide North Korea with energy have failed to keep up the food distribution system. Starvation in North Korea is partly owed to the regime's in-ability to deliver provisions from those regions which still produce grains to those areas which have suffered from the floods during the past three years.
- Calculated brinkmanship has also lent fresh news value to the "Golden Triangle" concept (a rather unfortunate label) which the North Korean leadership has put forward as an indigenous model of a "Special Economic Zone/Export Processing Zone", whereby foreign companies might establish joint ventures to make use of cheap North Korean labor and natural resources. The "Golden Triangle" is to be built near the delta of Tumen River by using the ports of Rajin and Sonbong.
- According to North Korean ideology, the idea of creating a Special Economic Zone leads to the high risk of being forced to open the country wider to the "evil influences" of anti-socialist ideas and "spiritual pollution". Even if the North Korean lead-ership might like to think that a special economic zone could be completely isolated against anti-regime ideas trickling out of the enclave and into the North Korean society, a point of no re-turn will soon be reached when the regime will no longer be able to control the clandestine influx of "subversive" ideas, namely, capitalism and its lure.

It is to be noted that both North and South Korea have worked on some sort of commonwealth model of cooperating economically (and to a certain degree also politically) during a transitory period of mutual "rapprochement". Up to 1993/94 there seemed to be no doubt that South Korea would be able to set the pace because North Korea's economy went from bad to worse year after year. The nuclear gamble obviously turned the table for some time. But with the obvious failure in feeding her people the North Korean power elite has completely lost this advantage, and at the same time has confronted South Korea with a number of new and totally unexpected problems before and after unification:

- For the time being South Korea will have to shoulder part of the burden to feed her Northern neighbor without trying to link this help to political conditions of the North. The Pyongyang leadership seems quite prepared to make the people suffer if only they do not have to admit that the "juche" ideology has failed. The present situation of dire need in the North will not cause the nomenclatura to give in.
- At the start of managing the huge task of unification ranks prominently the orderly dissolution of the organization of the Korean Worker's Party (KWP). To dissolve the lower echelons of the KWP will probably pose no great problems but will constitute a tremendous challenge to strip high-ranking functionaries and the military leadership of their privileges.

Dissolution of Northern mass organizations alone does not form the biggest obstacle; the most difficult problem is to offer an alternative. Only a gradual process of growing together will create a framework to integrate KWP cadres and members into the organizational structure of participatory democracy, Southern style in a united Korea. Political parties in the South, as well as other politically active mass organizations will have to face the task of absorbing and "re-educating" former KWP members.

Only a gradual process of unification will also make it possible to dissolve the armed forces of North Korea. A first step could be the use of the Northern model of "working soldiers", for example, to increase the number of units that do construction work and at the same time reduce the number of combat units. The North already has a vast number of "working soldiers" who have been engaged in many construction projects like the construction of the gigantic Mayday Stadium in Pyongyang or huge dam projects. A simple and quick dissolution of the North Korean people's army would create tremendous social problems since the Korean labor market (even after unification) will be unable to absorb literally millions of suddenly jobless soldiers from the North.

Unification can only work after years and years of close economic cooperation between the two parts of a divided country. This is perhaps another lesson from the German process of unification. Almost all German governments, both conservative and left-wing, have skillfully used economic interaction to promote the cause of good neighborhood and to tear down obstacles which mostly the Eastern side has erected. In a cynical sense, the West paid cash for good relations, even to the degree of bailing out political prisoners by paying ransom money which, in fact, was a fixed amount in the GDR budget.

Unified Korea: A challenge to other Asian countries?
Another lesson from the German experience is that unification should start with close economic cooperation but after unification it became obvious that the years of economic cooperation had not helped to create a competitive industrial structure in the GDR. Most companies were hopelessly outdated and would have never been able to compete internationally even after rigorous streamlining. Although Western economists and businessmen did keep a close watch on the East German economy, they were fooled by GDR propaganda. The East German economy turned out to be much more run down than expected. In fact, apart from some show-pieces of Eastern industry, most plants had to be simply dismantled. Transfer costs were (and still are) enormous. In the case of North Korea, however, there is no doubt about the catastrophic industrial (or general economic) situation. Even if South Korea, unlike Germany, manages to reduce the costs of unification, the financial burden will be so great that a unified Korea would rather become a competitor for those Asian countries which depend on cheap labor rather than challenge the other NIEs or even Japan. On the premise that South Korean conglomerates do invest in high-level industrial production, it will still take at least five to ten years to make these productions internationally competitive. Again there are problems of lack of capital. A labor force that has been trained on different (widely obsolete) machines, a lack of managerial personnel on the middle and lower level and a different work style. Of course, all these deficiencies can be overcome. That again will take time.

It is imaginable that the South Korea, unlike Germany, will take drastic measures to limit or even block free movement from the North to the South, invest in cheap labor production and exploit the North's potential of manpower and natural resources. This would result in an "interior colonization process" which would lead to increased resentment in the North and would, after all, postpone the necessity to pour money into the North.

It is highly doubtful whether South Korea would be able to raise the necessary transferable capital through increased taxes and additional levies. The tax raising potential of the South Korean government cannot compare with that of the German state. Even here the levies (like the "Solidaritätszuschlag" or solidarity tax) have met increasing opposition from the general population in the West.

Apart from the time factor, there can be no doubt that a unified Korea will quickly assert herself as one of the leading powers at least in Northeast Asia. The one common factor, or rather emotional platform between the two Koreas is a deeply rooted aversion against Japan. The government of a unified Korea would certainly be able to instrumentalize this aversion into some slogan like "let´s work hard together to beat the Japanese!" and galvanize both parts of the population into a united force of competition.

The arch-enemy Japan is not the only common denominator of Korean traditional heritage. During a unification process both Koreas could well make use of an uninterrupted cultural history, of which all Koreans are fiercely proud. Although North Korea has stopped to use Chinese characters in publications, the hangul-writing system is common to both Koreas. The North can fall back on the Chinese-trained elite while the South continues to work on reducing the use of Sino-Korean characters. Confucian values are still very much revered in both South and North Korea (cf. the fact that Kim Jongil carefully observed the traditional periods of mourning for his father). A new nationalism fueled by anti-Japanese feelings and xenophobia will help the two Koreas move closer together.

At the moment the South Korean government will have to go out of its way to help to stabilize the domestic situation in the North and aid the North's leadership in feeding its people. A sudden collapse of the North Korean system would lead to a development which would compare to the German experience. The South would have to completely finance both a run down system and the unification - a task greater than the South could shoulder. Peaceful coexistence and the medium term goal of creating a "commonwealth" between the two Koreas is the only way to a smooth unification process. Beware of the German example.

*   Prof. Dr. Manfred Pohl, Dept. of Japanese Language and Culture, University of Hamburg, Germany.

Notes

1. Toshimitsu Shigemura, "What is Happening in North Korea Today?", Foreign Press Center, Japan, June 1996; Shigemura takes a different position. He argues that in 1996 through international help and partly through domestic production the supply gap of grain was much smaller than generally assumed: North Korean grain production in 1995 was estimated at 2.0 million tons which in turn would have meant a shortfall of about another 2.0 million tons. Relief supplies from various international organizations and countries like China, Japan and South Korea were approximately 1.8 million tons, so starvation could not be based on insufficient supplies. The true reason probably lies with the very difficult transport situation which can supply the big cities with part of the necessary supplies while the peasant population in the countryside are apparently starving.
2. *The Japan Times,* 16 September 1996.
3. *South China Morning Post,* 25 May 1996.
4. Interview in Hamburg, 27 March 1997.
5. cf. New Korea Party lawmaker Hwang Byung-tai, former ambassador to China, *The Korea Herald,* 22 November 1996.
6. A model calculation based on the German model done by the Dresdener Bank estimates that if unification happens around 2000 and the supposed North Korean income level would be raised to 60% of the Southern level, South Korea would have to transfer 240 billion US $, more than half the country's annual GDP. "Putting Korea together again", *The Economist,* 10 May 1997, p. 84.
7. Johan Galtung and Dietrich Fischer, "Proposal for Korean reunification", *The Korea Herald,* 4 February 1997.
8. Kazuhiko Araki, "North Korea is like an airplane without a pilot", Modern Korea Institute, Tokyo, *The Nikkei Weekly,* 17 February 1997; reference to the separate visits of civilians and generals at the Kim Ilsong's shrine: *Vantage Point,* vol. XIX, no. 9, Sept. 1996, p. 23.
9. Kim Chang-kuk, "Uprooting Corruption: A Vital task", *Korea Focus,* vol. 5, no. 1, Jan./Feb. 1997, pp. 14-21.

Chapter 6

Leo M. van der Mey: "Securing Asia: From Nehru's 'Peace Zone' to the 'ASEANization' of Regional Security"

How is peace to be secured in Asia?(1) This is an important question as Asia has been the scene of a great number of conflicts since the end of World War II. In part, these were conflicts among or within Asian countries, in part, conflicts in which external major powers were involved. Some of them, like the wars in Korea, Vietnam, Afghanistan and Cambodia, can be rated amongst the most violent of the post-war period.

Although Asia is currently enjoying a period of relative calm, accompanied by a tremendous level of economic expansion, security is by no means guaranteed. The perceived threat of external danger, particularly from ambitious great powers or from problematic pariah states, rising defense expenditures in the region and the exertion of Chinese pressure on Taiwan, are just a few reminders of the pressing nature of security issues.

According to the picture painted by the realists or neo-realists, conflicts are the inevitable by-products of the struggle for power and influence in Asia. In proportion to their power capabilities and ambitions, states are motivated to strengthen, or at least, to con-solidate their positions, which results in confrontations with other states pursuing similar strategies. Even though the Cold War is a thing of the past, the realists are convinced that this process will continue albeit under changed international circumstances.

More optimistic are the neo-liberals, who propagate an inter-dependence scenario which envisages dynamic economic development advancing the cause of peace. They are convinced that the countries of Asia will benefit so greatly from further economic growth that the motto "war does not pay" will gain currency. Certainly after the end of the Cold War they predict that the irrepressible processes of economic development, which will make states more dependent on one another, and political modernization will contain conflicts in favor of international cooperation. Australia's Foreign Minister Evans echoed this optimism by observing in December 1995 that "everyone in the region seems far more bent on making money than making war".(2)

In the light of the unstable power relations and the unsolved international problems, a shadow of doubt must be cast on whether peace in Asia is feasible in the near future. It is equally questionable whether international politics in the region will run as antagonistically and discordantly as the realists would have us believe. For this reason, it is interesting to examine regional and sub-regional attempts that have been made to bring about peace in Asia and what the implications of these attempts are for Asian security.

This chapter examines the attempts that have been made to bring about peace in Asia so far. This is a trickier subject than one might think. To answer this question it is necessary to analyze what has been done or not been done by Asian countries themselves and by external major powers and international organizations to bring peace closer. This approach would be too unwieldy. Within the scope of this chapter it will be possible to tackle two Asian approaches at peace-making, namely:

- India's efforts, in collaboration with the People's Republic of China (China) and other like-minded countries, to bring about a peace zone in Asia;
- The endeavors of the Association of South-East Asian Nations (ASEAN) to realize a security regime in Southeast Asia.

This focus means that other approaches, like strategies to establish hegemony or balance of power arrangements, will remain beyond the scope of this paper.

The approaches to be discussed are both of Asian origin, but at first sight display great differences. The first difference is one of time. Nehru's ideal of a peace zone was applauded in the mid-fifties by other Asian countries. It proved to be short-lived because this security arrangement succumbed to the war between India and China (1962). The ASEAN countries started their experiments in 1967. They have continued to pursue these ends right up to the present day. Their domain proves to be a second difference. The peace zone propagated by Nehru revolved around India and China, in principle, covering the whole of Asia. ASEAN comprises countries from the sub-region Southeast Asia. In connection with the accommodation within their own sub-region, which has had and continues to have priority, this organization has recently extended its range of action to Pacific Asia. A third difference is to be found in the organizational design and the goals pursued, as ASEAN was more adept at handling international power relations than the movement headed by India.

The outlined differences, which will be examined later in detail, do not detract from the fact that there are striking similarities between both attempts at peace-making. These involve approaches formulated in the context of the Cold War, the aim of which was to create a security arrangement conceived in terms other than balance-of-power politics. The most important actors are the Asian countries themselves, that have tried to define a peace plan for their region or sub-region on a stage dominated by the international politics of major powers. Another common characteristic is the emphasis on independence. Within the framework of non-alignment with the superpowers, Nehru hammered home the importance of autonomy for the Asian states. From the ASEAN countries' side they have always argued for freedom from outside interference by the major powers. These are all variants on a common theme of independence. A third common feature regards the question of how to deal with China. In Nehru's view, a partnership with this major Asian power should help to shape a peace zone in the region. The ASEAN countries have pursued "constructive engagement" in order to promote a peaceful role for China in regional affairs.

These highlighted similarities and differences subject the two Asian approaches to analytical treatment. There is one other feature which makes this study all the more worthwhile; the Nehru model proved to be a failure and the ASEAN model a success, at least for the present. It is to be hoped that the following discussion will not only offer a review of these two approaches but

will also offer insight into the reasons for the different outcomes
and the consequences for current security in Pacific Asia.

NEHRU'S "PEACE ZONE"

After a long period of domination by the British, the Indians became responsible for their own foreign policy on 15 August 1947.
Having just been relieved of colonial status, the new government
succeeded in developing an independent foreign policy course in a
short period of time. This was a successful operation which put
India on the international map. The remark has been made that it
was not India that had a foreign policy, but Nehru, the first Prime
Minister and Minister of External Affairs. This is slightly exaggerated even if it does have an essence of truth in it: Indian policy was
closely intertwined with Nehru and was for a major part determined by his views. This is the reason why India's approach at
peace-making is called the Nehru model in this chapter. The
strategy of independence he formulated was directed at the following, related main points: adopting an aloof stance towards the
United States and the Soviet Union, promoting a policy of reconciliation in their East-West conflict and working towards the
creation of a peace zone in Asia.(3)

India set itself up as the advocate of independence for all countries in Asia and turned against the colonial powers who were not
prepared to relinquish their territories. Nehru condemned the
Dutch unwillingness to yield to the independence movement in
Indonesia and, in 1947, warned them that : "No European country,
whatever it may be, has any right to set its army in Asia against
the people of Asia. The spirit of new Asia will not tolerate such
things".(4) In Nehru's view imperialism, which originally had
been expressed mainly through colonialism, increasingly manifested itself in other forms, namely, the interference in the Third
World on the part of the United States and the Soviet Union. He
regretted this interference, a consequence of the competition between East and West, because the independence of the Third World
was endangered by it. From the very start, he criticized the superpowers who wanted to make new states their allies in order to
prevent alleged power vacuums. His policy was specifically directed towards safeguarding Asia from the rivalry between the
United States and the Soviet Union, and keeping China from becoming involved. Nehru's campaign against the penetration of the
superpowers in the Third World, which threatened to frustrate the

autonomy and development of the recently independent states, changed the course of the fight against imperialism.

Independence in international politics was for Nehru of prime importance. Building on the ideals propagated by the Congress Party during the struggle for independence, he based India's strategy on his assessment of the power balance in the post-war international system, and opted for an independent line in foreign policy. The independent line was not to be restricted to a distancing between East and West, but was also to include an active and positive involvement with international politics.

India's "special relationship" with China

In Nehru's view, friendly cooperation with China should have formed the basis for peace in Asia. Building on their centuries-old friendly relations, India and China would be able to find their rightful place in Asia, peacefully. As a shining example to the rest of the world, India and China were to demonstrate that Asia could step out of the history that had been determined by the European powers.

Long before the independence of India, Nehru had shown an interest in China and expressed feelings of empathy. Stimulated by his visit to China, Nehru launched the idea of "The Eastern Federation" in 1940, a sort of confederation with China and India as senior partners.(5) This federation would be able to give an impetus to further international cooperation. He was to express his future expectations in those years as: "a thousand million strong cooperative of the Chinese and Indian peoples as the base of a larger Asian-African cooperative and ultimately a new cooperative world order".(6)

At the Asian Relations Conference (March 1947) Nehru welcomed China as "that great country to which Asia owes so much and from which so much is expected".(7) The Asian identity was to gel their mutual relations. Nehru expressed this bond: "We are convinced that there is a keen desire on the part of Asian countries to work together, to confer together and generally to look to one another".(8) Nehru thought in terms of regional cooperation on an Asian scale. He summoned the Asian countries who were represented at the Conference on Indonesia (January 1949) to form a "more permanent arrangement" with a view to "effective mutual consultation and concerted effort in the pursuit of common aims".(9)

Above all, India's priority for friendly relations with China can be explained by the fact that this policy formed an essential part of the struggle for a peace zone in Asia. China's attitude was of vital importance for the success or failure of a peace zone in Asia. If Nehru wanted to be successful, then China's cooperation with this experiment was required. China was too important in the proposed Asian constellation to be left out. Should other, less important countries in the region drop out this would not prove to be an insurmountable obstacle, although it would be regrettable. Together with India, China was to be the axis around which the peace zone in Asia would revolve. The proposed peace zone gave a broader significance to India's ideal relations with China: it was not just a question of bilateral friendly relations, but also of peace in the whole of Asia. This underlined China's crucial role in India's Asia-policy. Sinha accurately summarized Nehru's strategy as "the cornerstone of the entire edifice of the vision and policy was China".(10)

India was keen to make China a partner in the Asian peace zone by snaring its northern neighbor, as it were, in a net of friendly relations. Good relations with China were essential for the establishment of peace in Asia. In his conversation with the diplomat T.N. Kaul, he emphasized the importance of India-China relations:

"The peace of Asia and, indeed of the world, can be affected one way or the other by the sort of relations that develop between new India and new China. If we can be friends and cooperate with each other, that will stabilize peace and prevent great power domination of Asia".(11)

Nehru also expected that the new relations in Asia would be radically different from the political relations between the countries in the "old world". In 1949 he described this difference in the following way: "The countries of Asia may have their quarrels with their neighbors here and there, but there is no basic legacy of conflict such as the countries of Europe possess".(12) According to Nehru, the Asian countries were not laboring under the weight of the legacy of traditional disputes and wars, and they were not infected with the power politics virus. The Asian countries would show the world how they could solve any difference that might arise in a peaceful way. Asia had a peace mission, as Nehru contended: "the whole spirit and outlook of Asia are peaceful, and the emergence of Asia in world affairs will be a powerful influence for world peace".(13)

In Nehru's plan, peace in Asia would be given a chance if the countries in this region were allowed to settle their own business ("Asia for the Asians"), and in so doing they would not be involved in the conflict between East and West. If these conditions were met, the countries of Asia would be able to develop and live in peaceful co-existence. Nehru propagated this type of peace zone in the first instance for Asia, but also cherished the hope that should this concept prove successful, it would be applied elsewhere in the world.

"Panch Sheel" and Bandung

In April 1954, India and China completed their negotiations on Tibet by signing the Agreement on "trade and intercourse", thus settling a question which had originally divided them. Due to the preamble, which included the principles of good neighborliness, this Agreement came to be known as "Panch Sheel" (five principles). In Nehru's view the importance of the Agreement with China lay not so much in the settling of the question of Tibet as in the inclusion of the five principles in the preamble to this document. These principles were formulated as follows: 1) "mutual respect for each other's territorial integrity and sovereignty", 2) "mutual non-aggression", 3) "mutual non-interference in each other's internal affairs", 4) "equality and mutual benefit", and 5) "peaceful co-existence".(14) In his explanation of the Agreement Nehru set out the implications in the following way:

"It is a matter of importance to us, of course, as well as, I am sure, to China that these countries, which have now almost about 1,800 miles of frontier, should live in terms of peace and friendliness and should respect each other's sovereignty and integrity, should agree not to interfere with each other in any way, and not to commit aggression on each other. By this Agreement, we ensure peace to a very large extent in a certain area of Asia. I would earnestly wish that this area of peace could be spread over the rest of Asia and indeed over the rest of the world".(15)

This passage summarizes Nehru's ideas in a nutshell. He considered the principles in the preamble as a jointly supported code of behavior for good neighborliness. The establishment of the Agreement implied for him a special relationship based on mutual trust between India and China, thanks to which peaceful relations could be realized. With this Agreement India's security was safeguarded, and it would serve the ends of peace in Asia. Furthermore, Nehru saw in the agreed code of behavior an example for other countries to follow which would further the ends of peace in the world.

Impressed by the announcement of "Panch Sheel" and this shift in the right direction for India-China relations, many other countries considered the Agreement of 1954 significant. The formulated principles found a willing ear in the Third World as the conference of Bandung (1955), a summit of Asian and African leaders, demonstrated.(16) The Asians dominated the conference: they had taken the initiative and in terms of numbers they formed a majority. In addition, leaders like Nehru, Sukarno and Zhou Enlai were the foremost speakers. The conference of Bandung was therefore significant because for the first time countries from the Third World raised their voices in unison in international politics. They acted together as a collective with a message to the world and presented themselves as a political factor. International politics dominated by the established major powers was not to run without them, but with them, in the future. The message of Bandung must be seen in the context of growing anxiety in the Third World about the competition between the United States and the Soviet Union and the accompanying alliance formation, which was seen as a serious threat to world peace. The leaders of Asia and Africa made it quite clear to the superpowers that no further escalation in the conflict between East and West was to be laid at their door as they did not want to be frustrated in their political and economic development.

As far as the peace zone in Asia was concerned, Bandung was important for two reasons. The participation of China was an important facet of this conference. The initiative to invite Peking had come from Burma and India. For Nehru, China was more of an Asian than a communist power and should therefore take part. The Chinese leaders were glad to use the opportunity presented by the conference to force an entry into the Third World. Moreover, Bandung signified a confirmation of the "Panch Sheel" doctrine announced by India and China in 1954. At the conference, Asian countries like Indonesia, Nepal and Thailand were to endorse conciliation between India and China and embrace the principles they had established with open arms. They committed themselves to this by adopting a "Final Communiqué", in which these principles were formulated in a more detailed form.(17) In this way the five principles were elevated to an alternative for traditional foreign policy and a model for the regularization of relations between countries in the Third World.

Nehru's belief and misperception

Nehru saw his belief in the India-China friendship endorsed in the Tibet Agreement (1954), in which both countries subscribed to principles of good neighborliness. For him this served as a guarantee for peace-loving Chinese behavior and as proof that India had no military threat to fear from the north. In his view, the expressed consent of the Chinese leaders definitely demonstrated their Asian solidarity, which he had assumed to be present from the start. Full of Pan-Asian sentiment he believed that India could depend on the relationship of mutual trust which had been established with China. Nehru's expectation was that both countries would act in the spirit of the principles of good neighborliness, which they had underwritten, and that any eventual problems would be sorted out in a reasonable way.

It was questionable whether China imbued the preamble with such important and far-reaching significance as India, and whether both parties would arrive at the same interpretations in political practice, particularly if their own security was at risk.(18) The endorsement of the five principles entailed no more than a moral obligation to obey a code of behavior, which they could interpret in their own way or even ignore if they so wished. Nehru was not to be turned from his idea that India in its relations with China should seek security primarily through friendship. This policy, which was based on the idealization of these relations with China rather than on actual relations, was a projection of Indian priorities onto the leaders in Peking. The initial lack of Chinese response to India's overtures followed by halting cooperation only served as an extra stimulus for him to make every effort to achieve his proposed aims. He was optimistic about the eventual result: "I firmly believe that what one gives others, one gets back. If our approach to others is friendly, others are friendly to us".(19)

By basing his policy towards China on firm intentions of friendship and cooperation, Nehru ignored the possibility that India could be confronted with a situation in which the principles of good neighborliness would no longer hold. In a situation like that, India would no longer be able to react adequately to a Chinese threat because their military forces would not be suitably equipped. In 1962 this eventuality became a reality. China resorted to violence in order to force through a decision in the border conflict; India was not prepared for this change in the "rules".

It is bitterly ironic that in 1962 India became embroiled in a war, despite Nehru's valiant effort to secure peace. After the tragedy of the division of the subcontinent, which burdened the relations in South Asia, the war with China was to bring the pursued zone of peace in Asia to a tragic end.

THE "ASEAN WAY" TO PEACE

With the proclamation of the Bangkok Declaration in 1967, ASEAN became a reality. Five states from Southeast Asia (Indonesia, Malaysia, the Philippines, Singapore and Thailand) decided to close ranks and to aim at cooperation. Later, in 1984, the newly independent Brunei was to join them, followed by Vietnam in 1995.

ASEAN did not have to start from scratch since it was preceded by earlier exercises in intergovernmental cooperation, like the Association of Southeast Asia (ASA) and Maphilindo (Malaysia, the Philippines and Indonesia).(20) Whilst these earlier attempts floundered because of disputes, ASEAN was to mark a new beginning in cooperation in Southeast Asia. In the case of this organization the motto "third time lucky" would apply as they are now successfully coping with problems which brought about the collapse of their predecessors. ASEAN continues as a viable, working organization that has celebrated its thirtieth anniversary in 1997.

Several converging factors prompted the states in Southeast Asia to renew their attempts at cooperation. In brief, the leaders in the region recognized the desirability, if not the necessity, to strengthen their country through cooperation. In the Bangkok Declaration they proposed a multipurpose organization with emphasis on commitment to economic, social and cultural cooperation. Perceptions of threat were, in fact, a stronger stimulus than the desire for economic integration. As Evelyn Colbert so rightly observed: "Beneath the bland Bangkok Declaration, a shared view on security issues was the driving force behind ASEAN's organization".(21) These perceptions of a foreign threat stemmed primarily from China, where the "Cultural Revolution" was in full force, and from Soviet-supported North Vietnam. This perception of threat was strengthened by a perceived decline in American power in Asia, which manifested itself in the Vietnam war. In the future aggressive communism would meet less resistance. Against this background, the feeling started to grow in Southeast Asia that the ASEAN countries would be stronger if they formed an association, or that they would at least be less vulnerable than if they operated independently. In retrospect, the Indonesian Sadli was to refer to this feeling as follows: "the major motivation for setting up ASEAN was some kind of fear, that is, fear of a triumphant and expansive communism in Asia".(22)

In addition, the perceived threat in ASEAN countries had a counterpart within their own borders, namely, internal disorders caused by communist and separatist insurgencies and potential subversion by Chinese minorities. Closer cooperation was to help to keep these in check. Furthermore, the ASEAN countries wanted to limit their mutual differences of opinion on matters like conflicting territorial claims for the future in the hope of preventing any repetition of highly charged confrontations such as that between an ambitious Indonesia and Malaysia.

Finally, the new start for cooperation in this sub-region was promoted by the unanimity between the leaders of the countries involved. In this respect, the takeover in Indonesia in the mid-sixties was important, as this halted Sukarno's radical foreign policy. Suharto's redirection of Indonesian foreign policy had barely started when he began to promote cooperation in 1966: "A cooperating Southeast Asia, an integrated Southeast Asia, to constitute the strongest bulwark and base in facing imperialism and colonialism of whatever form and from whatever quarter it may come".(23)

In some respects ASEAN was a product of international circumstances and conditions, in other respects it was the creation of leaders who saw in it a window of opportunity. They saw its potential as a joint venture which would strengthen them in their relationships with the outside world and thought it would offer a multilateral framework for national policies as well. From its inception ASEAN was imbued with a complementary character whereby national interests continued to prevail over regional interests. Thambipillai underlined this in the following way: "Collective strength is only sought where the benefits are associated with a unified stand...In the ASEAN case the whole is subservient to the parts".(24)

ASEAN and international security

When ASEAN was founded, the member states gave foremost priority to cooperation in economic, social and cultural areas. No matter how much they may have been driven by the perceived communist threat, for tactical reasons the "founding fathers" did not want to present their new organization as primarily a political-military alliance. However, in the Bangkok Declaration they did establish the promotion of "regional peace and stability" as their second aim. For the ASEAN countries this meant they would observe restraint in their mutual relations. According to Buszynski this encapsulates the maintenance of peace within ASEAN in "its ability to affirm a commitment to regional order based upon the territorial status quo".(25)

The ASEAN countries determined their position on matters of international security in a far more detailed and explicit way in the Kuala Lumpur Declaration (1971) which stated their intent to establish a "Zone of Peace, Freedom and Neutrality" (ZOPFAN) in Southeast Asia. With the changed international conditions, such as the American "détente" with China, the ASEAN leaders thought it was necessary to go somewhat further than in 1967. The initiator of the ZOPFAN idea was Tun Abdul Razak, Prime Minister of Malaysia, who stated: "This region has been convulsed by war essentially because of the involvement of major powers in our affairs. It is clear from this therefore that peace and stability can only be safeguarded by a policy of neutralization which will ensure that this region will no longer be a theater of conflict for the competing interests of major powers".(26) Although opinions were divided within ASEAN about the effects of ZOPFAN, members still rallied around the banner of reducing external influence.

The acceptance of the ZOPFAN idea is important for two reasons.(27) The ASEAN leaders with this first pursuit of external policy wanted to prescribe a joint line in opposition to the major powers. They realized that by pursuing peace and stability in Southeast Asia they were partially dependent on a sympathetic response from outside great powers. With ZOPFAN, they asked for their support in promoting stability through non-interference. Furthermore, ZOPFAN provided a base for subsequent, more detailed, security arrangements. An example of this is the Manila Declaration (1987), in which a "Southeast Asia Nuclear Weapon Free Zone" (SEANWFZ) is the proclaimed aim. After many years of discussion, SEANWFZ was eventually sealed with a treaty in December 1995. Another development arising from ZOPFAN was the "Treaty of Amity and Cooperation" (TAC, 1976). In combination with the "Declaration of ASEAN Concord", both launched at the Bali Summit, the TAC was to give a new impetus to regional stability and cooperation. Shocked by the American withdrawal from Vietnam and the triumph of communism, the ASEAN countries decided to commit themselves to the promotion of peace through a code of conduct for good neighborly behavior. In essence, TAC signified a codification of the security principles developed since 1967. The most important principles were non-interference in each other's internal affairs, resolution of disputes by peaceful means and renunciation of the threat or use of force. Apart from endorsing these principles in the treaty, its non-exclusive character was typical of TAC. It is an example of open regionalism in that other countries can also sign the treaty. Later, in the nineties, the countries of Indo-China would do so, and in endorsing it they have become more involved in ASEAN aims.

ASEAN's security performance during the Cold War

How has ASEAN fared in practice, bearing in mind these aims? Mutual relations have steadily improved since 1967.(28) Compliance with the aim of restraint and the frequent contact between ASEAN leaders have led to good relations. Regional cooperation that has taken place has brought with it a process of accommodation, whereby conflicts do not get out of hand. Where countries once allowed their differences of opinion to escalate, since 1967 they have refrained from interference in the internal affairs of others and have not threatened or used force against one another. This does not mean that all the problems have been solved and that disputes are a thing of the past. Lingering conflicts in Southeast Asia include territorial disputes, like the clashing claims to Sabah and the Spratly Islands. However, the ASEAN states respect the territorial status quo, and they tend to agree to disagree over intractable issues. More important still is the fact that they concentrate on issues on which they can come to an agreement.

In this way they have succeeded in making headway in many areas, including military cooperation.

The formulation of an external security policy caused ASEAN more difficulty, as did the implementation of ZOPFAN. The member-states might have been in agreement about the general aim of non-interference by outside great powers, but they disagreed on the consequences. This was true of some ASEAN states' external links with the great powers, in particular the military role of the United States in the region (bases, treaties). In view of the apparently impossible task of developing a uniform policy, they sought refuge in a typical "ASEAN solution". This far they have allowed one another to decide for themselves to what extent they consider external bonds necessary for their national security and compatible with the ZOPFAN idea.

In addition to this disagreement within ASEAN on the consequences of ZOPFAN, the great powers had their own ideas about the desirability of it. In general, they were not prepared to relinquish their hold on Southeast Asia in order to comply with the expressed desire for neutrality. Of the superpowers, it was the Soviet Union that wanted to protect the military relation with Vietnam, whilst the United States condemned ZOPFAN on the grounds of the existing strategic bonds with countries in the region. Japan did not adopt an official policy on ZOPFAN, but in practice supported American views. Only China was sympathetic towards ZOPFAN, particularly because its realization would reduce the influence of the United States and the Soviet Union in Southeast Asia.

The consequences of the differing opinions within ASEAN and the dismissive reaction of the major powers just mentioned was that the ZOPFAN idea was discussed but not implemented. Apart from that, the discussion on ZOPFAN was to shift from neutrality and non-interference to respect for regional stability and opposition to any hegemonic power. It is not so much a question of excluding great powers, as much as commitment to conditions which are acceptable for ASEAN.

From the mid 1970s ASEAN has aspired to a dialogue between interested partners. This dialogue started with talks with Australia, New Zealand and Japan, formally initiated in 1977, and was extended to cover the other major trading partners (Canada, the European Union, South Korea and the United States). The dialogue offers ASEAN countries the opportunity to exchange ideas with the countries important to them, including major powers. The agenda mainly comprises economic issues, but from 1979 discussions on the Cambodian issue were to lead to an extension to political issues.(29) After the end of the Cold War it was decided that this would include regional security. The discussion on political and security issues was to be continued in 1994 in the specially created ASEAN Regional Forum, about which more later.

The discussion of the Cambodian issue revealed the importance the ASEAN countries attached to international concern for this area. No single political topic has led to feelings running so high as that of the Vietnamese oppression of Cambodia. In response to the Vietnamese invasion of this country (December 1978), the ASEAN countries adopted the joint standpoint that the occupation should cease and that the puppet regime should be replaced by an independent government. The reason this situation was of such importance was that Cambodia formed a test case for their external security policy. Firstly, they saw this as a violation of the principle of restraint and respect for the territorial status quo and, as such, as a barrier to the implementation of ZOPFAN. Secondly, this threat to peace and stability in their "own" region provided the opportunity to use their collective voice in international forums.

Once again, when it came to developing a jointly supported position, there were diverse views based on differences in geographical position and political persuasions. Thailand, as a "front-line state", wanted to follow a harder, and more active line than a country like Indonesia, which was to gradually play a more mediatory role. This does not detract from the fact that, at crucial moments, the ASEAN countries succeeded in continuing to form a closed front on diplomatic matters. With tenacity and flexibility they channeled their efforts into the establishment of an internationally recognized government within Cambodia. Here, they not only succeeded in keeping this subject on the agenda of the United Nations, but also, in the end, on that of the major powers. This led to the 1989 International Conference on Cambodia, on the basis of which the Paris Peace Agreement (1991) could be drawn up. The end of the Cold War was a godsend for the ASEAN countries to prove their diplomatic usefulness in tackling the Cambodia issue. With this issue settled, a great barrier for peace and cooperation in Southeast Asia was swept away.(30)

ASEAN in the post-Cold War era

The end of the Cold War and the preceding disintegration of the Soviet Union brought about an international shift to a mixture of unipolarity and multipolarity.(31) The former indicates that one major political power with a global strategic reach is left, and the latter that a number of power centers dominate international economic relations. In addition to increased international interdependence and a tendency towards economic globalization, uncertainty about the changed power configuration proves to be an important consequence of the ending of the Cold War. In this new stage of international relations there are at least three challenges for ASEAN: consolidation and strengthening of cooperation within ASEAN, the expansion of ASEAN in Southeast Asia and the development of a security dialogue in Pacific Asia. Of these challenges the central focus will be on the "ASEANization" of regional cooperation.

In the first place there is the challenge of continuing along the well-trodden path within ASEAN, also within the changed international context. In view of the successful sub-regional cooperation up to the present, that will be more difficult than it might seem. It remains to be seen whether the international situation, which is both more complex and more fluid, will provide the same amount of cohesion as the common perception of threat during the Cold War. The same holds for the crucial role the leaders of ASEAN have played in the development of the organization. Will the new generation of leaders be as dedicated and unitarian as their predecessors? This is all the more important in that growing interdependence in Asia has not reduced the role of the state, but instead has been accompanied by the political strengthening of the state apparatus with continuing emphasis on national economic performance and by growing nationalism.

Currently, there is a willingness among ASEAN countries to strengthen cooperation within the stated framework. This also holds for areas like that of economic integration, where the progress being made leaves much to be desired. At the Singapore Summit (1992) it was decided that an ASEAN Free Trade Area (AFTA) would be created within 15 years. Afterwards the target date was brought forward to 2003. Another aspect of cooperation, which is even more important in this discussion, concerns political integration. There is no doubt that in ASEAN a security regime of which TAC forms the core has been brought about. This regime, which can be described as a set of "principles, norms, rules and decision-making procedures",(32) does not seem to have reached the stage of a security community. In Deutsch's view such a community has only been reached if integration has progressed so far that the chance of the outbreak of a violent conflict has been reduced to practically zero.(33) This assumes limited conflicts between countries in a region and a multilateral framework that is strong enough to deal with eventual conflicts in a peaceful way. It is questionable whether ASEAN as an international organization has generated enough absorption power for conflict management in cases of lingering territorial disputes and other points of friction. The matter is even further complicated by the rise of "new disputes", such as transnational environmental problems, which are difficult to resolve. The positive side of ASEAN is its concentration on "comprehensive security", which covers more than just military security alone.(34) Possibly, increased interest in this will contribute to the transformation from security regime to security community.

A second challenge is formed by the enlargement of ASEAN to include the countries of Indo-China. This extension, which can be seen as a window of opportunity to further mutual understanding, can also hamper this challenge of strengthening cooperation within ASEAN, by bringing with it increased diversity and more contradictions which will need ironing out.

In July 1995 Vietnam was formally accepted as a new member of ASEAN. Previously perceived as an aggressive antagonist, Vietnam was given the opportunity to join the organization which was its former adversary. The entrance of Vietnam marks the solution of the conflict over Cambodia and signals the end of a Southeast Asia split into two parts: ASEAN and Indo-China. This step is important because Vietnam is, as it were, encased in this regional organization. Furthermore, Laos, Cambodia and Myanmar (Burma) have been given the encouragement to follow the example of Vietnam. Due to this extension, ASEAN not only became bigger but also more powerful in relation to other countries and in international forums. As a result, ASEAN is now in a stronger position with respect to China than it was before. The less positive side of the development is obviously that the joining of Vietnam has put the relations within ASEAN and the decision-making process to the test. No matter what direction this may move, the "ASEANization" of Southeast Asia seems to be an irreversible process. The Indonesian Foreign Minister Alatas described this historic development in the following way: "For the first time in the history of Southeast Asia, we are going to be united and not divided. This part of the world has long been the arena of the large powers, who have used different Southeast Asian countries as their pawns".(35)

"ASEANization" of security in Pacific Asia?

Finally, the third challenge is that of promoting security cooperation in Pacific Asia. Under the influence of the changes in international relations, a discussion has taken place at ASEAN meetings from 1990 onwards to include regional security on its formal agenda.(36) Initiatives were taken by the dialogue partners Australia and Canada, with assistance from Japan. Initially there was some reticence within ASEAN, particularly from Indonesia, to pursue the proposed extension of the consultations. Nevertheless, the discussion went ahead and eventually resulted in a decision which was acceptable to all parties, namely, to start up a security dialogue with a modest agenda. At the Singapore Summit (1992) it was decided that the so-called Post-Ministerial Conference (PMC), in which talks are held between the ASEAN countries and their dialogue partners, would be used as a forum for such an exchange of views. This Conference takes place annually after the ASEAN Ministerial Meeting (AMM). After the dialogue had begun, it soon became clear that there was a preference for a separate consultation organ directed specifically towards regional security. This led to the decision by the AMM in July 1993 to conduct discussions in the ASEAN Regional Forum (ARF) from 1994 onwards. Meanwhile, this idea had gained American approval because the Clinton administration wanted to follow a more multilateral course in Asia. The AMM formulated the aims of the proposed forum as follows: "It is important for ASEAN to work with its dialogue partners and other regional states to evolve a more predictable and constructive pattern of political and security relationships in the Asia-Pacific".(37) An important function of this new forum, although not specifically mentioned, is the inclusion of China, as a guest in the consultations.

The creation of the ARF meant a regular security dialogue between ministers of foreign affairs of the seven ASEAN countries and their seven partners in the PMC (Australia, Canada, the European Union, Japan, New Zealand, South Korea and the United States), two guests or consultative partners (China and Russia) and three observers (Laos and Papua New Guinea plus Cambodia). Later, in July 1996, China and Russia were to become full-fledged dialogue partners, India a new dialogue partner and Myanmar an observer. The ARF forms the third stage of the annual ministerial talks which begin with the AMM, are followed by the PMC and are rounded off with the ARF. At a lower level talks take place periodically at Senior Official Meetings (SOM) partly as a form of preparation for the ministerial talks. In addition to these official meetings, informal get-togethers are organized within the framework of the ARF. An example of this is the series of workshops organized by Indonesia on the South China Sea. In all cases the ASEAN countries are the pivot of the pursued security dialogue.

Furthermore, it is worth mentioning that in addition to the governmental track, a non-governmental track has been established to support regional security in a changing Asia. This is the result of the establishment of the "Council for Security Cooperation in Asia Pacific" (CSCAP), in 1993, which was given an initial impetus by a number of strategic "think tanks".(38) A European counterpart of CSCAP is the "European Council for Security Cooperation in Asia Pacific" (ECSCAP), which has the stimulation of consultations between Europe and Asia as a part of its remit.(39) Here lies a rewarding task since the first, long overdue, summit of leaders from both regions, Asia-Europe Meeting (ASEM), only took place in March 1996 in Bangkok.

ASEAN has an important role to play in consultations on security issues in Asia. Southeast Asia both geographically and strategically takes on a special role in East Asia and South Asia. At the same time this region also takes part in the economic development in Pacific Asia, through which it has gained in international significance and status. In addition to this, ASEAN can boast of a thriving level of development, and this organization has had the necessary experience with security cooperation between the countries of Southeast Asia and in leading a security dialogue with external countries, including major powers. For these reasons, ASEAN is the appropriate actor to take the leading role in the consultations in ARF. Some countries, like Canada and Australia, have even argued for an institutional upgrading of ARF and for measures far more extensive than those hitherto pursued. The ASEAN countries do, however, maintain the view that ARF should develop gradually. Koh, Singapore's "ambassador-at-large",

emphasizes this: "The Asian preference, unlike the Western preference, is to take a very non-legalistic approach to things. We take
actions step by step and allow things to evolve".(40)

For the time being, ARF continues to be restricted to a security
dialogue between ASEAN and other Asian countries and major
powers. This forum is seen as an opportunity to exchange information and to show respect for each other's views. Information and
respect are to contribute to more transparency in relations and lower
levels of threat perception. In addition to the promotion of these
security consultations, the ARF is particularly focused on the constructive engagement of the major powers. In recognition of the
involvement of these powers, a role which is impossible to disregard, the ASEAN countries are aiming at a channeling of external
influences in favor of regional stability. This can be seen in relation
to the United States where they are trying to keep the most powerful country in the world committed to Asian security and also in
relation to supporting Japan's military-strategic low-profile.
Probably the most important feature, is their effort to prevent
China from adopting a threatening, hegemonic role in Asia. An
example of this is the consultations on the South China Sea, where
a number of countries have laid claims to the Spratly Islands. As a
result of their talks, which resulted in the AMM "Declaration on
the South China Sea" (1992) the ASEAN countries have opened
talks with China. For them this would seem to be a litmus test
directed at precluding the likelihood of China acting unilaterally
and using force against these islands. Should China not comply, she
would risk the good relations it enjoys with ASEAN countries.
China has not yet agreed to commit itself to the ASEAN declaration. ARF has succeeded, however, in eliciting pledges from China
in support of a multilateral peaceful resolution of maritime claims
in the area.

Thanks to ARF, there is now a security dialogue in a region
where, with some exceptions like the Asia Pacific Economic Cooperation forum (APEC) and the East Asian Economic Caucus (EAEC),
multilateralism has barely come into existence. This is in striking
contrast to other regions, and in particular Europe, where a number
of multilateral institutions have been established to promote
cooperation. For the time being ARF is an extremely fragile consultative structure, which may easily crumble under the contradictions
and pressures both internally and externally. The latter explains
the felt need for additional security measures, like the "Five Power

Defense Arrangement" (linking Malaysia and Singapore to the United Kingdom, Australia and New Zealand) and the defense agreement between Indonesia and Australia (December 1995), as a strategic counterweight to the threat of force by China in the region. Such defense measures and the bilateral security links with the United States emphasize that ASEAN countries are not willing to base their security on dialogue alone. To paraphrase Cromwell's statement "Trust in God, but keep your powder dry", ASEAN's motto is: trust in dialogue, but make sure you have military backing. It is important to remember that the success of "ASEANization" of security cooperation in Pacific Asia is not so much dependent on the efforts of ASEAN, however valuable these may be, as on the attitude of the major powers, who are still in the process of seeking a new balance.

EVALUATION

Having completed the discussion on Nehru's zone of peace and the ASEAN way to peace, I would now like to evaluate these approaches. The ASEAN way to peace has proven more successful than Nehru's approach. Since they started out in 1967, the ASEAN countries have been successful in strengthening their mutual cooperation. In the early days the new organization was sometimes scathingly portrayed as a "talk-shop" or, even more negatively, as a "joke". Many an author wrote ominous passages on the impending demise of this organization, like the preceding collapse of Nehru's peace scheme. Despite the gloomy prophecies ASEAN has prevailed and has found responses to internal and external challenges which it has been confronted with. The purpose of this evaluation is to indicate why the Indian attempt at peace-making failed and why the ASEAN approach has been relatively successful up to now. In order to explain the evolution of these attempts at peace-making, the following factors will be discussed: the international context, the institutional development and "the rules of the game". The first factor is a general one, namely, the influence of the international power structure on the genesis of these approaches and on their further development. The other factors are specifically linked to the respective approaches. These factors concern on the one hand the institutional design and imbedding and on the other the style of operation, including the principles upon which the *modus operandi* is based.

International system conditions provide the key explanation for the foundation and subsequent consolidation of ASEAN. In the mid-sixties there was a common perception of communist threat in Southeast Asia, which gave a certain impetus to cooperation. In the late seventies the Vietnamese occupation of Cambodia gave a new stimulus to joint action. After the Cold War had finished, uncertainty about the changed international power relations, in particular, the future role of China in Asia, once again provided the spark for increased cooperation. This common perception of external threat was complemented by a commonly felt need for "resilience". The ASEAN countries wanted the sub-region to become more resilient in international politics, thus making it less dependent on the major powers.

In this respect there is a similarity with the ideal of a peace zone. As in the Nehru model independence from both camps was the central focus; in the ASEAN approach the emphasis was laid on independence which had to be respected by the external powers. A great difference is that in the fifties no common perception of threat existed among the signatories of the Bandung Declaration. In the case of ASEAN, the perception of threat was not a divisive but a unifying power. Moreover, the start of this new organization was restricted to only a part of Asia, which made cooperation easier.

With the advantage of hindsight, it can be concluded that Nehru's aim of a peace zone for the whole of Asia which would be respected by the superpowers was an extremely ambitious strategy. A number of Asian states sought refuge in security guarantees from the United States or the Soviet Union, whilst these superpowers made conflicts in the region their bones of contention. The reason why creating a peace zone for the whole of Asia was too ambitious, must be sought in the underestimation of the effects of the Cold War. The American government was very hostile to India's initiatives, and the region became more involved in the East-West conflict than Nehru had hoped.

Another major reason for the success of ASEAN is to be found in the way in which its further design came about. As a sequel to the Bangkok Declaration, institutionalization gradually took place. The principle behind this was that the process is more important than the structure. It was not until the Bali Summit of 1976, almost ten years after its foundation, that the ASEAN countries came to an agreement on further cooperation and decided on the installation of a permanent secretariat.

The discussion with the dialogue partners (from 1977) was also gradually extended, both in the sense of participants and topics, and subsequently institutionalized. The gradual piecing together of ASEAN's design did not detract from progressing on a steady course. Also, as ASEAN developed, they made sure that intergovernmental cooperation did not take place at the expense of national policies. ASEAN is based on the principle that it is a multilateral framework within which, ultimately, national interests of participating countries prevail over sub-regional interests. They work collectively just as long as it is in their own interests. This leads to obvious limitations, but the advantage is that ASEAN does not form a threat to the participating countries. Over the years this organization has become increasingly institutionally anchored and this happened at moments when there was consensus on further cooperation.

This is in stark contrast with the peace zone pursued by India which was merely declaratory. An important drawback of the Nehru model was that it got no further than underwriting general principles, which in practice could be interpreted in various ways. "Panch Sheel" and "Bandung" received neither political follow-up nor any institutional imbedding which would have committed the Asian countries involved to the propagated peace zone in a more definite way. This could have been achieved by intensifying contacts, more in-depth cooperation and more explicit guidelines for conciliation of eventual conflicts. The lack of such measures can be partly explained by the implicit assumption that the declarations of 1954 and 1955 spoke for themselves and did not need to be worked out in greater detail. In particular, "Bandung" was seen as the seal of an assumed harmony of interests. This calculation was based on a belief in Pan-Asian identity and solidarity, which were to form the building bricks of the peace zone.

A final explanation for ASEAN's success involves its style of operation, namely, a general acceptance of "the rules of the game". These rules can be captured by the concepts of consension and pragmatism. In the first instance, the ASEAN countries try to reach an agreement with one another. If this succeeds, then they start up a process which can be consolidated after a certain period of time. If this does not succeed, they then hold over the decision-making on such a contentious issue. After a period of restraint, they can make a

new attempt to reach agreement, hopefully under better circumstances.

The rules of the game as outlined here emphasize the crucial
role of the leaders of the ASEAN countries as promoters of cooperation. In 1967 they were prepared to subordinate existing problems to
accommodation within the new cooperative body. Subsequently
they ensured that ASEAN as an organization kept up its momentum
by taking new steps at important moments. Characteristic of this
mode of operation is that the ASEAN countries engage in an almost
permanent dialogue, progressing step by step and subsequently
implementing the aims advanced.

This too is in contrast with the envisaged peace zone in the fifties, when the countries involved were expected to promote the
maintenance of this zone of their own accord. Furthermore, at that
time there was absolutely no compulsion for the leaders to make an
effort to make the peace zone work through mutual consultations.
The weakest spot in Nehru's security scheme was the belief in the
"special relationship" between India and China as a basis for a
peace zone. In the early sixties the escalation of the border conflicts
and the related increase in rivalry between both Asian powers
provoked so much momentum that "Panch Sheel" was put under
very great pressure. The lack of rules for conflict management and
the worsened personal relations between Indian and Chinese leaders stood in the way of accommodation. The underestimated
destructive dynamism of national antagonisms, regional rivalry
and personal friction led to the war of 1962, as well as to the collapse of the peace zone in Asia.

All in all, the ASEAN countries knew how to make good use of
the opportunities available to improve their mutual relations and
to improve the position of the sub-region. They understood that
they were partly dependent on the great powers to realize external
security policies. This is all the more true for their new aim to
extend the security regime to Pacific Asia. If the ASEANization of
Pacific Asia is to succeed, then the security dialogue instigated by
the ARF must be constructively supported by the major Asian powers and the United States.

*   Dr. Leo van der Mey is Assistant Professor at the Department
    of Political Science, Leiden University, The Netherlands.

Notes

Earlier versions of this chapter were prepared for presentation to the workshop on "International Relations and Security in Pacific Asia" of the Netherlands Institute for Advanced Study, The Hague, 2-3 April 1996, and to the panel on "Military and Intellectual Foundations of Security in Asia" at the Joint Convention of the International Studies Association and the Japan Association of International Relations, Makuhari, 20-22 September 1996. For comments on these versions I would like to thank the participants in these meetings, as well as Mary Heidhues, Wil Hout and Michael Leifer. I am also greatly indebted to my NIAS colleagues in the research group "Pacific Asia and Europe: Developing Interfaces" for making valuable suggestions on the topics covered in this chapter and to Kate Williams for her creative editorial assistance.

1. The use of the word secure and the paraphrased title of this chapter were inspired by R.H. Ullman, *Securing Europe*, Princeton, 1991.
2. *International Herald Tribune*, 22 December 1995. For further analysis of these views with respect to Asia see A.L. Friedberg, "Ripe for Rivalry: Prospects for Peace in a Multipolar Asia", in: *International Security* (18, 3) 1994, pp. 5-32, B. Buzan and G. Segal, "Rethinking East Asian Security", in: *Survival* (36, 2) 1994, pp. 3-21 and S.W. Simon, "Alternative Visions of Security in the Asia Pacific", in: *Pacific Affairs* (69,3) 1996, pp. 381-396.
3. The following analysis of the Nehru model is partly based on my study *Nehru's Droom Voorbij. 1962 als keerpunt in India's verhouding tot China* [Nehru's Lost Dream. 1962 - a turning point in India's relations with China], Leiden, 1990. See also L.M. van der Mey, "The India-China Conflict: Explaining the Outbreak of War 1962", in: *Diplomacy & Statecraft* (5, 1) 1994, pp. 183-199.
4. Nehru quoted in: D.R. Sardesai, "India and Southeast Asia", in: B.R. Nanda, ed., *Indian Foreign Policy. The Nehru Years*, New Delhi, 1976, p. 81.
5. *National Herald*, 28 October 1940, in: J. Nehru, *Collected Writings 1937-1940*, London, 1941, p. 389.
6. Nehru quoted in: R.K. Karanjia, *The Philosophy of Mr. Nehru*, London, 1966, p. 111.

7. Nehru, 23 March 1947, in: *Jawaharlal Nehru's Speeches I*, 1946-1949 [further referred to as *Speeches I*], New Delhi, 1967 (3rd ed.), p. 299.
8. Nehru, 22 March 1949, in: *Speeches I*, p. 254.
9. Nehru, 20 January 1949, in: *Speeches I*, p. 328.
10. Sinha, "China: Making and Unmaking of Nehru's Foreign Policy", in: *China Report* (15, 2) 1979, p. 53. See also A.R. Basu, "India's China Policy in Historical Perspective", in: *Contemporary Southeast Asia* (13, 1) 1991, p. 103.
11. Nehru quoted in: T.N. Kaul, *Diplomacy in Peace and War. Recollections and Reflections*, New Delhi, 1979, p. 29.
12. Nehru, 8 March 1949, in: *Speeches I*, p. 236.
13. Nehru, 23 March 1947, in: *Speeches I*, p. 302.
14. *Notes, Memoranda and Letters Exchanged and Agreements Signed between the Governments of India and China* [White Paper I], New Delhi, 1959, p. 98.
15. Nehru, 15 May 1954, in: *Jawaharlal Nehru's Speeches III, 1953-1957*, New Delhi, 1958, p. 263.
16. Appadorai, *The Bandung Conference*, New Delhi, 1955 and G. McT. Kahin, *The Asian-African Conference. Bandung, Indonesia, April 1955*, Ithaca, 1956.
17. Jankowitsch and K.P. Sauvant, eds., *The Third World without Superpowers. The Collected Documents of the Non-Aligned Countries I*, New York, 1978, pp. LVII-LXVII. See also F. Godement, ed., *Problem Solving in Asia. Exception or Example?* [Reference Paper Asia Europe Forum], Venice, 1996.
18. Gupta, "Indian Approaches to Modern China. A Socio-Historical Analysis I", in: *China Report* (8, 4) 1972, pp. 48-49. See further Y.Y.I. Vertzberger, *Misperceptions in Foreign Policy Making: The Sino-Indian Conflict, 1959-1962*, Boulder, 1984 and S.A. Hoffmann, *India and the China Crisis*, Berkeley, 1990.
19. Nehru quoted in: S. Gopal, *Jawaharlal Nehru: A Biography III, 1956-1964*, London, 1984, pp. 275-276.
20. For basic documents covering this period see *ASEAN Documents Series 1967-1988*, Jakarta, 1988 and for an analysis of Asia and the ASEAN model see M. Haas, *The Asian Way to Peace: A Story of Regional Cooperation*, New York, 1989.
21. Colbert, "Southeast Asian Regional Politics: Toward a Regional Order", in: W.H. Wriggins et al., *Dynamics of Regional Politics: Four Systems on the Indian Ocean Rim*, New York,

1992, p. 234.
22. Sadli, "ASEAN: a Personal Reflection", in: H. Soesastro, ed:, *ASEAN in a Changed Regional and International Political Economy*, Jakarta, 1995, p. 236.
23. Suharto quoted in: M. Leifer, *Indonesia's Foreign Policy*, London, 1983, p. 119.
24. Thambipillai, "Continuity and Change in ASEAN: The Politics of Regional Cooperation in South East Asia", in: W.A. Axline, ed., *The Political Economy of Regional Cooperation: Comparative Case Studies*, London, 1994, pp. 124 and 130.
25. Buszynski, "Southeast Asia in the Post-Cold War Era: Regionalism and Security", in : *Asian Survey* (32, 9), 1992, p. 830.
26. Razak quoted in: D. Wilson, *The Neutralization of Southeast Asia*, New York, 1975, p. 4.
27. For further information about ZOPFAN see Wilson, op. cit., and M. Alagappa, "Regional Arrangements and International Security in Southeast Asia: Going Beyond ZOPFAN", in: *Contemporary Southeast Asia* (12, 4) 1991, pp. 269-305.
28. Broinowski, ed., *Understanding ASEAN*, New York, 1982, M. Leifer, *ASEAN and the Security of South-East Asia*, London, 1989 and D.F. Anwar, *Indonesia in ASEAN: Foreign Policy and Regionalism*, Singapore, 1994.
29. Colbert, op.cit., p. 251.
30. Frost, "The Cambodian Conflict: The Path towards Peace", in: *Contemporary Southeast Asia* (13, 3) 1991, pp. 119-163 and P. Raszelenberg et al., *The Cambodia Conflict: Search for a Settlement, 1979-1991*, Hamburg, 1995.
31. For Asia and ASEAN after the Cold War see J.C. Hsiung, ed., *Asia Pacific in the New World Politics*, Boulder, 1993, A. Mack and J. Ravenhill, eds., *Building Economic and Security Regimes in the Asia Pacific Region*, Sydney, 1994 and A. Acharya, *A New Regional Order in South-East Asia: ASEAN in the Post-Cold War Era* [Adelphi Paper, no. 279], London, 1993.
32. Krasner, "Structural Causes and Regime Consequences: Regimes as Intervening Variables", in: S.D. Krasner, ed., *International Regimes*, Ithaca, 1983, p. 2.
33. Deutsch et al., *Political Community and the North Atlantic Area: International Organization in the Light of Historical Experience*, Princeton, 1957, p. 5.
34. Parnwell and R. Bryant, eds., *Environmental Change in South-*

east Asia: People, Politics and Sustainable Development, London, 1996 and M. Alagappa, "Comprehensive Security: Interpretations in ASEAN Countries", in: R.A. Scalapino et al., eds., *Asian Security Issues: Regional and Global*, Berkeley, 1988, pp. 57-62.

35. Alatas quoted in: *Far Eastern Economic Review*, 8 February 1996, p. 36.

36. Wanandi, "Asia-Pacific Security Forums: Rationale and Options from an ASEAN Perspective", in: D. Ball et al., *Security Cooperation in the Asia-Pacific Region*, Washington, 1993, pp. 8-17.

37. *Joint Communiqué of the Twenty-Sixth ASEAN Ministerial Meeting* [23-24 July, 1993], Singapore, 1993, p. 3. For an analysis of the ARF see M. Leifer, *The ASEAN Regional Forum.* [Adelphi Paper, no. 302], London, 1996.

38. Ball et al., op.cit., pp. IX-XI and 36-38.

39. ECSCAP statement by F. Godement et al., *An Agenda for Euro-East Asian Security*, London, 1995 and G. Segal, *Thinking Strategically about ASEM: The Subsidiarity Question*, London, 1996.

40. Koh quoted in: *The New York Times*, 17 August 1993.

Chapter 7

John Groenewegen: "Changing Japanese Technology Policies"

This contribution focuses on the recent changes of technology policies in Japan. After a short introduction on the role of government in a market economy and a discussion on the history of Japanese policies until the 1970s, I will examine the changes in the environment which have forced the government to adopt its policies. The most important changes, which include increasing internationalization and pressure from outside (especially that of the US) to change the trade balance, growing independence and confidence of Japanese firms, and the entry of Japan into the new edge technologies, demand a completely different policy than hitherto pursued. The shift from applied to basic research and the consequences for the effectiveness of the policy instruments of MITI will be the focus of attention.

I will then analyze some cases in the high-tech sectors in which firms and government have worked together in order to stimulate R&D. From the case studies I draw conclusions about the conditions for effective technology policies and reflect on expected changes in the near future.

Government in a market economy

Japan has been a modern market economy from the 1950s onwards; that is to say, autonomous firms decide on investments and markets coordinate transactions of labor, goods and capital. In the 1950s, however, the intervention of government in Japan has been so directive (some preferred to characterize Japan as the most intelligently centrally planned economy in the world, see McMillan 1985) that the autonomy of firms could be doubted. It is beyond doubt that the independence of firms has strongly increased from the mid 60s onwards, and that Japan has been a market economy from those years onwards. Market economies, however, can differ fundamentally from each other, and Japan is generally considered to be a special case (Groenewegen 1993). Since markets in the Japanese economic system used to be more organized than elsewhere, government had a special role in the economy. Before discussing the particularities of the Japanese market economy, I will first briefly list the general arguments for government intervention in market economies in order to have a benchmark for explaining the specific position of government in Japan.

In all market economies government intervenes because of market failures such as collective goods, externalities and so-called natural monopolies. In the case of *collective goods* (like defense or dikes) markets cannot coordinate transactions, because goods cannot be individualized and no one can be excluded from consumption when the good or service is produced (everyone has to consume defense protection once it is installed, and an individual unwilling to pay a price cannot be excluded from protection). In this situation government replaces the market and decides on the production of the collective goods and finance is taken care of through taxes. In case of *externalities* the market does not register all scarcities. A well-known negative externality is pollution due to the absence of a market of clean air. Then the price of the good produced by air pollution has to be corrected by government through taxes, so the price reflects the "real scarcity". *Natural monopolies* are specific situations, in which the production technology is such that the most efficient scale of production equals total demand. So only one production plant produces at minimum costs per unit, and in that case a monopoly is most efficient. Government has to regulate those monopolies in order to prevent high consumer prices, or bad quality (for instance, in the case of water, gas, telecommunication services).

Like every other government in a market economy the Japanese government also intervenes because of these market failures. Besides market failures, markets can also be imperfect, which gives rise to government intervention in the form of competition policies. Those policies aim at the prevention or elimination of market concentration, which can have far-reaching consequences for technological development. Here we see large differences between market economies with the US and Japan often being the extreme cases (Yamamura 1986). A *market imperfection* is a situation in which the market in principle can coordinate efficiently, but firms have changed the market structures in such a way that competition is eliminated and the market cannot do its job adequately. Cartels are a case in point. The starting point is the idea that markets perform efficiently when a large number of firms compete with each other. Then firms are pressed to minimize production and transaction costs and to produce according to customers preferences. If firms make agreements to set prices, or divide markets, or to calculate prices according to specific cost plus pricing rules, then they reduce competition and customers get products at higher prices, or lower quality. American competition policy (anti-trust law) forbids in principal every type of collusion among firms (Groenewegen 1994). From the 1950s onwards (see below) Japan has had a different approach towards the blessings of competition. This view is based on a different idea of how markets function and how performances are evaluated. In short, Japan has been critical towards the capabilities of markets to coordinate behavior efficiently in the long run. When uncertainty and the need for information are introduced into the discussion, then Japan has defended the position that markets have limited capabilities in dealing efficiently in the long run. It is considered the responsibility of government to create an environment that reduces uncertainty for firms. This is exactly what Japanese industrial and technology policies is all about. Such policies are closely related with competition policy because the policies are based on the same view on the functioning of markets. In order to highlight Japanese technology policies two contrasting views on markets with respect to R&D of firms must be discussed.

These two views can be labeled as the "market efficiency hypothesis" and the "guided market hypothesis" The former considers the market as an efficient allocation mechanism, provided some crucial conditions are fulfilled: the presence of a large number of suppliers and customers, flexibility of prices, high mobility of goods, services and production factors, no distortion from firms and government. The latter view claims that firms and markets are suffering from short-sightedness in the sense that competition forces them to make profit in the short run. Moreover, prices reflect scarcities at this moment, and not future demand and supply. This is especially troublesome when we look at investment decisions like R&D. Firms make investment plans and compare returns on investment. Then uncertainty about future demand and supply which determines future prices, is crucial. If markets do not provide that kind of information, who does? In case of high uncertainty firms will apply a shorter horizon and postpone or eliminate investment plans resulting in a so-called "underinvestment" in R&D. This can be fatal for the competitiveness of the firm, the sector, and ultimately for the total economy. Japanese government has recognized this shortcoming of markets from the 1950s onwards and by means of a system of indicative planning, of industrial and technology policies, government has complemented the market mechanism.

From direct to indirect intervention in Japan
In the 1950s and 1960s government intervention has been very direct. The first plans of the Ministry of International Trade and Industry (MITI) were developed in an environment, in which firms had no foreign currency to finance the import of materials and technology. The firms were wholly dependent on government: specific target sectors were selected ("production priority system") and applied to sectors such as electric power, coal, iron and steel, and chemical fertilizers. The import of the necessary technology was financed by MITI and directed to the selected sectors. Exporting firms had to change foreign currency with MITI. Also, special financial institutions like the Japan Development Bank, supported investments in selected industries. Private banks were willing to lend money to firms in the target sectors. The home market was protected against foreign competition. Finally, if cooperation between firms was necessary to develop a targeted industry, then competition law was overruled by MITI. The Fair Trade Commission (FTC), a body responsible for the execution of the Anti Monopoly Law, was clearly the weaker agency in government. Those were the days of well coordinated industrial policies (Johnson 1982). Most policies in the 1950s and 60s were effective

because MITI controlled the basic resources: credit, technology, raw materials, markets and regulations of other ministries (like Ministry of Finance, Ministry of Transport, and the like).

From the middle of the 1960s onwards that situation began to change due to internal and external developments. When Japan grew economically, she was accepted as member of GATT (1955), IMF and the OECD (mid sixties). From then on the game had to be played according to the international rules of "free" trade. At the same time Japanese firms made higher profits and became more independent from especially the financial incentive of government. Johnson (1982) describes how MITI was unpleasantly surprised by Mitsubishi making a joint venture with Chrysler in the late 1960s without MITIs permission. The "Developmental State" (a State which guides economic structural development) began to lose its glamour and was forced to change policies of indirect guidance.

MITI did not want to lose control over industry because it feared stiff foreign competition when it would liberalize the markets. Japanese firms were considered too weak to compete successfully with the American and European giants. An attempt of MITI to have Parliament accept the so-called "Special Measures Law", which would have given MITI enormous legal power to intervene in specific industries, failed. The opposition of other ministries, notably the Ministry of Finance, of the employers association (*Keidanren*), of the large business groups (*keiretsu*) and of the FTC, was so strong that MITI had to be satisfied with a set of more indirect means of intervention. These have become known as the "Administrative Guidance", which was used to implement the objectives published in the so-called *"Visions"*. This is not to say that MITI was trying to violate the principles of the market economy; on the contrary, MITI viewed intervention as complementary to the market and aimed at strengthening the market principles. In official documents specifically the importance of information production and diffusion as complementary to the market was stressed:

> To...maintain and advance private sector's vigorous development...it is necessary to provide adequate information concerning the trends of domestic economy, international economy and industrial structure. It is particularly important to present a picture of the desired industrial structure, to achieve a national consensus on this, and to provide guidelines which facilitate the

distribution of resources. These steps will spur creative technological development and pioneering plant investment and will
thus invigorate the market structure by encouraging effective
competition (Industrial Structure Council, 1980, quoted from
Aldershoff, 1982).

This was the official argument for MITI to guide the industries in
the direction of the targets of the indicative plan("*Visions*"). From
the publication of the first "*Visions*" in 1963 onwards MITI tried to
reassure members of the OECD, notably the US, that their guidance was nothing more than information production and that
measures did not differ from the ones used in other market economies. MITI claimed that there is nothing mysterious about
administrative guidance: the directions, recommendations, suggestions and warnings of MITI do not reduce the autonomy of firms, but
help them to develop a long-term view which stimulated R&D
investments in specific directions. In the first "*Visions*" of 1963 the
optimal industrial structure for the future was grounded on two
criteria: income elasticity and productivity. Japan should concentrate industrial activities in sectors in which strong growth in
productivity was to be expected. Heavy and chemical industries
were presented as key sectors. The visions of the 1970s and 1980s,
which took changing comparative advantages into account,
stressed the importance of high-tech knowledge intensive sectors
(computers and numerically controlled machine tools). Together
with a change in focus in the visions, MITI changed its method of
intervention from a rather direct one in the fifties into a more
indirect approach from the mid-sixties onwards.

It would be a mistake to believe that all government intervention of MITI has been effective. Kikkawa (1983) shows that the
industrial policy in stagnating sectors (shipbuilding) can be very
effective, but that interventions in the expansion stage are of little
use (automobile, computers). This has to do on the one hand with
the lack of need of firms to be assisted by government and on the
other hand with the conflicts that such policies raise between
MITI and other ministries. With respect to the former it is clear
that firms are in need of a neutral outsider to organize the "orderly
retreat" in stagnating, mature markets. When a price war threatens the well-being of the whole sector, the firms find themselves in
a prisoners' dilemma and are often unable to restructure the market
efficiently by themselves. In such a situation firms are willing to

be guided by government in exchange for governmental services as a neutral arbitrator. However, when markets are in the expansion stage of the life cycle then firms are not very interested in "administrative guidance". On the contrary, examples in Kikkawa (1983) and Goto and Odagiri (1996) show that also Japanese firms have their private interests and develop their own strategies irrespective of the wishes of the government (the automobile sector is a clear case in point). With respect to the introduction stage of the life cycle the case is mixed. The second source of ineffectiveness of industrial policies involve conflicts between MITI and other ministries and agencies. Conflicts between MITI and the Ministry of Post and Telecommunications are reflected in cases concerning computers and telecommunication, with the Ministry of Health and Welfare in cases on pharmaceuticals, and more generally with the Ministry of Finance in cases of Keynesian demand policies, and with the FTC about strategic alliances and depression cartels which MITI has organized with industry. It would be misleading to present Japanese industrial and technology policies as a harmonious relation between government and firms. On the contrary, policy in Japan, as elsewhere, can be best characterized as a struggle between different interest groups among which government itself is certainly not a harmonious whole. Recent developments in technology policy in which "research associations" were central illustrate this.

Technology policies in the 1990s

In market economies firms generally "underinvestment" in R&D, which is due to the costs involved, the lack of complementary knowledge and the risk of not being able to sufficiently appropriate the benefits of the R&D investment. Firms can try to solve these problems themselves by means of cooperation. An alliance with other firms can, for example, increase funds available for R&D, or joint ventures can link complementary knowledge of different firms into one R&D project. Underinvestment can also be caused by the risks involved in the expansion phase of the life cycle. What are the dangers that others will imitate the innovation and enter the expansion stage without the burden of heavy R&D costs? Then competitors can offer the new product at such a low price that the firm which made the original investments cannot earn their investments back. Patents often solve that "appropriability problem", but certainly not always. Firms can try to reduce the "appropriability risk" by making agreements with competitors, suppliers and customers. Agreements on standards, on production facilities, on long-term supply, on the common use of R&D results, on not selling knowledge to others, and the like, are all examples of how firms can deal with appropriability problems themselves. This does not mean government is an outsider then. Agreements between firms imply reduction of competition, and government has to decide whether the gain in an increase in R&D investments counterbalances the reduction in competition: the issue of cooperation against collusion.

If firms are not able to solve the underinvestment problems themselves due to lock-ins, prisoner dilemma, or other barriers, then government as a broker can organize cooperation in so-called "research associations". The initiative of government and her monitoring role make it a typical Japanese way of government intervention.

Examples of these high-tech consortia (independent organizations that bring together competing firms with the purpose to start joint R&D), are the VLSI, Supercomputer, and the Fifth Generation Computers (Callon, 1995).

With the institutional arrangement of research associations it became possible to undertake R&D projects jointly that were too common, too costly, too risky and/or too difficult for a single firm to tackle alone, thus solving the underinvestment problem inherent in R&D investment (Goto and Wakasugi, quoted from Audretsch). MITI often takes the initiative to organize a research association and negotiates with the Fair Trade Commission to exempt the association from the Anti-Monopoly Law.

A large part of undertaken R&D in those associations is financed by government; for example, in 1985 half of the R&D programs were subsidized, implying that government claimed the resulting innovations as property of government. R&D can be organized in one of the sixteen public laboratories under the direction of the Agency of Industrial Science and Technology (AIST) of MITI. MITI can also finance projects carried out in private research associations for 100 per cent. But in that case patents also belong to MITI which can distribute the information to any firm willing to pay a fee. R&D can also be financed with conditional loans, which firms have to repay when the R&D leads to profit-making activity within a seven-year period (for example, the project on large integrated circuits: VLSI). The results of Japanese technology policy with respect to the research associations are mixed, which can be illustrated with the following cases.

Very Large Scale Integration (VLSI)
The VLSI consortium involved the private firms: NEC, Toshiba, Fujitsu, Hitachi and Mitsubishi and also Nippon Telegraph and Telephone (NTT) and MITI. It targeted the development of semi-conductors for computer use. Japan had to catch up with the US and for that reason a joint effort was considered necessary. The immediate reason for MITI to launch the VLSI project was information about plans of IBM to develop a new type of chip far beyond what the Japanese could produce at that time. In 1975 MITI launched the idea of a joint laboratory for the development of large integrated circuits. Firms were interested because the costs were too high for them individually, but the idea of cooperation of scientists from different firms seemed a nightmare to them. With a substantial subsidy MITI convinced firms that something like a joint lab had to be created (Figure 1 shows the organizational structure of the labs). Electrotechnical laboratory (ETL), a MITI's research lab, was one of the heads of the sub-labs. There were two group-labs, the Cooperative Development Laboratories (CDL) and NTIS (NEC-Toshiba Information Systems).

But the lab was something firms were forced into and was not wholeheartedly supported by them. The firms gave the joint lab a peripheral rather than a central part of the program. Firms, not fully convinced of the benefits of joining research, were not forced to support the program. Those firms which sent scientists to the joint lab, were given special instructions not to send their top people and to keep the core knowledge for themselves. The VLSI project is generally considered a success, but not because of the joint research. In fact, 85 percent of the research was undertaken by separate private laboratories of the participating firms. Most of the information exchange cooperation was not the result of the joint lab, but a matter of interest of the private firm and historical relations.

"In sum, even at the small joint lab, where MITI put tremendous effort into the design and promotion of a setting conducive to joint research, it was extremely difficult to get researchers from competing companies to work together. Patent data reveal that joint research was minimal" (Callon 1995,91).

Figure VLSI Consortium Lab Structure

Source: Callon 1995, 18

It is considered more successful because subsidies pushed investments of firms in specific directions. "Thus the VLSI consortium was
more an example of high-tech subsidies than of high-tech joint
R&D." (Callon 1995,16).

Although the VLSI project is characterized by conflicts between MITI and NTT, Callon (1995,116) evaluates the VLSI
positively: the goals were met, positive spill-overs in promoting
Japanese production of semiconductor equipment existed, and opportunity costs were minimized.

Supercomputer

This project aimed to build the world's fastest computer. It was not
well funded (20 percent of VLSI), and the participating firms were
the VLSI ones and Oki. The reluctance of firms to participate with
the project has been the problem from the beginning. MITI continued to press them, but the lack of enthusiasm is reflected in the
absence of a joint lab and corporate funding. There are only separate
labs and MITI funding, which can hardly be called a joint R&D

consortium. The idea was that participating firms would share the results of each others separate research. Through a registration and information system, conferences and reports, MITI tried to facilitate information exchange. However, Fransman (1991) and others conclude that knowledge sharing was minimal.

In assessing the Supercomputer project Callon (1995,129) concludes that the goals were partly realized and partly not. "In sum, the Supercomputer consortium was unable to achieve its goals of creating new systems and new device technologies that would leap frog the status quo."

Fifth generation

The fifth generation project started in 1982 and involved more firms and more money than the Supercomputer. Also Matsushita, Sharp and NTT participated; other firms and labs were also involved. The project aimed at a radical change in computer technology, and a joint lab had to become the heart of the project. Again MITI had difficult problems in getting the firms committed. Although a joint lab was created, it was responsible for only 20 percent of the funds. Another problem concerned the relationship between the MITI's civil servants and the top managers. Within MITI career positions are reserved for the general officials (*jimukan*) from the University of Tokyo in contrast to the scientists with a technical background (*gikan*). Callon (1995,50) describes how the MITI *jimukan* had a completely different idea about the project than the *gikan* of Fuchi, for instance. In assessing the results of the consortium these were very bad in meeting the objectives, spillovers and opportunity costs. MITI had conflicts with other bureaucracies about the projects: with the Ministry of Post and Telecommunication (MPT) which supervised NTT that was a state monopoly until 1985; with the Ministry of Education (MOE) and the Science and Technology Agency (STA) about basic research issues (Callon 1995, chapter 3). With Japan moving to technology frontiers conflicts concerning basic research became more intense. "Science" has traditionally been the area of the MOE and STA and not of MITI. In the VLSI project the programs of MITI and NTT differed on a number of aspects (time period, length, budget, participating firms), likewise in the Supercomputer project.

With respect to the Fifth Generation it was the conflict between the MOE and MITI that blocked university participation. In that project basic research was crucial, and firms were neither willing nor able to be involved in basic research. Because of Japan moving more and more towards the edges of technology, MITI tried to become increasingly involved in fundamental research. However, that was the domain of universities and the bureaucratic domain of the MOE.

A closer look at the cooperation in the consortia makes one skeptical about how real the cooperation was. True, all of the invited firms did join the consortia but often joining was more a matter of tactics than commitment. If possible, firms did not contribute to the funds and refused to create a joint lab. A qualification of "minimal" or "hostile" cooperation seems to be appropriate.

Recent changes and conditions for effective policy

Understanding and evaluating a country's policy demand detailed knowledge of the institutional structure in which the policy is embedded, and of the internal and external changes that take place.

Institutional structure

A country's institutional structure consists of values and norms, formal and informal regulations and the structures and organizations at meso and micro-level. In the case of Japan values of group orientation, long-term trust relations between firms, internal labor markets inside firms, are among others, elements which make Japan a "relational capitalist state"(see Groenewegen 1997). This is in contrast with "market capitalism" with individualistic values that characterize, for instance, the American world. In its specific institutional setting Japanese government was able to develop an industrial policy of setting priorities and organizing investments in the 1950s and 60s. The internal and external developments did not obstruct such intervening actions: the *keiretsu*, internal labor markets, subcontracting system, and the like, supported strong governmental guidance, whereas external developments did not put much pressure on Japan to change policies in those days.

The institutional structure remained more or less the same, but internal and external changes forced government to adopt her policies. The direct industrial policy had to be replaced by a more indirect technology policy based on Visions and Administrative Guidance. Later the research associations became important instruments.

Today Japan faces new challenges with large potential impli-cations for government policies. We will discuss the further shift to basic research, the further liberalization of markets, and the extension of Japan's role as an economic and political leader.

Basic research

Japan is now already quite a few years at the forefront of techno-logical development. The years of learning and applying Western technology are far behind Japanese firms. A shift from catch up to fundamental research demands a large role for public institutions, like universities. However, Goto and Odagiri (1996,266) point out that universities "are suffering from obsolete equipment, poor funding, and the loss of talented researchers to companies". They show that researchers at universities spend only 12 per cent of the nation's R&D expenditure; a percentage that is dramatically declining. Compared to Europe and the US, the support of univer-sity researchers in Japan is much poorer. Significant is the financial support universities get from business by means of grants, joint projects and subcontracting. Goto and Odagiri write:

> "Such an increase can be beneficial in fostering industry-university collaboration. Yet, if the increase is the result of uni-versity researchers desperately seeking industry funds to compensate for the shortage of government funds, one may worry whether truly basic research can be maintained."

Another problem raised by Goto and Odagiri (1996) concerns the lifetime employment at universities. A more flexible employment system that allows for changes in new research areas, joint projects between industry and universities, and temporary exchange of personnel is needed to stimulate projects in basic research.

The shift from applied to more basic research will in itself have large implications for the position of MITI (Callon 1995,170). First, the directly visible return from R&D funded by MITI will decrease when the research becomes more basic. Second, the con-flicts between MITI and the Ministry of Education will increase and finally, basic research demands a longer time span, which makes the control of research associations more difficult.

In short, to push Japan further into areas of basic research re-quires changes in the allocation and organization of funds, as well as changes in the employment relations.

Further liberalization and deregulation

Japan regularly announces programs of liberalization and deregulation of labor, capital and product markets. Often these programs seem to be meant for propaganda especially for the US market. However, recently analysts regularly point out that important actors in Japan seem convinced of the necessity to start fundamental changes. Why? There is no alternative. From the 1970s Japan has experienced a decreasing growth (average 1955-1973:10 percent; 1973-1991: 4 percent; 1991-1996: 1 percent). Keynesian demand stimulation ($300 billion in the last five years) does not seem to have any impact on the real economy (*The Economist*, January 1997). To stimulate exports as an engine of growth is politically unrealistic. Moreover, owing to increased overseas production facilities, exports are no longer easily stimulated. What about lowering interest rates in order to stimulate investments? Interest is as low as low can be. Government spending does not seem to be a good alternative either because public debt is already very high. More and more businessmen, politicians and bureaucrats in Japan seem to opt for the only remaining alternative: deregulate markets, stimulate competition so production and transaction costs will decrease and growth will result from increasing productivity and decreasing costs. It is not only the Economic Planning Board (EPA) that favors deregulation; also MITI, *Keidanren* and the *keiretsu* openly plea for deregulation. At the same time other changes can be observed: life-time employment is under attack. In recent years firms have openly reduced their work force and seem to rely more on smaller groups of core workers. Also there have been changes in shareholding and the functioning of the capital market as a market for corporate control (Groenewegen 1997). Elements from American "market capitalism" are imported into Japanese "relational capitalism". All this strengthens the idea that something is changing, but that does not necessarily mean changes are so fundamental that the characteristics of "relational capitalism" itself are under attack. Take the change in lifetime employment and the relation with R&D as an example. Imai and Itami (1984) discussed the relation between the internal labor market and the type of R&D in Japan: long-term commitments push for incremental innovations along existing lines of competencies. Changes in the internal allocation can have implications for long-term commitments of labor as well as management, but how fast and how deep these consequences will be is hard to tell. It is likely that all actors involved realize well the blessings of the internal labor market, but at the same time are convinced of the fact that more flexibility and cost reduction is needed. It is likely to expect a solution, which fits into the Japanese institutional structure and which will allow for an internal labor market for a smaller group of core employees and a larger external labor market for employees with less firm specific capabilities.

Foreign investment, Trade and ODA
Japan has become an economic leader in Asia and is an emerging political leader. The interdependencies of not only the economies in East Asia make it impossible for Japan to return to any kind of protectionism. The interdependencies are a fact of life with large implications for government policies. Take the industrial networks and R&D investments as an example. Japan is well known for its industrial networks (Groenwegen 1993) which stimulated investments in R&D substantially. Aoki (1990) among others points out how important relations between production and R&D departments are with respect to innovations. When large parts of the production are placed overseas then that relationship is at least partly broken. Technology policies of governments that were related to those networks will change when foreign direct investments increase in such a way as in the Japanese case.

Conclusion
We have seen that the nature of technology (more basic and the leading edge), the autonomy of firms (having their own resources and need to survive in a turbulent competitive world market), and pressure from abroad (not to protect and to intervene), form together a strong pressure to change policy. Given the institutional structure and the history of the actors involved, this certainly does not mean that Japanese government will withdraw from the market and let private interest rule. All actors, including firms, expect government to act, but in a different way than before. It is expected that intervention will be less channeled through research associations and will be directed to the stimulation of basic research. This implies a growing importance of business groups and networks and a decreasing role for government.

* Dr. John P.M. Groenewegen is Associate Professor of Economic Organization, Erasmus University Rotterdam, The Netherlands.

References

Aldershoff, W.G. (1982), "Anticiperend economisch-structuur beleid in Japan", *ESB*, 28 July, pp. 768-771.

Aoki, M. (1990), "Toward an Economic Model of the Japanese Firm", *Journal of Economic Literature*, XXVIII, March, pp. 1-27.

Callon, Scott (1995), *Divided Sun; MITI and the Breakdown of Japanese High-Tech Industrial Policy 1995-1993*, Stanford, California: Stanford University Press.

Fransman, Martin (1991), *The Market and Beyond: Cooperation and Competition in Information Technology Development in the Japanese System*. New York, Cambridge University Press.

Goto, A. and Hiroyuki Odagiri (1996), *Technology and Industrial Development in Japan*, Clarendon Press: Oxford.

Groenewegen, J. (1993), *Dynamics of the Firm*, J. Groenewegen (ed.), Aldershot: Edward Elgar.

Groenewegen, J. (1994), "About Double Organized Markets: Issues of Competition and Cooperation. The Dutch Construction Cartel: An Illustration", *Journal of Economic Issues*, pp. 901-908.

Groenewegen, J. (1997), "Institutions of Capitalism", forthcoming in the *Journal of Economic Issues*, June.

Imai, K. and H. Itami (1984), "Interpenetration of Organization and Market", *International Journal of Industrial Organization*, 2, pp. 285-310.

Industrial Structure Council (1980), *Industrial Structure Policy for the 1980s (excerpt)*, March.

Johnson, Chalmers A. (1982), *MITI and the Japanese Miracle: The Growth of Industrial Policy, 1925-1975*. Stanford, California: Stanford University Press.

Kikkawa, M. (1983), *Shipbuilding, Motorcars and Semiconductors, the Diminishing Role of Industrial Policy in Japan*, in: G. Shepherd, F. Duchène and Ch. Sanders (eds.), *Europe's Industries: Public and Private Strategies for Change*. London: Pinter.

McMillan, Charles (1985), *The Japanese Industrial System*, De Gruyter: Berlin, New York.

Yamamura, Kozo (1986), "Joint Research and Antitrust: Japanese vs. American Strategies", in: *Japan's High Technology Industries*, edited by Hugh Patrick and Larry Meissner, University of Washington Press: Seattle.

Chapter 8

Joop A. Stam: "Technology Transfer of Japanese Enterprises in Pacific Asia: The Case of the Electronic Industry"

Since the early eighties we can observe a growing tendency among Japanese enterprises to gradually shift their focus of attention and activities from Western markets to those of Pacific Asia. In Japan this is often referred to as *datsu-ô nyû-a*, which can be translated as "goodbye West, here we are Asia", a reverse of the movement after World War II when Japan distanced herself from Asia and sought shelter with the West.(1) There are a number of reasons which contributed to this shift.

First of all, the worsening trade friction between Japan and her American and European partners. Japanese products exported to American and European markets were not equally matched by Japanese imports of Western goods. Japan was univocally blamed for the subsequent huge trade surplus because of its alleged closed markets and barriers towards foreign products. The trade dispute escalated even to a point that American senators reverted to bashing Japanese products in front of television cameras to underline their argument and relieve their frustrations. The Japanese were shocked and deeply insulted. Secondly, the growth and development of the NIEs, the newly industrializing economies in the region, South Korea, Hong Kong, Taiwan, Singapore and in their wake also the so-called ASEAN-4 countries like Malaysia, Thailand, Indonesia and the Philippines, created new markets and business opportunities for an expansionary Japanese industry. Thirdly, the increasing prosperity and soaring labor cost in Japan made it attractive to transfer labor-intensive, dirty and dangerous production processes to Pacific Asia. The respective countries of the region in turn stimulated direct foreign investment and tried to attract all type of industrial activities with tax benefits and location incentives.

An extra stimulus to expatriate part of the production to the Pacific Asian region were the Plaza Agreements of 1985, when the G-7 decided to realign the major currencies. Within a short period of time the Japanese yen appreciated from ¥ 205 to the dollar in 1985 to ¥ 130 in 1991 and finally even below ¥ 90 in 1995. The effect of the appreciation has been dramatic. Japanese products suddenly lost their competitiveness in export markets, and companies were forced to cut costs. Simultaneously, with their high-priced yen Japanese companies could easily afford to invest abroad, a condition which even improved when the so-called "bubble economy" created an unexpected potential to borrow money.

Finally, the Japanese government under Prime Minister Nakasone, introduced an active policy of *kokusai-ka*, internationalization. Japan with a low percentage of offshore production of its total production, should reduce its export and produce more abroad. This would decrease the trade surplus but also contribute to the economic and industrial development of the recipient countries. The developing economies of Pacific Asia were the most natural target for investment. In addition, Japan's Official Development Assistance (ODA) money which generously flowed to the region, was often linked up to designated public utility and infra-structure projects. Since many of these projects were assigned to Japanese industry, their growing preference for Pacific Asia can be understood.

During the last two decades the economies of Pacific Asia have almost all taken off one after another. They are all in different stages of development but strongly interlinked through trade and investment.(2) Berri and Ozawa refer to a process of "comparative advantage recycling", i.e. as the industrialization of the region proceeds, a structural upgrading of technological sophistication, from low-tech, labor intensive to hi-tech, capital intensive, takes place.(3) In particular foreign direct investment has facilitated significant increases in domestic Asian business and contributed to the improvement of the economic performance of the respective Asian economies. Consequently, the Pacific Economic Cooperation Council, the PECC, concluded in its 1995 report "Advancing Regional Integration", that "FDI may provide an even stronger stimulus to economic development than increased trade". One of the obvious reasons is the expected spill-over effects of technology-related-investment in local production facilities.

Technology transfer and regional development

In recent years governments in Pacific Asia have all converted from an import-substitution policy of industrialization to an export-led industrialization policy.(4) This policy shift coincided with an active acquisition of foreign direct investment because the new factories would create employment and income, tax revenues and foreign reserves but above all because foreign direct investment would contribute to economic and industrial development through technology transfer.

Technology transfer is a concept with a multitude of definitions. We follow Agmon and Glinov and define technology transfer as the process of acquisition, development, utilization and maintenance of (technical) knowledge, both hardware, software and human ware, which occurs in transactions between governments, institutes, enterprises and individuals.(5) Technology transfer can be the result of aid agreements between governments or exchange arrangements between institutes like universities. We will concentrate on technology transfer at the enterprise and individual levels and look in particular at the effects of interaction between foreign enterprises and domestic firms, partners, suppliers or subcontractors in the host country. Technology transfer between a foreign and domestic firm directly affects the individual employees involved as well, most obviously through (in-company) training and education.

In this chapter we will concentrate on technology transfer of Japan's electrical and electronic industry and try to assess its effects on the development of the recipient country. We have chosen this sector because during the last decade and a half Japanese electronic enterprises have substantially expanded their manufacturing capacity in the region and produce now more than 60 percent of their total world output in Asia (Table 1). In addition, not only large assembling companies have set up shop in Pacific Asia but also medium and small size Japanese manufacturers of parts and components have followed their masters to the developing economies of Pacific Asia. Another reason for choosing the electronic industry is the tradition of technology transfer between the core firm and its suppliers and subcontractors and the strong cooperation within the manufacturing networks.

This technology transfer in Japan can be located in the vertical production chain, *sangyô keiretsu*, the pyramid of loyal small and medium-sized companies supplying the parts and components to the final assembler. This dominant structure of mass-production in Japan provides the possibility for the core firm to reap the benefits of specialization and flexible manufacturing, in particular in terms of reduction of production costs. One of the primary conditions for realizing these benefits has been the close cooperation between the core firm and its main suppliers. Although the relationship cannot be labeled egalitarian, the interdependence between core company and suppliers has had a beneficial effect on inter-company technology transfer.

Table 1   Japanese Electronics Manufacturers Abroad (%)

%	consumer electronics	industrial electronics	parts & components	total
Asia/world	**59.3**	**48.2**	**68.4**	**62.2**
ASEAN/world	29.8	17.6	28.1	26.3
NIEs/world	17.9	18.7	31.4	25.4
China/world	9.1	10.9	8.3	9.3

Source: EIAJ, 1995 foreign investment list

In order to secure the required quality and quantity of parts, components and subassemblies, Japanese electronics makers have resorted to investment in training and education of the personnel of the supplying companies while often also taking care of the co-financing of their equipment. Thus not only knowledge about production techniques but also production management has been shared. Within this structure long-term relations are adamant. These long-term relations are a precondition for joint product design and development of new markets as well. Sharing all necessary information available within the network, enables the cluster of companies to enter new markets and reduce risks. Often collaboration in research and development follows.

Within this cooperative structure technology transfer between the core enterprise and its suppliers is intensive and transactions costs are reduced. Consequently, high quality, competitive products designed, developed and produced in an integrated way, have become the hallmark of Japanese industry and created their competitive edge in the market. It is obvious that Japanese enterprises manufacturing in Pacific Asia seek to transfer this model of cooperation. How successful are they? From an extensive study of the available literature and field studies we can make the following analysis.(6)

Stages of internationalization and contribution to local development

The internationalization of Japan's electronic industry towards East and Southeast Asia can roughly be divided into three stages. The first stage concerns the substitution of imported Japanese products in domestic Asian markets by local production of those products. The second stage comprises the mass-production of luxury electric and electronic household goods, mainly for export markets like Europe and the United States and partially to accommodate a growing domestic demand. The third stage is an extension of the second one and contains the production of high-tech electronic equipment, predominantly for export to advanced markets.(7)

This strategy of internationalization of production of Japanese large electronics manufacturers has coincided with changes in development policy of the respective countries in Pacific Asia as well. In particular the transition from an import substitution type of industrialization policy, stimulating local production of previously imported goods, to an export oriented industrialization, i.e. attracting foreign capital and technology by offering tax free zones, tax exemptions or cheap locations, to produce goods for export, spurred Japanese investments in the region, especially in the ASEAN countries. Malaysia which developed the ambition to become an important production center for electronics has been a target country of Japanese electronics makers. Once these companies were firmly established they almost naturally evolved to the next stage, expanding their scope of activities by utilizing their competitive advantage, and fending off newcomers.

Stage one

The import substitution stage usually constitutes the establishment of a local factory, either as a 100 percent daughter or subsidiary company or as a joint operation with a local producer.(8) The products are commonly technologically simple and have a limited added value as, for instance, rice cookers, toasters, fans and small radios. As local demand for these products increases it becomes more efficient to produce them in the proximity of the market rather than export them. For these types of electro-mechanical products procurement of parts and components in the local market is not a serious problem. Product and production technology required for manufacturing these goods usually matches the available domestic sources and technical capabilities.

As a matter of fact product improvement and adaptation to the local requirements are easily achieved, while autonomy to develop an own market strategy or even technology policy is relatively large. Local employees are taught how to operate in an authentic Japanese production environment and become familiar with modern production methods, tools and techniques. The same applies to local producers of parts and components. Japanese high quality standards demand support from the Japanese manufacturing company, and their active assistance stimulates improvement of product and production technology.

In this stage of import substitution of simple products the technology transfer of the Japanese manufacturing company both in terms of training local personnel in modern manufacturing techniques and upgrading of local technical capabilities, is relatively high. From the early nineteen eighties on we can observe this type of investment cum technology transfer of Japanese electronic industry in the ASEAN countries. The NIEs experienced this stage somewhat earlier and nowadays proceed themselves to transfer technology to ASEAN as well.

Stage two

The second stage concerns the mass production of luxury consumer electronics. We refer to products like mid-sized color TV's, audio equipment, video recorders, air conditioners and the like. These products are mainly manufactured for export to foreign markets but also meet a growing demand among domestic consumers who have reached the level of prosperity to afford them. Incentives for Japanese manufacturers to produce these products off-shore are the attractive fiscal climate and the ready support of the host government in the wake of their export-oriented-industrialization policy, but above all, the rising labor costs in Japan itself and the lower wages in the region, particularly in the ASEAN-4 countries. The Plaza Agreement of the G-7 in 1985, resulting in the rapid rise of the yen, made export of these mass products less competitive and stimulated the manufacturing of this category of products abroad. Thus a new phase started in the internationalization strategy of Japanese enterprises.

The production systems put in place in the region are highly standardized and strongly automated. They have been completely tested in Japan and are able to produce high quantities of products of a constant quality, an inevitable requirement when the competitive markets of Europe and North America are the destination of these products. The technological knowledge of these systems is embedded in the machines which present themselves as black boxes and hardly accessible. Technology transfer in this stage of internationalization is mainly related to the training and education of local personnel to operate and maintain the machines. Routinized production runs and prescribed handbook operations do not allow for meaningful local autonomy. Production schedules are dictated by distant marketing and sales departments.

Standard parts and components are procured at the local market but only to the extent that domestic producers can deliver them in the right quantities, of the right quality and at the right time. As Japanese electronics manufacturers have expanded their factories and increased their investment in mass production facilities all in a short period of time, domestic suppliers were often unable to meet the required criteria. Consequently small and medium-sized Japanese parts and component makers followed the assemblers abroad and created supply chains in Southeast Asia in order to fill the gap and meet the demand. In the hierarchy of suppliers they obviously rank higher than the domestic companies. With their technological capabilities, honed in Japan, they can easily outperform the local entrepreneur who is often relegated to the production of simple things like wire, connectors, body panels or packaging materials.

Japanese part and component suppliers have spread all over the region but are operating in a hub and spoke structure with Singapore and Hong Kong as a hub. The intra-company procurement of the Japanese electronics networks pose a formidable competition to the budding local enterprises. And yet these local enterprises do associate themselves actively with both the Japanese assembling company and the Japanese suppliers in order to get access to advanced production technology and upgrade their own capabilities.

At the end of the nineteen eighties when the yen had soared sky-high, most Japanese electronics makers had expatriated a substantial part of their production of mass-consumer goods to the ASEAN countries, skillfully utilizing the low-cost structure of the host countries, the incentives of the local authorities and the availability of experienced Japanese suppliers.

Table 2   Procurement of Japanese Industry in ASEAN
(% of total procurement)

	electronics industry		
	1986	1989	1992
local procurement	31.1	34.3	39.7
import from Japan	55.3	40.3	42.2
import from third countries	13.6	25.3	18.1
North America	*0.2*	*0.2*	*8.7*
Asia	*98.3*	*98.1*	*90.5*
Europe	*0.1*	*0*	*0.2*

Source: MITI, 1988, 1991, 1994

Stage three
A third wave of overseas investment starts in the early nineties when also the manufacturing of high-tech products like computers, computer peripherals, video cameras, pocket telephones and the like, is transferred to Southeast Asia. The competitive environment, the booming Asian economies, the well-developed infrastructure and the recessive Japanese home market spurred most Japanese electronics makers to complete their internationalization policy and integrate Asia in their production strategy.

These high-tech products are all designed, developed and tested in Japan and then assembled in ASEAN member states in an automated or robotized production system, to be exported to the regional markets but above all those of Europe and the Americas.

The production processes are usually closed systems which do not allow local management to intervene. The high level of technical sophistication leads to a high percentage of Japanese technicians in key positions and limited possibilities for local technical staff. The remaining routine jobs in this highly automated environment are performed by locals. After all technology transfer in this type of production processes is very limited. Recently some Japanese companies have reluctantly set up schemes for training loyal Asian staff in their factories in Japan. The reluctance to invest in large scale training can be understood from the perspective of the market value of these employees after training and the high labor mobility.

Subassemblies and core components are usually directly imported from Japan of ordered from Japanese suppliers in the region. Local companies provide the additional parts. Of course they can learn from their role as subcontractor in a Japanese production chain and upgrade their technical and organizational capabilities, but the impact of this high-tech manufacturing on the industrialization is limited. And yet national and local authorities are very eager to attract these type of investments.

Table 3   Japanese Investments in Electronics in ASEAN and Technology Transfer: Stages and Gross effects

Import Substitution '80 local content 90 %	Mass Production '85 local content 40-60%	Hi-tech Production '90 local content 10-30%
rice cookers	color TV's	CD players
toasters	video recorders	PC; peripherals
radios	audio equipment	video cameras
electric fans	air conditioners	cellular telephones
autonomy high	autonomy medium	autonomy low
TT high	TT medium	TT low

Observations

The rapid expansion of Japanese electronics industry into the region, in particular the ASEAN countries, has revealed a number of problems.(9) First of all, there is an increasing lack of local suppliers which are able to meet the quality standards of Japanese assemblers and can produce the required numbers. Concurrent with the growing demand of supplies they should expand their enterprises but lack of capital available to these medium- and small-sized companies seriously hampers these plans. Local banks and investors prefer to fund the big companies and large projects above the risky business of small companies. Family capital remains the principal source of funding.

Secondly, the booming electronics industry in ASEAN has created a growing demand of adequately trained and educated technical personnel. Although investment in education is expanding, the scarcity of qualified technicians is becoming evident. In addition, young people with advanced education prefer the office to the factory. Within Japanese companies in the region local personnel with a technical background often experiences competition from Japanese expatriated technical staff. Consequently, they frequently change jobs when promotion to higher-ranked positions is not feasible. In itself this might be considered positive for spreading knowledge and experience, but often the feeling of an interrupted, incomplete technology transfer remains.

The interlinkage between foreign direct investment and the needs of local economy and industry is highest in the stage of import substitution. However, the contribution to the improvement of local skill levels decreases as the level of sophistication of product and production processes increases. Apparently the required time to adjust to the necessary technology and skill levels does not coincide smoothly with international market developments and production strategies of transnational corporations.

Japanese international electronics companies have replicated their integrated production system in the NIEs and in ASEAN in a typical hub and spoke structure. They utilize the long-term inter-corporate and intra-conglomerate relations for sourcing the parts and components in the ASEAN region among Japanese suppliers, in a similar way they are used to in Japan. Local companies can only benefit technologically and commercially to the extent that they are prepared to establish long-term relations as well.

In general Japanese transnational companies with production facilities in Pacific Asia strongly control the technology which is transferred to Asian countries. First of all, they transfer step by step and only within the framework of a long-term relationship. Secondly, the predominant way of transfer of skills and techniques is through on-the-job training of local personnel. This entails company-specific training and an increased level of dependency. In addition, key technical and managerial positions are occupied by Japanese expatriate personnel.

Local suppliers to Japanese assembling companies who are engaged in a long-term relationship can move up from one market to another and from one technological niche to the following. However, they become very dependent on their Japanese buyers through adaptive engineering. Jointly developed technologies bind companies to each other and have a restrictive effect on further expansion, particularly when patents and licenses are involved. Their dominant position allows Japanese companies to dictate conditions. This situation is particularly prevalent in the ASEAN countries; the NIEs which have had an equal share of Japanese production companies, have been able to overcome this dependency through strong local competition of enterprises active in the same product markets or through government intervention and regulation.

It is clear that with the advent of Japanese production facilities in the region many technological and organizational innovations have been introduced. The arrival of computer based manufacturing and the adoption of zero-defects, just-in-time delivery have changed suddenly the nature of production processes in the region. In order to fully benefit from this, host countries must develop their own indigenous technological capabilities as quickly as possible. Only on that basis they can prevent debilitating dependency and gain leverage in more advantageous technological transfer arrangements. An active role for government in building an infrastructure and setting priorities for development is needed since it is highly unlikely that private initiative will do so. Footloose international companies are moving along with the opportunities in sight.

Active government support in strengthening the financial basis of local small and medium enterprises is necessary to guarantee an independent development of the industry. In addition, a stimulus for research and development is needed in order to upgrade the technological capabilities and generate indigenous innovations.

Ideally, investing transnational enterprises and host country industry should cooperate in the joint development of hardware, software and human ware but corporate attitudes, market conditions and plain competition seem to prevent a complete technology transfer.

* Prof. Dr. Joop A. Stam, Department of Modern Japanese Studies, Faculty of Economics, Erasmus University Rotterdam, The Netherlands.

Notes and reference

1. Tadashi Yamamoto. "Grass-roots exchange in a new era". *Japan Review of International Affairs.* Volume 10, no. 2 Spring 1996, p. 137. See also Koji Taira. "Workplace productivity, macroeconomic performance, and world history", in: *Human Resource Management and Economic Development in Asia.* Proceedings of the 1994 Asian Regional Conference on Industrial Relations. Tokyo: The Japan Institute of Labor, 1994, p. 240.
2. Yamazawa Ippei. *Economic Development and International Trade. The Japanese Model.* Honolulu: East-West Center, 1990.
3. Berri and Ozawa. "Pax Americana and Asian exports: revealed trends of comparative advantage recycling". *The International Trade Journal,* Volume XI, no. 1, Spring 1997, p. 39-67.
4. Edward K.Y. Chen. "The Asia Model of Economic Development: Policy Implications for the 21st Century" in: *Asia's Challenges in the Coming Century. New Ways for Japan to Cooperate in Regional Development.* Tokyo: Institute of Developing Economies. 1997, p. 45-54.
5. Agmon and Glinov. *Technology Transfer in International Business.* Oxford: Oxford University Press, 1991. p. 64.
6. Shojiro Tokunaga (ed.). *Japan's Foreign Investment and Asian economic Interdependence. Production, Trade, and Financial Systems.* Tokyo: University of Tokyo Press. 1992. Shoichi Yamashita (ed.). *Transfer of Japanese Technology and Management to the ASEAN Countries.* Tokyo: University of Tokyo Press, 1992. Ministry of International Trade and Industry. *Prospects and Challenges for the Upgrading of Industries in the ASEAN Region.* Tokyo: Tsûshô Sangyô-sho, 1993. Kaigai Rôdô Hakusho. *NIEs, ASEAN Shokoku no Keizai Hatten to Chingin Henka.* Tokyo: Nihon Rôdô Kenkyû Kikô. Seki Mitsuhiro. *Beyond The*

Full-set Industrial Structure. Japanese Industry in the New Age of East Asia. Tokyo: LTCB International Library Foundation, 1994. Jomo K.S. (ed.). *Japan and Malaysian Development. In the Shadow of the Rising Sun.* London: Routledge, 1994. Imano Kôichiro, Uchida Masaru. "Gijutsu idô to Nihonjin shukkôsha" in: *Taiwan no Rôdô Jijô to Nihonkei Kigyô.* Tokyo: Nihon Rôdô Kenkyû Kikô, 1992. Hiromi Ohki. "Japanese Processing and Assembly Industries in Asia are Building Regional Division of Labor", in: *Digest of Japanese Industry and Technology,* No. 262, 1991, p. 22-34. Yoo Soo Hong. *Leveraging Technology for Strategic Advantage in the Global Market: Case of the Korean Electronics Industry.* Korean Institute for International Economic Policy: working paper no 93-07, December 1993. Toru Sunada ea. *Japan's direct investments in East Asia. Changing division of labor and technology transfer in household electric appliance industry.* MITI Research Institute, 1993. Van Tran. *Japanese Style Management and Technology Transfer in Thailand.* Tokyo: Japan Center for Economic Research. 1993.

7. Edward K.Y. Chen distinguishes four stages and types of industrialization in the Pacific Asian region: Import Substitution type 1, producing consumer goods, using protectionist measures to groom infant industries; Import Substitution type 2: producing capital goods and consumer durables; Export Orientation type 1: producing labor-intensive light manufactured goods; Export orientation type 2 and Export Orientation 2 Complex: producing technology/capital/knowledge-intensive products. He argues that economic growth in East Asia can be explained by the linkage of direct foreign investment and trade based on networks of companies and industries. Our Japanese example is a point in case. See: "The Asia Model of Economic Development: Policy Implications for the 21st Century" in: *Asia's Challenges in the Coming Century. New Ways for Japan to Cooperate in Regional Development.* Tokyo: Institute of Developing Economies. 1997, p. 45-54.

8. See Suthiphand Chirathivat and Giovanni Capannelli. "Experience of Japanese Firms in ASEAN: Electrical Machinery and Transport Equipment Industries in Thailand and Malaysia". Paper presented at Bocconi University Workshop: Integration Dynamics among ASEAN Economies. The Role of Europe and Japan. March 22-25, 1995. Giovanni Capannelli. "Technology Transfer through Subcontracting Relationships from Japan to

Malaysian CTV Industry". Appendix to workshop paper "Experience of Japanese Firms in ASEAN: Electrical Machinery and Transport Equipment Industries in Thailand and Malaysia". Bocconi, March 1995.

9. Atipol Bhanich Supapol (ed.). *Transnational Corporations and Backward Linkages in Asian Electronics Industries.* New York: United Nations, 1995. Shujiro Urata. "International Technology Transfer by Japanese Multinationals in East Asia". Unpublished paper, Waseda University, Tokyo. February 1997.

Chapter 9

Hafiz Mirza, Kee Hwee Wee and Frank Bartels:
"Towards a Strategy for Enhancing ASEAN's
Locational Advantages for Attracting
Greater Foreign Direct Investment"

The Association of South East Asian Nations (ASEAN) is in many respects a pioneer. As the premier regional organization of the developing world it has for many years played the role of leadership by example. The ASEAN Free Trade Area (AFTA), although not the first agreement of its type, represented a goal and a vision which struck a chord internationally and inspired others to follow this lead. The free trade provisions of the Mercosur treaty are an example in point. With the ASEAN Investment Area (AIA), the Association has struck boldly into the political and economic wilderness, for no regional grouping - whether in the industrialized or developing worlds - has yet created the fully-integrated investment-supporting environment that is envisaged by this proposal. The goal of an AIA was first declared by the ASEAN Heads of Government at the Fifth ASEAN Summit in 1995:

> ASEAN shall work towards establishing *an ASEAN investment region* which will help enhance the area's attractiveness and competitiveness for promoting direct investment. The promotion of direct investment into and amongst ASEAN Member Countries will help in the development and growth of ASEAN economies.

In this regard, ASEAN shall implement, among other investment measures, an ASEAN Plan of Action on Cooperation and
Promotion of Foreign Direct Investment and Intra-ASEAN Investment.

After this declaration the ASEAN Investment Region (AIR) was
defined as a concept covering cooperation, promotion and liberalization initiatives; this was distinguished from the ASEAN
Investment Area (AIA) whose scope was narrower, principally
related to liberalization activities. In practice it is not possible to
so easily separate the two concepts, although most of the discussion
below will be in the context of the AIA. Since the Fifth Summit,
ASEAN has created a number of committees and bodies to oversee
the development of the AIR/AIA, including the Senior Officials
Meeting on Investment (SOM-I), a Working Group on Investment
Cooperation and Promotion (WGICP) and a strengthened ASEAN
Secretariat to handle the increasing level of Investment Cooperation.

This paper seeks to help develop a "strategy for enhancing
ASEAN's location advantages for attracting greater foreign direct
investment (FDI)" in the context of the AIA by reporting on some of
the findings of a recent survey of Transnational Corporations
(TNCs) with FDI in ASEAN countries (the survey was conducted by
the Bradford Management Center in cooperation with the ASEAN
Secretariat). Clearly marrying the views of potential beneficiaries of FDI policies to the goals of the AIA should ensure that the
strategy developed is highly appropriate, but full regard should be
given to:

• The social, political and economic aspirations of ASEAN
  Member Countries and ASEAN as a whole. The provisions of
  the AIA must be subsidiary to these.
• The "rules of the game" as defined by ASEAN Member Countries' membership of international bodies such as the World
  Trade Organization (WTO). In other words international laws
  and agreements to some extent circumscribe what is permissible
  in terms of policies and actions.(1) Having said this, if developing countries' reactions to the UNCTAD Global Investment
  Forum (2) were as hostile and cynical as reported by the press,
  there is still a long way to go before international rules

directly affecting investment are agreed on a global basis, whether within the WTO or other organizations.

- ASEAN's broader political and economic goals, for example within APEC or in terms of the eventual incorporation of Laos, Cambodia and Myanmar to create the ASEAN-10 (the existing member countries of ASEAN are Brunei, Indonesia, Malaysia, the Philippines, Singapore, Thailand and Vietnam).

- Trends in international capital flows and the extent to which ASEAN Member Countries' need to compete for capital.

- Finally, it is not possible to practically distinguish between policies aimed at non-ASEAN TNCs with regional headquarters in ASEAN and those TNCs domiciled in an ASEAN Member country. It is therefore important to recognize the implications of FDI policies for ASEAN TNCs, especially because non-ASEAN TNCs are pressing for measures to encourage intra-ASEAN FDI (see section 2).

Section 2 of this paper will present empirical findings from the survey, while section 3 will discuss the implications for strategy, followed by our conclusion.

TRANSNATIONAL CORPORATIONS IN ASEAN

Motivations, obstacles and policy preferences.

This section analyses three issues examined in the survey because of the light they may throw on factors which TNCs' find attractive about ASEAN and how these factors are evolving: the historical (original) motivations underlying the decision to invest in ASEAN; the current obstacles to effective local operations in ASEAN, as perceived by the TNC parent company (an all-important perspective if further FDI from overseas is to be encouraged); and the policies which TNCs regard as particularly valuable in encouraging their further involvement in the region.(3) The analysis is based on a postal response by 248 non-ASEAN TNCs (20 European, 36 USA, 140 Japanese, 37 Taiwanese, 13 Australian, 2 Other) who were asked to express their views on a series of issues. The questions related to motivations, obstacles and policies was composed of likaert scale variables to which the firms were asked to reply, e.g. the policy questions (one each for FDI in the host, intra-ASEAN and trans-ASEAN) consisted of 22 possible policies which could be ranked from "will increase attractiveness to will decrease attractiveness". The actual results reported below are based on a statistical process known as factor analysis through which the responses of firms to each question have been grouped in order to determine the most important underlying factors of relevance. Although there is no space to go through the methodology here, suffice it to say that the results are, on the whole, very reliable in that firms are consistent in their responses and significant

Figure 1. Targeting Foreign Direct Investment:

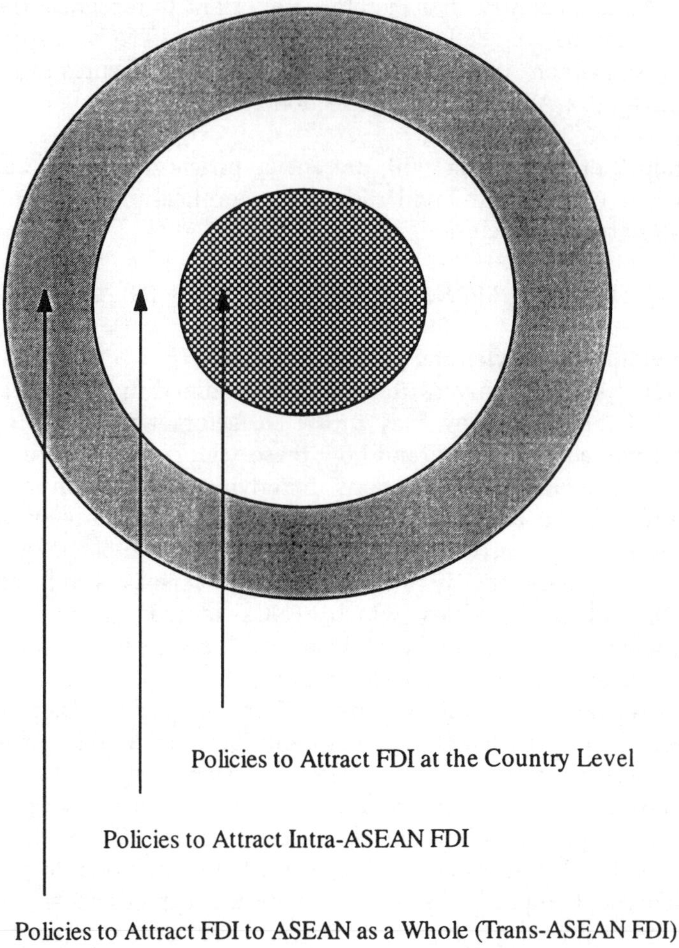

Policies to Attract FDI at the Country Level

Policies to Attract Intra-ASEAN FDI

Policies to Attract FDI to ASEAN as a Whole (Trans-ASEAN FDI)

(i.e. not the product of chance associations). Although factors extracted through factor analysis techniques are traditionally difficult to interpret, this was not the case here. Nearly all factors were readily explicable.

As figure 1 indicates, the results below (figures 2 to 5) are presented in terms of motives etc. at the host country level, the intra-ASEAN level and the trans-ASEAN level. This is because

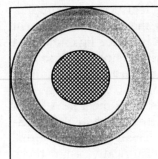

Figure 2. Historic Motives for
Foreign Direct Investment in
ASEAN Countries

- Host Country Level
- Partner Availability (2)
- Conducive Regulatory Environment (3)
- Good Logistics and Supplier Industries (4)
- Commitment to Customers (5)
- Circumvent Protection (Tariff Barriers) (6)
- Financial Privileges (8) (*Negative Correlation*)

- Intra-ASEAN Level
- ASEAN Schemes (1)

- Trans-ASEAN Level
- ASEAN Market (7)

Note: The numbers in brackets denote the order of importance
assigned to each factor or category by responding firms.

the strategies which need to be evolved must be directed at each of these levels; furthermore this form of presentation shows how the interests of TNCs has changed over time from an early orientation towards particular host countries to a much more ASEAN perspective at the present time.

Historically TNCs were primarily concerned with investments in particular ASEAN economies and this comes over very strongly in figure 2. Six of the eight significant motives for FDI in ASEAN are host country related.(4) Thus local partner availability, a conducive regulatory environment, good logistics and supplier industries, a commitment to customers and the need to circumvent tariff barriers were the most important reasons for investment at the host country level. This is also the order of importance, so host country governments could prioritize their policies if these motives were still operative. It is worth mentioning that statistically the single most important historical motive for investment in ASEAN was ASEAN schemes (AIJV, BBC etc.) which operate at the intra-ASEAN level. In fact only a relatively small number of firms regarded ASEAN schemes as important historically - but these firms were very strongly motivated indeed by this factor, hence its strong showing. The potential of the ASEAN market was also important, but less so for firms which were initially interested in specific local markets or a low cost base. It may at first seem strange that financial privileges appear to have a negative impact on motivation. However, the principle variable in the factor is "exclusive licensing privileges" which presumably were not readily available to foreign TNCs. In addition, when one of the authors (Hafiz Mirza) spoke to TNC subsidiaries and ASEAN firms in a separate interview based survey he was told that although a few firms benefited from such exclusive treatment, most did not: hence the generally negative attitude towards such state policies. From the point of view of strategy, TNCs prefer transparency and predictability to exclusive, non-transparent privileges.

In terms of future motivations (Figure 3), factors remaining to the fore are those relevant to the ASEAN countries in which TNCs already invest. However, it seems that both intra- and trans-ASEAN are likely to be more important: ASEAN Schemes are the second most important motivating factor mentioned (a view supported by a large number of firms), and the large emerging ASEAN Market is the fourth most important factor. In addition, the local market will be more important for future investments and "gaining insider status" and "acquire local firms" are motives which also underscore the significance of the market. Local presence presumably also helps companies get around non-tariff barriers, tariff barriers being less significant. Firms are also impressed by the improving local physical and commercial infrastructure. The fact

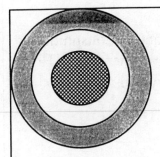

Figure 3. Likely Motives for Future Foreign Direct Investment in ASEAN Countries

- Host Country Level
- Low Production Costs (Tax Breaks, Cheap Labor, Good Local Suppliers) (1)
- Viable Local Market (3)
- Good Physical and Commercial Infrastructure (5)
- Gain Insider Status (6)
- Local Partnership and Resources (7)
- Circumvent Protection (Non-Tariff Barriers) (8)
- Acquire Local Firms (9)
- Utilize Schemes and Privileges (10) (*Negative Correlation*)

- Intra-ASEAN Level
- ASEAN Schemes (BBC, AIJV etc.) (2)

- Trans-ASEAN Level
- Large Emerging ASEAN Market (4)
- Falling Transport Costs (11)

Note: The numbers in brackets denote the order of importance assigned to each factor or category by responding firms.

that cost reduction appears as the single most important factor probably implies that TNCs in particular host countries are moving to *other* ASEAN countries; if so, this suggests that more effective intra-ASEAN infrastructure is necessary if FDI in the region is to be sustained.(5)

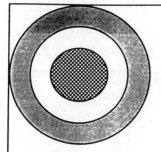

Figure 4. Factors Constituting Barriers to Investment in the Host Country and ASEAN

- Host Country Level
- Political Instability and Restrictions (1)
- Poor Physical Infrastructure and Non-Transparency of Regulations (Bureaucracy, Rules Volatility) (2)
- Lack of Good Quality Management and Skills (3)
- High Labor Costs (4)

- Trans/Intra-ASEAN Level
- Lack of Potential Partners (1)
- Poor Physical and *Commercial* Infrastructure and Non-Transparency (Rules Volatility, Bureaucracy) (2)
- Economic Instability and State Intervention on Socio-Economic Grounds (3)
- Lack of Good Quality Management and Skills (4)
- Intra-ASEAN Non-Tariff Barriers (5)

Notes: (1) The numbers in brackets denote the order of importance assigned to each factor or category by responding firms. (2) Two separate questions were asked, one regarding barriers in the host country, the other about barriers in ASEAN.

Having said this, there are still a number of barriers or obstacles to investment in ASEAN (Figure 4). At the country level (firms were asked about barriers at the host and trans-ASEAN in separate questions) four major obstacles emerge: political instability and restrictions, poor physical infrastructure and non-transparency of regulations (ASEAN is an economically diverse region: good infrastructure in some countries or regions attracts; in others it repels), lack of good quality management and skills and high labor costs.

At the trans-/intra-ASEAN level, poor infrastructure and a lack of good quality management and skills are again important, implying that these are significant factors in many parts of ASEAN: particular heed should be taken of these obstacles.

Very significantly, a lack of potential partners features very strongly at the trans- or intra-ASEAN level: this implies that although TNCs are actively considering other ASEAN countries for future investment, it is difficult for them to find suitable partners. This may simply be due to a lack of information in some cases, although in one or two ASEAN member states there may be a genuine dearth of prospective local partners. Non-tariff barriers are also clearly matters for concern.

What then should ASEAN governments do to encourage FDI at the host-country, intra-ASEAN and trans-ASEAN level? The views of firms are expressed in figure 5. Interestingly, apart from the provision of information about markets and policies, firms are looking for ASEAN-wide measures and schemes, even at the host country level. It seems most firms with existing investment in ASEAN really are looking in regional terms. With this in mind they are very keen to see regional political and economic stability. They also seem to be very keen on intra-ASEAN FDI: AFTA should be extended especially in terms of reducing NTBs, ASEAN-wide schemes such as the former AIJV are regarded as valuable, and an ASEAN-wide harmonization of FDI policies would encourage FDI in other ASEAN countries. It is worth noting that ASEAN-wide FDI policies might result in a *relative* reduction of FDI at the host or trans-ASEAN level, but there would be gains at the intra-ASEAN level: in general this parallels the political wishes of ASEAN governments and the tendencies of ASEAN firms.

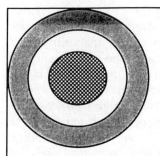

Figure 5. Policies which would Increase the Attractiveness of the Host Country and ASEAN to Foreign Direct Investors

- <u>Host Country Level</u>
- More Provision of Information on the Local Market and Government Policies (1)
- Extend the ASEAN Free Trade Area (include NTBs in AFTA) (2)
- Enhanced ASEAN-wide Schemes (BBC, AIJV) (3)
- ASEAN-wide Arbitration, Financial and other Services (esp. for SMEs) (4)
- ASEAN-wide FDI Policies (5) *Negative Correlation: see Intra-ASEAN Level*
- Increased Regional Political and Economic Stability (6)

- <u>Intra-ASEAN Level</u>
- ASEAN-wide Information and Market Services (esp. for SMEs) (1)
- ASEAN-wide Trade Liberalization (2)
- Increased Regional Political and Economic Stability (3)
- ASEAN-wide Harmonization of FDI Policies (inc. Establishment of Complementary FDI Regimes) (4)
- Enhanced ASEAN-wide Schemes (BBC, AIJV) (5)
- ASEAN-wide Arbitration, Financial and other Services (esp. for SMEs) (6)

- <u>Trans-ASEAN Level</u>
- Enhanced ASEAN-wide Schemes (BBC, Project Assistance, AIJV) (1)
- Increased Regional Political and Economic Stability (2)
- ASEAN-wide FDI Policies (3) *(Negative Correlation: see Intra-ASEAN Level)*
- Extend the ASEAN Free Trade Area (include NTBs in AFTA) (4)
- ASEAN-wide Arbitration, Financial and other Services (esp. for SMEs) (5)
- ASEAN-wide Information and Market Services (esp. for SMEs) (6)

<u>Notes:</u> (1) The numbers in brackets denote the order of importance assigned to each factor or category by responding firms. (2) Three separate questions were asked, one regarding barriers in the host country, the other about barriers in ASEAN.

TOWARDS A STRATEGY TO FACILITATE FDI
INTO AND WITHIN ASEAN

The results of the research discussed in section 2 imply that ASEAN's best strategy to attract non-ASEAN TNC FDI is to facilitate intra-ASEAN FDI. This makes sense at a number of levels. Firstly, ASEAN is a region which is having to compete with other regions and growth zones, including Mercosur, "Greater China" and India in the developing world alone: it therefore needs to stress its critical mass as a community of closely cooperating economies as opposed to a club of individual and individualistic nation states. Secondly, ASEAN - or at least parts of ASEAN - is maturing and represents a growing market to which TNCs are responding, often by taking advantage of the regional division of labor: this is a natural process and needs to be encouraged. Thirdly, as ASEAN matures, so does its home-grown TNCs which, apart from also pursuing a regional division of labor, are potential targets or partners for non-ASEAN TNCs or their subsidiaries in the region. These tendencies explain the success of the ASEAN Free Trade Area (AFTA); they also require that the ASEAN Investment Area (AIA) must provide the broad physical and commercial infrastructure within which intra-ASEAN trade and investment may occur. Together they perforce encourage increased inward investment from outside the region.

Table 1 (see page 207) provides a strategic framework to encourage FDI in ASEAN as indicated by the analysis provided in section 2. A number of points can be made. First, although the strategy is based on the needs of non-ASEAN TNCs, much of it is relevant to ASEAN TNCs as well. Secondly, generally the framework is market-supporting and therefore in line with the provisions international institutional arrangements. Thirdly, if ASEAN follows these priorities then essentially it is creating the infrastructure for a modern economy and the opportunity exists for the Association to use the latest world-best technology: this will result in a broad-based competitive advantage. Finally, a number of relevant ASEAN cooperation programs already exist. These include, the Brand-to-Brand Complementation Scheme (BBC), the ASIAN Industrial Cooperation Scheme (AICO, the successor to the ASEAN Industrial Joint Venture Scheme), ASEAN Intellectual Property Cooperation, ASEAN Cooperation on SME Development, ASEAN Cooperation in Services, the ASEAN Plan for Action on Infrastructure Development, ASEAN Cooperation on Standards and

Quality etc. What this study adds, however, is (i) confirmation that many of ASEAN's initiatives are truly supported by non-ASEAN TNCs; (ii) an indication of the specific priorities of transnational firms which may enable governments and officials to finetune the emphasis they give to various policies; and (iii) some suggestion of new potential priorities or extensions of existing priorities.

CONCLUDING REMARKS

By analyzing survey responses by 248 non-ASEAN TNCs to questions relating to motivations, obstacles and policies, this chapter has been able to outline the broad priorities of these companies in terms of their future operations in ASEAN. By showing that these priorities are especially related to intra-ASEAN investment activity it has been shown that considerable scope exists for ASEAN to pursue a FDI-encouraging strategy which simultaneously facilitates the internationalization of ASEAN TNCs, furthers the region's development objectives and is broadly in accord with the provisions of the international institutional framework within which the ASEAN Member Countries operate. ASEAN needs to develop specific measures which further the strategy delineated above. For instance, ASEAN is a vast region and certain localized trajectories of infrastructural development may be more appropriate than others. For instance, which ASEAN "complementaries" need attention first? Better communication structures with Indo-China, a stress on the industrial "spillover" from Malaysia and Thailand into Vietnam or a "revamping" of the three existing "growth triangles"? At the practical level many further decisions need to be made.

* Hafiz Mirza is Professor of International Business at the University of Bradford Management Centre, United Kingdom. Kee Hwee Wee is Assistant Director, Investment Finance and Banking, ASEAN Secretariat, Jakarta, Indonesia. Frank Bartels is lecturer in International Business, Nanyang Business School, Nanyang Technological University, Singapore.

Notes

1. Some of these issues are covered quite well in the context of regional bodies by the WTO Secretariat (1995), *Regionalism and*

the *World Trading System,* World Trade Organisation, Geneva. See also, UNCTAD (1996), *World Investment Report 1996: Investment, Trade and International Policy Arrangements,* United Nations, New York and Geneva, as well as Arvind Panagariya, M.G. Quibria and Narhari Rao (1996), *The Emerging Global Trading Environment and Developing Asia,* Asian Development Bank, Economic Staff Paper No 55, Washington.

2. Held on 10 October 1996 in the Palais des Nations, Geneva.
3. These issues represent only some aspects of the survey.
4. The variables in the question distinguished between "levels" and only the "host-level" variables are to be found - *largely* - in the factors extracted.
5. A recent study by the Japanese Institute of Overseas Investment (JOI) details specific infrastructural requirements in ASEAN countries. JOI (1996), "Current Status and Problems in the Financial Situation of Supporting Industries in Asia", *JOI Review,* September, No 29.

Table 1   **Priority Policies to Encourage Foreign Direct Investment Into and Within ASEAN (Based on Figures 3-5 and Broader Considerations)**

Policies and Measures	Policies *Applicable* at the[1]			Comments
	Host Level	Intra-ASEAN Level	Trans-ASEAN Level	
Policies to Ensure Regional Political and Economic Stability	++	++	++	Clearly concerns about some countries and the general regional scenario
Trade Related Measures				
Extension of AFTA	++	++	+	Already in Progress
Attack on NTBs	+++	+++	+	Esp. Some Countries
Reduction in Restrictions on Foreign Investors				
Removal of Barriers on Participation by Foreign Corporations	+++	+++	++	Esp. Some Countries
Ease Restrictions on *Outward* FDI (esp. for Domestic Firms)	+++	++	+	Assists both ASEAN and non-ASEAN TNCs with Subsidiaries in the Region
National Treatment for Foreign Firms	+++	+	+	

Table 1 continued.

Creation of an Enabling Environment for FDI				
Establish Good Quality Support Ind.	+++	+++	+	Includes Services, Capital Markets etc.
Establish Good Physical & Comm. Infrastructure	+++	+++	+	A Prime Opportunity to Establish World-Best Infrastructure and Comms.
Predictability and Transparency of Laws & Rules	+++	+++	+	Esp. Some Countries
Develop Good Quality Manpower	+++	+	+	
ASEAN-Wide Harmonization of FDI Policies	+	+++	+++	Will Ease the Creation of the ASEAN Investment Area
Harmonization of ASEAN Corporate Laws and Reg.	++	+++	++	Will Ease the Creation of the ASEAN Investment Area
Incentives for FDI				
Information and Technical Services	+++	+++	++	Could Utilize the Latest Web Technology
Assistance in Finding Partners & Contacts	+++	+++	+++	Could Utilize the Latest Web Technology
Enhanced ASEAN Schemes (AICO etc.)	++	+++	+++	
Joint Promotion of FDI	+	++	+++	Esp. Significant for Encouraging TNCs unfamiliar with ASEAN
ASEAN-wide Arbitration and Other Services	++	+++	++	
Tax Concessions, Grants and Other Incentives for Inward *and* Outward FDI	++	++	+	
Complementary ASEAN FDI Regimes/Schemes	++	+++	+	Will Ease the Creation of the ASEAN Investment Area

Note: 1. +++ = High Priority; ++ = Medium Priority; + = Low Priority or Unnecessary.

Chapter 10

Takuo Akiyama: "International Diversification of Investment in Newly Emerging Securities Markets in Asia"

Equity investments in developing countries have expanded rapidly in the period from the early eighties until 1993, and set off an investment boom which has now quietened down due to the rise in US interest rates and the crisis of the Mexican currency. However, from a middle or long-term perspective, investments in newly emerging markets are very attractive due to the fact that they are situated in growth markets. For advanced countries aiming towards international diversification of investments these emerging markets cannot be overlooked as a market for investments. This means that in the mid and long term these regions more than others are regions with the highest probability for economic growth.

RISK SPREADING AND INVESTMENT RETURNS

The reason for the diversification of international investment lies in the aim of risk reduction through spreading investments. As a result, investment behavior tends towards buying in markets where price rises are likely, and towards selling in markets where a drop in prices can be anticipated. The degree of independence of various equity markets is directly linked to the degree of independence of the economy and governmental economic policy of the countries concerned. It goes without saying that there are also factors which to a certain degree influence share prices round the world. But

purely local and regional factors give rise to a considerable varia-
tion. This holds in particular for the advanced countries on the one
hand and the emerging markets of Latin America and Asia on the
other.

The aim of international diversification of investments does
not only lie in spreading of risk. Investment in foreign shares results
from the fact that there is• a high probability that while the
domestic share market falls, markets in other countries may rise,
owing to a low interdependence of each national market. Assuming
that markets in one country will invariably outperform others, the
best investment policy is that the investor only invests in well
performing markets. However, predictions are often highly uncertain. By diversifying investments in markets with an anticipated
equal profitability, the investor may lower portfolio risks. The
result is an achievement of a higher rate of anticipated profitability on the basis of a better relation between risks and returns.
The interdependence of markets is much lower between emerging
markets and those of advanced countries compared to the interdependence of advanced markets. By means of a sufficiently
diversified portfolio investors are in a position to absorb the high
volatility of share prices among the various emerging markets.

Investments in markets with strong economic growth potential
Global capital markets are divided into those of North America,
Europe and Japan. Most recently emerging markets have been expanding rapidly, resulting in an increase of opportunities for foreign
investment. In the past, from the sixties to the eighties, European
and American investors invested actively in Japanese shares because Japan was able to sustain an economic growth rate which
surpassed that of Europe and America (the annual average rate of
growth for the GDP during the period of twenty five years from
1960 to 1985 was 3.4 percent for America, more than 4 percent for
Europe, and 7.5 percent for Japan).

These gaps in the growth rates were sustained over a relatively long period. At present (1996) the growth rate of the
advanced countries has tapered off while their economies are beset
with severe structural problems. On the other hand we are confronted with regions with emerging economies, among which there
are countries with an economic growth rate exceeding 10 percent. In
some countries investment risks may be high, but they display

economic growth and an expansion of equity markets, and possess attractive investment opportunities.

According to research by the World Bank the GDP of emerging countries rose by 5.1 percent in the period between 1965 and 1989 compared to 3.1 percent for the OECD countries and is expected to continue surpassing the growth of America, Europe and Japan for the next decade and beyond. The projections of the IMF also predict that the combined growth rate of the emerging countries in Asia and Latin America will reach 6.5 percent by the year 2000, and maintain a growth rate of 6 percent for the next two decades. In addition, emerging countries possess 85 percent of the global population while producing less than about 30 percent of global GDP; however, they occupy only 12 percent of the aggregate current value of global securities markets (1993 figures). If those newly emerging countries continue their growth and development, they are expected to occupy 50 percent of the current aggregate value of global securities markets.

Points of interest and concern

However, in order to expand investments smoothly in securities markets in newly emerging countries, there are numerous tasks to be tackled by investors from advanced countries and emerging markets. Most of those markets, in general, are of a small scale, display violent changes, low liquidity of shares and high volatility of share prices. Trading is focusing on one kind of shares and often operating an outdated market system. In addition, investors from advanced countries become once more aware of currency risks and capital loss sustained by developing countries as a result of the Mexican currency crisis of 1994/1995.

This requires a comprehensive evaluation of circumstances beyond the analysis of the characteristics and structure of such securities markets, and an appraisal of the fundamentals of those countries, including the overvaluation of share prices and currency values peculiar to developing countries, movements of international currencies, and international financial markets. Emerging markets themselves drew lessons from the Mexican economic crisis mentioned above. For their political authorities it is necessary to be constantly prepared to adopt sober and appropriate measures to deal with the effects of global financial changes, while at the same time making efforts towards a proper adjustment of overvalued share prices and currencies, an improvement of the fundamentals, and a reform of problematic features of markets.

Continued growth of emerging markets can be expected to be supported by four important factors:

1. the transfer of technologies from advanced countries through which developing countries acquire a considerable amount of industrial and engineering skills;
2. spread of education and a rise in the level of education;
3. liberalization and deregulation of systems;
4. expansion of capital flows from advanced countries both in the areas of direct and indirect investment.

THE ECONOMIC STATE OF AFFAIRS OF ASIA'S EMERGING MARKETS

Following the "burst of the bubble" in the nineties the Japanese economy continues its slow growth, Europe remains afflicted by high unemployment, and America, also continues to run double digit budget and trade deficits in a period of economic recovery. Prospects for the economies of the advanced countries are not bright. While growth in advanced countries continues at low levels, Asian countries continue to display high levels of growth.

Growth strength of Asian countries

The table below shows the effective economic growth strength of Asian countries, developing at levels surpassing those of the advanced countries.

The high growth of Asian countries can be traced to the following developments:

1. In the wake of the Asian NIEs (Newly Industrializing Economies: South Korea, Taiwan, Hong Kong, Singapore) of the seventies, the ASEAN-4 countries (Malaysia, Thailand, the Philippines and Indonesia) promoted policies of export led industrialization;
2. in this process they endeavored to attract foreign capital in order to obtain capital for industrial development, while at the same time sponsoring domestic financial capital markets;
3. this in turn enabled new developments towards an economic structure characterized by "export plus domestic demand" which

released them from the traditional export dependent economic structure.

Table 1   The Economic Growth of Asian Countries (GDP)
unit: %

	81-85	86-90	1991	1992	1993	1994	1995*
Hong Kong	5.6	7.6	4.1	5.3	5.5	5.4	4.6
Singapore	6.2	7.9	6.7	6.0	9.9	10.1	8.9
Taiwan	6.5	8.9	7.2	6.0	5.9	6.5	6.3
Korea	8.4	10.8	9.1	5.1	5.5	8.4	9.2
Malaysia	5.1	6.8	8.7	7.8	8.5	9.2	9.3
Thailand	5.0	9.9	8.2	7.4	7.5	8.7	8.6
Philippines	1.0	4.6	0.7	0.1	1.7	4.4	4.8
Indonesia	4.7	6.3	6.6	6.3	6.5	7.5	7.6
China	11.2	7.8	8.0	13.2	13.4	11.8	10.2
India	--	--	1.2	4.2	5.4	6.1	6.2
Japan	4.2	4.7	4.3	1.1	0.1	0.5	0.8
US	2.6	2.8	0.7	2.6	3.0	3.9	2.9

* *Estimation*
Source: Economic Planning Agency, [Overseas Economic Data], ADB Outlook: 1996.

Traditionally, Asian countries had raised overseas capital in the form of loans. Numerous countries had gone through bitter experiences as a result of problems of foreign indebtedness due to exchange rate and interest fluctuations, and this acted as an incentive to attract direct investments which are free from the burdens of interest payments. In addition, Japanese enterprises had a difficult time to reduce production costs resulting from the rapid appreciation of the Yen following the Plaza Agreement of 1985, and proceeded to relocate production towards Asian countries which possess a cheap and well trained labor force in abundance.

The increase of Japanese direct investments in Asia produced a snowball effect of investments producing investments, with positive effects for the real economy in terms of growth, employment, trade expansion and export competitiveness but also an increase in personal income and living standards.

Growth until the middle of the eighties owed most to the expansion of export of manufactured goods to the advanced countries, in particular the United States, with a concomitant increase of the influence of the economies of the advanced countries. In recent years there has been an increase of personal consumption in the region underpinning domestic demand; the center of gravity of trade patterns as well has moved away from advanced countries to the region itself. In other words, economic development has changed towards a pattern of autonomous growth, away from the dependence on advanced countries.

The Asian region has increased its scope once more by the rapid growth of direct investments by the NIEs and ASEAN wishing to accelerate growth into China and Vietnam by tackling the huge markets of China, Indo-China and India which have come to the fore since the end of the Cold War, and increased mutual dependence within the region.

Huge infrastructural investments
In the nineties Asian countries mobilized plans for the improvement of infrastructure on a large scale; the majority of countries plans for economic development centering on all kinds of social infrastructure investments (harbors, roads, communications, electricity, airports, motorways, high-speed trains etc.) in order to strengthen their industrial base and living standards.

It is estimated that these projects require investments to the tune of one trillion 500 billion US dollars until the beginning of the year 2000. In order to meet this demand it is necessary to complete the establishment of adequate regional capital markets.

The accumulation of foreign currency reserves
The policies of external liberalization of Asian countries has promoted the influx of long-term capital, which in turn greatly reduced external debts. As shown in Table 2 below, there has been a rapid increase in foreign currency holdings by Asian countries. This

in turn has led to an increase in the volume of domestic currency. As an example, excess capital resulting from excess volatility entered stock markets in Taiwan, and the share index rose by a fifteen fold from 835 at the end of 1985 to 12,495 by February 1990. This was followed by a collapse to one-fifth of that value by October 1990, namely 2,560. Such excess liquidity is absorbed through copious consumption and investment in capital goods.

Table 2   Shifts in Foreign Currency Reserves of Asian Countries (in 100 mln US dollars)

	1985	88	89	90	91	92	93	94	95
Hong Kong		170	204	252	304	374		430	554
Singapore	128	171	203	277	341	399	484	550	694
Taiwan	266	739	732	724	824	823	836	923	913
Korea	29	123	152	148	137	171	202	257	332
Malaysia	49	65	78	98	109	172	271	326	240
Thailand	22	61	95	133	175	204	245	288	367
Philippines	6	10	14	9	32	44	47	62	64
Indonesia	49	50	55	75	93	104	113	132	137
China	127	185	180	296	437	206	212	516	754
India	59	42	34	22	56	64	151	190	167
Japan	265	977	849	771	690	687	956	1229	1833

Source: *Asian Statistics Annual Report 1995*, published by *The Economist*

Consolidation of capital markets
Asian financial markets are generally still characterized by the existence of a large amount of regulations. Indirect finance - bank loans - are the center of capital procurement, with a high share of short-term finance. Long-term financial markets are as yet under-developed.

The share of direct finance - capital procurement in capital markets centering on bonds and shares - is still exceedingly small. Apart from a few countries, low interest financing and credit supply provided by government-linked financial institutions play a great role. Various countries have implemented policies to foster capital markets in order to change the structural preference for indirect finance and aim for the introduction of a long-term stable capital market. The following policies were adopted:

a) relaxation of currency controls and investment regulations to ease the introduction of foreign capital;
b) modernization of the system of securities trading and the economic system in general;
c) privatization of state enterprises and public offering of shares;
d) strengthening of the supervision of markets;
e) expansion of the number of individual investors;
f) fostering institutional investors;
g) fostering securities trading companies and improving their quality;
h) changes and strengthening of standards for entering the share market.

It is expected that these measures for consolidating the securities capital market and strengthening its structure will greatly improve the environment for investing. In particular, they will increase confidence of overseas investors and further promote the influx of capital from advanced countries into the Asian region by contributing to the attractiveness of future Asian equity investors.

PECULIARITIES AND PROBLEMS OF THE ASIAN SECURITIES MARKETS

Although Asian securities markets have attracted the attention of global investors, individual Asian markets are still small scale and display numerous weaknesses typical for emerging markets, compared to securities markets of America, Europe and Japan. However, Table 3: A Comparison of the scale of Asian share markets shows an expansive growth of Asian securities markets during the past ten years; they display a growth that deserves our attention, in particular when we analyze aggregate value of shares entering the market, the aggregate size of trading, and the number of companies listed.

Table 3   The Asian Securities Markets, A Comparison

Countries	Listed companies number		Current prices 100 mln $		Stocks traded 100 mln $	
	End '85	End '93	End '85	End '93	End '85	End '93
Hong Kong	279	477	345.1	3,352.7	71.5	1,321.1
Singapore	316	331	110.7	3,046,7	28.5	742.0
Taiwan	127	285	104.2	1,928.8	49.5	3,430.0
Korea	342	693	73.8	1,394,2	41.6	2,081.4
Malaysia	284	410	162.3	2,146,5	24.8	1,504.5
Thailand	93	347	18.4	1,301.9	5.5	129.8
Philippines	137	180	6.7	393.1	0.8	31.9
Indonesia	24	172	1.2	328.4	0.93	91.4
China		218	20.3	423.4	8.2	652.3
India	1,529	3,263	143.6	979.8	49.6	213.8
Asia 10 Total	3,131	6,376	986.3	15,796.8	289.0	10,902.4
Japan	1,476	1,667	9,482.6	20,999.3	3,299.7	7,813.8
US (New York)	1,541	2,362	19,500.0	45,450.0	9,807.7	22,833.9
UK (London)	2,116	1,803	3,534.9	10,454.1	634.1	4,235.4

Notes:
Singapore data include the foreign spot market. The total of listed current total and stocks traded is for China 1991 instead of 1985; 1993 is an estimate. The figures for India only include the Bombay Stock Exchange; US figures include foreign stock, UK excludes them. The number of listed enterprises in the UK, and the total current listed enterprises for 1993 are the figures for September 1993.

Source: IFC Emerging Securities Markets Fact book 1994.

Peculiarities and problems of the primary equity markets
Asian share markets attract global attention due to the high equity investment performance against the background of strong economic growth potential. Consequently, shares show vitality especially in

secondary markets rather than in primary markets. This means that they cannot fully function as a means of raising capital, normally a characteristic of a primary market, for the following reasons:

a) Family management by owner-managers still prevails, and they tend to strongly dislike public access to shares and spreading of share ownership, aware as they are of the chance of interference in management by a third party with public access to shares.
b) It is easy to obtain bank loans for the procurement of enterprise finance. In addition, there is a financial market dominated by indirect finance where the banks, too, aim for supplying finance to superior enterprises.
c) There is a high degree of volatility of prices on share distribution markets. There is an insufficient number of domestic investors, and their investment behavior is distinguished by short-term considerations; also, it is a market highly aware of investments by foreign investors, heavily influenced by foreign short-term investors such as America's Mutual Fund.
d) Domestic investors have insufficient investment capital, but also lack knowledge in the area of securities investments. Apart from some NIEs such as Singapore and Hong Kong individual investors mostly belong to the affluent classes or have received higher education.

Nevertheless, securities markets in Asia have fulfilled a definite role through the increase of listed enterprises, the privatization of state enterprises, and the diversification of financial sources for enterprises, and the increase in the number of individual investors. The number of listed companies in ten Asian countries doubled from a total of 3,131 listed companies in 1985 and their number increased to 6,376 by 1993. The current tasks of fostering securities markets lie most importantly in establishing policy guidelines to provide facilities for enterprises to raise capital and to increase the number of listed companies in order to expand the number of objects for investment.

Peculiarities and problems of secondary trading markets
As Table 3 indicates the aggregate current value of shares listed in 1993 ranks third after the New York Stock Exchange and the Tokyo

Stock Exchanges with a value of 1,579.6 billion US dollars, if we regard the share markets of these ten Asian countries as one market and compare them with each other. In terms of trade volume it is in second place with 1,090.2 billion US dollars second to the NYSE, and globally first with 6,376 companies listed. One may say that the securities market of the Asian Ten forms the fourth pole of a four-polar global securities market next to New York, Tokyo and London. A comparison of the situation in 1985 and 1993 indicated a twofold increase in the number of listed companies, a sixteen fold increase in current aggregate value, and a thirty-nine fold increase in trade volume; these increases suggest the enormous growth of Asian share markets in this eight-year period. As for individual markets, the aggregate current value of shares listed in Hong Kong and Singapore surpassed 300 billion US dollars (in 1993), ranking next to France and Germany.

Asian share prices continued to rise since the middle of the eighties against the background of strong economic growth, registering their highest value in the period between the second half of 1993 and the beginning 1994. With the rise of American interest rates in 1994 the trend went towards adjustment, and aided by the Mexican currency crises (end of 1994 until the beginning of 1995) continued a certain downward trend.

Peculiarities of share prices
Databases on emerging markets show that the investment performance of Asian share markets is high. There are of course countries displaying extraordinarily high performance values in Eastern Europe, Latin America and the Middle East, but of the twenty countries whose 1993 index showed an increase of more than 50 percent, about half of them were Asian. This development is accompanied by structural problems such as the fact that share prices are normally fixed at a higher level due to the tight relationship between supply and demand of shares in the market, the relatively small size of the market compared to markets in advanced countries, and a high-price volatility.

SYSTEMIC PECULIARITIES

a) Regulations applying to investments by foreigners
As a rule, most countries restrict the ratio of foreign shareholdings while there are also markets such as Hong Kong and Singapore

without any restrictions. Yet even Hong Kong and Singapore have restrictions concerning some categories of enterprises or specially designated enterprises. In addition, some countries determine a maximum amount for (foreign) investment, or else limitations on the acquisition of shares per investor. Almost no country has local currency exchange regulations, but some require permits.

b) Investors

Most recently the rate of individual investors has increased in the majority of countries. This has to be seen against the background of some countries having implemented a conscious national policy of fostering the growth of individual investors (Taiwan, South Korea, Thailand, Singapore). On the other hand, Asian emerging markets share the feature of underdeveloped institutional investors. Originally, a long-term financial market did not exist, or was not developed in Asian countries where short-term finance dominated. At present, there is a conscious fostering of capital markets aiming for the formation of long-term financial markets. A significant part of the financial flows is expected from overseas investors, in particular from those of advanced countries, and thus there is a tendency towards relaxation of investment regulations. At the same time fostering domestic investment by large-scale investors such as pension funds, trust funds, investment management, securities houses, and banks is an important task.

c) Tax system for securities

Some countries in Asia such as Hong Kong do not apply taxes to either residents or non-residents, but the majority distinguishes between residents and non-residents and applies source taxation at a certain level. Further, the majority of countries does not apply capital gains taxes (however, Thailand applies a 15 percent tax to foreign corporations, but no tax to individual investors).

d) Introducing computerized securities markets

Only India and Indonesia still operate according to the modus of Open Outcry without computerization. Indonesia is planning to do this at the same time as moving to a new securities trading institution. Stock clearing systems have not yet been introduced in the Philippines, Indonesia and India.

The NIEs have promoted computerization for trading and settlement, and this is proceeding according to plan. Except for Indonesia the ASEAN countries are in the process of tackling and developing computerization. One may also appreciate that China makes efforts in this direction when she establishes a securities trading institution. India is still in the planning stage, and will require some time before a new system will be in place.

Asian bond markets are still underdeveloped, while share markets are becoming more complete and expanding. This applies in particular to the secondary bond market, where one can hardly speak of a market except for national bonds and public bonds in some countries.

As opposed to the lively picture in the stock markets, there is little in these to attract the investor. One may cite the following as reasons:

a) The majority of countries has controls on interest rate levels; since the price of bonds runs counter to the actual market situation, there are few incentives for investors to own bonds.

b) There is little need for the issuance of bonds by the public sector in a period of positive development trend with regard to the financial income of Asian countries. Even when they are issued, they are issued *en bloc* to be digested by governmental financial institutions, and not thrown onto secondary markets.

c) Nearly all private enterprises raise finance through the issuance of equities without relying on the issue of corporate bonds; the number of such bonds reaching the bond market is exceedingly low. Thus, the bond markets are lifeless both in the issuance and trading of bonds in contrast with the lively equity markets.

In Asia, there is a comparatively large primary market for the issuance of bonds in South Korea, Taiwan, China and Singapore; the majority is national bonds and public bonds, and most of them are issued as short-term government securities. However, since 1993, one should notice that some private Asian corporations have issued convertible bonds and warrant bonds in the Euro market and the Swiss market.

SHARE MARKETS IN TEN ASIAN COUNTRIES

Hong Kong

Hong Kong has started to carry strong weight as an international securities market through the listing of China's H (Hong Kong) shares and the consolidation of a futures trading market. The number of listed enterprises rose rapidly from the beginning of the nineties to third place in Asia after Japan and South Korea, if we disregard India. The aggregate total of current prices was only second to Japan, with 385.2 billion US dollars at the end of 1993. The strong attraction of this market for overseas investors lies in the stability and reliability of its economy.

At the time of "Black Monday" (the great crash at the New York Stock Exchange) in 1987 markets were closed for four days; to prevent a reoccurrence, the SFTC (Securities Futures Trading Committee) was set up in 1989. It did not close trading even during the Tiananmen Incident (June 1986), when trade continued as usual.

The Hong Kong market is highly valued as a core market for Asian shares portfolio trading. After the rapid rise of share prices in the second half of 1993 these fell again as a result of interest rise in America, the canceling of Mutual Fund in America, and selling pressure exercised by overseas investors, and the market now shows a strong trend towards adjustment.

Investment trends by foreigners, and in particular changes in America's financial situation have a great impact on share prices, and at the same time Hong Kong is a market that requires substantial caution in connection with events on the Chinese mainland; during the transitional period, when Hong Kong reverts to China, market trends will enjoy the attention of investors worldwide.

Singapore

The Singapore securities market is under the control of the MAS (Monetary Authority of Singapore) and is the most advanced market in Asia as far as the consolidation of its infrastructure and internationalization is concerned.

The Disclosure System and regulations concerning insider training are in place. The government encourages private possession of shares by its citizens and carries out a policy of preferential treatment for investing. With the public offering of shares of Singapore Telecom the number of private shareholders rose in one go from 300,000 to 1,500,000 individuals.

The Singapore Securities Exchange is composed of its three markets, the Main Board, SESDAQ and CLOB International. Despite the decree by the Malaysian government in 1990 canceling the listing of Malaysian shares in Singapore, trading in Malaysian shares is continuing, as well as trade in other Asian shares. CLOB International was created exactly for that purpose.

Singapore is a city state of 3,000,000 people. There are limits to the expansion of the scale of the national economy, and Singapore's aim - including the aim of its government is to expand the vitality of Singapore's securities market by promoting further internationalization. Attempts to attract listing of enterprises from neighboring ASEAN countries and the like are important for the continued promotion of efforts towards a more convenient and open market for overseas investors.

Taiwan

There was a consistent increase in listed enterprises during the second part of the eighties. In Taiwan with her large number of private corporations, the number of managers with an interest in securing profit for the owner increased with the vitality of the distribution of shares, and this fact was the main reason for the increase in listed enterprises.

The aggregate amount of current prices of Taiwanese shares was the biggest among Asian countries with the exception of Japan at the height of the "bubble" (the beginning of 1990), but according to the figures for the end of 1993 ranked fourth behind Hong Kong, Singapore, and Malaysia. The percentage of individual shareholders is high, and since trading fees are cheap, trade turnover is exceedingly high, an important factor for the way share prices fluctuate.

Regulations concerning investments by foreigners are gradually being relaxed. From March 1996 investment in Taiwan shares was completely opened up to overseas private investors, and at the same time, the upper limit for the total of investments by foreigners per kind of share was lifted to 20 percent from 15 percent. Regulations concerning the transfer of money in connection with investments in share were also relaxed, and the abolition of regulations in the future are presently under consideration. However, the market requires attention in its sensitivity towards relations with the mainland and in the Taiwan Independence movement.

South Korea

In terms of value of share trading Seoul ranks third after Japan and Taiwan, and in terms of listed enterprises second after Japan if India is excluded. The separation of capital (ownership) and management does not proceed well, and there is a strong tendency by owner-managers to avoid lowering their share of share ownership.

Therefore, capital increase through paid in capital is almost exclusively carried out by the allocation to existing share owners. On the issue of new shares a limit of 20 percent of shares issued is preferentially allocated to members of the employee's share owners association. Before January 1992 investment regulations concerning foreigners prohibited such investments in principle, but liberalization of the capital market has proceeded step by step. After 1994 the maximum share of shares owned by foreigners was expanded to 15 percent. The abolition of these rules limiting investment by foreigners has been planned for 1998.

Price fluctuations of the South Korean share market are characterized by its strong link with the major factors of the domestic economy, at variance with securities markets of other Asian countries which strongly reflect the financial situation in the United States. As an external factor one should point to the strong degree of interdependence with the Japanese Yen exchange rate, a high Yen pushing up South Korean share prices.

Malaysia

Until the first half of the 1980s the Malaysian securities market did not leave the realm of a local market, and as a result of the active fostering of a capital market by the government the scale of the securities market now ranks behind that of Hong Kong and Singapore. Trading is conducted at Kuala Lumpur and Bumiputra Stock Exchange. However, the majority of trade is carried out at Kuala Lumpur. Participants in trading at Bumiputra are limited to Bumiputra (ethnic Malaysians), and trading volume is small. There is administrative guidance to set public subscription price levels lower than market levels due to the Bumiputra policy, and raising of capital by issuing shares at current prices after the public listing of shares is difficult. As a result, problems remain owing to the Bumiputra policy whereby almost all of Malaysia's paid in capital increase is effectuated by additional share issues allocated to shareholders through intermediate prices.

Thailand

The Thai capital market ranks at about the same level as that of South Korea with listed aggregate current prices of 130.2 billion US dollars, and in terms of listed enterprises (347) surpasses that of Taiwan and Singapore (1993 figures). This is a result of the promotion of share listing after 1989. The composition of enterprise categories used to be dominated by financial and construction sector, but recently the listing of new categories of shares - of estate companies, communication, transport, and various manufacturing enterprises - increased, and there is much more variety in enterprise categories.

Since the reform of the securities trading law of 1984 Thailand implemented an expansionist policy of the capital market; until then there were problems such as the lack of consolidation of the securities system, an excess supply of shares that accompanied the rapid increase of newly listed companies, as well as insider trading.

However, as a result of increased efforts in the management of markets by the establishment of the Securities Exchange Committee (SEC) in 1992, the raising of the level of listing standards, the participation of foreign investors in the market who showed a positive appraisal of the reforms, resulted in a fundamentally upward trend in the market. The ratio of foreigner in trade volume has rapidly increased to 20 percent by September 1994 from 4.8 percent in 1985, and increased the influence of foreign investors.

The Philippines

Of similar size to the Indonesian market, the Philippines is the smallest market in Asia. In terms of aggregate current value the Philippines capital market is about one-tenth of that of Hong Kong. Since mining, oil and raw materials related shares are in the majority, and the size of enterprises is small, the market often displays speculative moves.

The market expanded together with economic recovery and more stable politics in 1993, as the biggest rise in share prices in Asia (133 percent) has reflected. Furthermore, both trading places, in Manila and in Makati were linked on-line. There is also a 40 percent upper limit for foreign holdings of shares, but currency management is basically free if one registers at the time of investing. The securities market is however still very immature, and the securities system needs further refinement and strengthening.

Indonesia

There were hardly any listed enterprises in Indonesia before 1985, and the securities market did not function as the place where enterprises raise capital. In 1989 the government thrashed out a policy to foster a capital market, and advanced the · refinement of the securities system, and the opening of the securities market to the outside world.

However, influenced by the immaturity of the securities system and the excess supply of shares that accompanied the rapid rise of newly listed enterprises, the market continued at low level beyond the second half of 1990. To deal with it the government raised the standards for listing enterprises at the Jakarta securities exchange in order to improve the quality of listed enterprises. The Indonesia government is advancing the refinement of the securities market and other reforms at great speed, but there are still many problems to be solved, such as the disclosure of the financial situation. In addition, there is the problem that the immaturity of domestic investors allows the market to be dominated by investing trends of foreign investors.

China

The Chinese securities market has only recently been created, and the size of the market is still small. Foreigners may invest in "B" shares listed in Shanghai and Shenzhen, and in "H" shares listed in Hong Kong. Trading in Shenzhen and Hong Kong is based on the Hong Kong dollar, in Shanghai on the US dollar.

In the beginning of 1995 there were 28 kinds of "B" shares, and 12 kinds of "H" shares. Compared to "B" shares foreign investors could obtain information about "H" shares more easily, and since volatility was high, "H" shares enjoyed a higher popularity than "B" shares. However, foreigners were not willing to invest as much in "B" and "H" shares as China had hoped. There were several reasons: a) the backwardness of the securities market system, b) the insufficiency of the disclosure system, and c) the small size of the market and high price volatility.

During the share investment boom at the time of the establishment of a share market in 1991 and 1992, demand outpaced supply and share prices rose. In order to achieve a better balance the government granted permissions to enterprises to issue new shares on a grand scale, and as a consequence of large scale new emissions share prices dropped to a low level in 1993. The Chinese securities market continues to be consolidated but needs further consolidation through the implementation of consistent policies.

India

Among the listed enterprises the Indian securities market ranks number one in the world, but in reality the listed enterprises are almost all medium and small scale. It is estimated that there are more than 30 million share owners, second to the United States only.

As a result of the opening up of the securities market to foreigners in February 1992 foreign institutional investors may invest freely in shares owned by foreigners if they receive the approval of the Securities Exchange Commission of India (SECI). The economic reforms since 1991 have produced positive results in changing the attitude of the world towards the Indian economy, but it is a market which still needs many reforms, including improvement of the securities market infrastructure, such as rules on trading and settlement.

* Takuo Akiyama is senior researcher at the Long Term Credit Bank. Tokyo, Japan.

Chapter 11

Roger van Hoesel: "New Challenges: Korean Investment in Europe"

The recent surge of Korean investment in Europe means new challenges, for both Europe and the Korean companies involved. After the wave of Japanese investment in the 1980s, Europe in the 1990s again faces new competition on home grounds from companies that were hitherto unknown here. By the end of 1980 Korean firms invested only a very modest US $ 5 million in Europe (Table 1). The importance of Korean investment for Europe as a source of inward investment was correspondingly negligible (0.002 percent).(1) By the end of 1995, however, Korea's total investments amounted to more than US $1.5 billion whereas the relative share in total inward investment in Europe increased no less than 70 times. Examples given in this chapter will clearly indicate that these figures will continue to rise at a very rapid pace in the coming years.

From a Korean perspective, large-scale foreign direct investments (FDI) in such "distant" regions as Europe have ushered in a new era in the internationalization of its companies. Until the 1980s, the international business activities of Korean companies were almost completely confined to the export of goods from the home economy; by the end of 1980, for instance, the total of outstanding FDI amounted to only US $127 million - most of which was invested in neighboring developing countries. By the end of 1995, however, more than US $10 billion has been invested abroad by

Korean companies. At the same time we note from Table 1 that during the last fifteen years Europe, having received 15.1 percent of total Korean FDI by the end of 1995, has become a much more important destination for Korean companies.

Table 1 **Importance of Korea and Europe as source and destination of FDI, respectively (in US $ million; %)**

	1980	*1985*	*1990*	*1995*
(a) Korean FDI in Europe	5	60	148	1544
(b) Total FDI in Europe	203348	245075	761250	1120884
(a)/(b)	0.002%	0.024%	0.019%	0.14%
(c) Total Korean FDI	127	461	2301	10225
(a)/(c)	3.85%	13.00%	6.42%	15.10%

Sources: Bank of Korea (1996), UNCTAD (1996)

The literature dealing with the emergence of Korean multinationals is still rather modest;(2) discussions on their operations in Europe are almost absent. This paper therefore aims to shed some light on this phenomenon. To begin with, we investigate the nature of these investments. We will subsequently attempt to explain the sudden rise of investment activities by distinguishing a first and second wave of Korean FDI. And finally, we will evaluate the investment activities of these new multinational enterprises (MNEs) and conclude with some thoughts about how European companies ought to perceive their new competitors.

Characteristics
In this chapter we confine ourselves to the manufacturing sector to which more than half (54.5 percent) of total outstanding Korean FDI in Europe has been directed by the end of 1995.(3) These investment projects in particular have evoked many questions and have received considerable media coverage. Who are the companies behind those FDI figures and what activities do these data represent? Table 2 (see appendix p. 241) lists the most important production activities of Korean companies in Europe. From this table, a number of interesting observations can be made. In the

1980s, the first projects that were initiated in Europe primarily concerned the assembly of final consumer electronic goods (such as color TVs and microwave ovens). Although some smaller electronic firms like Carmen and Haitai also set up modest assembly operations in the European Union (EU), the most important ventures were undertaken by the Korean conglomerates (*chaebol*).(4)

Recently, however, this picture of the electronic sector has changed considerably. By increasing the number of factories as well as the size of individual investment projects, Samsung, Daewoo and LG (formerly Lucky-Goldstar) have drastically extended their presence in Europe. In addition, their production activities are no longer confined to the assembly of final consumer electronic goods. Now Samsung also produces color picture tubes in Germany and together with Texas Instruments, DRAMs in Portugal. Daewoo manufactures color picture tubes and cathode ray tubes in France. Also, in cooperation with Texas Instruments Daewoo announced the establishment of a semiconductor plant in Northern Ireland. In 1996 LG announced a US $2.65 billion investment in Wales (the biggest Korean investment in Europe to date) where the company will establish two factories producing semiconductors and color TV components. In addition to the intensification of activities by the *chaebol*, various smaller firms recently decided to shift the production of intermediate products to Europe. While companies like Poong Jeong and Fine Electromechanics will initially supply only Samsung, they hope to expand to serve European companies as well.

Another major change compared with earlier ventures concerns the sectors in which Korean companies invest in Europe. Next to the electronics industry, all of the "big four" (Samsung, Hyundai, Daewoo and LG) have invested recently in excavator plants in the EU.(5) Especially noteworthy, however, are the huge amounts Daewoo committed to invest in the production of vehicles ranging from cars to heavy trucks. The company's rather aggressive entrance of the European market is quite remarkable given the US $400 million losses Daewoo Motors incurred in the first half of the 1990s. In all cases, Daewoo acquired majority stakes in existing local firms. Interestingly, all of these investments were made in former state companies in Poland, the Czech Republic, and Rumania. In the case of the Polish FSO factory, for instance, the production of the outdated Polonez cars will gradually be replaced by Daewoo models which, incidentally, are based on products from other car manufacturers. Although Daewoo expects to sell cars successfully in Central and Eastern Europe, the company intends to export an important share of its production to Western Europe.

This brings us to our final observation, namely, the increased importance of Central and Eastern Europe as a destination of Korean FDI. In 1990, no less than 86.2 percent of FDI stock could be found in the European Union, whereas the former East Block (including CIS) received only 1.3 percent. By the end of 1995, however, the share of the EU decreased to 68.1 percent of total outstanding Korean FDI, whereas the CIS and other countries in Central and Eastern Europe attracted 13.7 percent and 16.7 percent, respectively.(6)

The most intriguing question is how to explain the emergence of Korean MNEs on European soil. For this purpose, we distinguish between the "first wave" of Korean FDI in the 1980s and the new, or "second wave" of investment activities in more recent years.

The first wave
First of all, the growth in FDI flows would not have been possible without a major change in government policy in outward investment (UNCTAD, 1995). For a long time the main policy was one of capital export restrictions to keep investments at home. This attitude changed in the second half of the 1980s when the Korean economy was confronted with eroding traditional comparative advantages. Shortage of low-skilled labor started to push wages up, a trend that was reinforced by tendencies of democratization which gave more room for wage demands by labor unions.(7) These wage increases were not matched by productivity growth. The gradual upgrading of the domestic economy from one primarily based on labor-intensive ("Heckscher-Ohlin") manufacturing such as textiles and other light industry goods as the leading export sectors, to more "undifferentiated Smithian" industries (based on scale economies) such as heavy and chemical industries and "differentiated Smithian" industries (assembly based, subcontracting dependent) such as electronics and automobiles, has also led to more intense direct competition with producers from major trading partners (Ozawa, 1995). As a response to their success in exports, the US authorities (for Korea strategically the most important market) forced the local currency to appreciate.(8) This clearly made exporting from the home economy less attractive. As a result, the Korean authorities decided to drastically liberalize their policy of capital outflows, thus freeing the way to shift production overseas.

During the first wave, most Korean FDI took place in neighboring (cheaper) developing countries, however. Investments in the industrialized world - and certainly in the relatively unknown EU - were still very modest. A major motivation to shift production operations to countries of the EU was the threat of protectionist measures such as anti-dumping duties against Korean electronic companies. These market seeking/retaining investments have not been without problems. Jun and Yoon (1995) concluded that these investments were of a "life or death decision". They reported that the firm-specific assets that MNEs from early industrialized economies possess (such as an innovative lead or strong marketing capabilities) were not present in the case of these Korean companies. How then were these companies able to start up their production activities in such a highly competitive environment as that of the EU? Especially in the 1980s, the local content of the assembly operations in Europe was rather low implying that a substantial share of intermediate products was still imported from Korea or elsewhere in Asia. This suggests that for the most part the firm-specific assets of the companies involved were based on country or region specific competitive advantages, such as those related to manufacturing capabilities (Hikino and Amsden, 1994). Furthermore, by supplying primarily the lower end of the European market these consumer electronic producers avoided direct competition with MNEs of more advanced economies.

The second wave
The second wave of Korean FDI in the 1990s witnessed a rapid increase of investments in Europe. This trend coincided with a greater diversity of motivations to invest in the region. In the 1990s, the motivations of Korean firms to invest in Europe became more diverse. This does not mean that early explanations lost their relevance, however. Korea's objective to become a member of the OECD, for instance, has led to an overall liberalization of its economy which *inter alia* implied a further relaxation of foreign exchange controls in recent years. The threat of protectionist measures of the EU remains an important consideration. In fact, Korean firms have been so sensitive to complaints of European manufacturers that plants of the Korean excavator producers, for example, have been set up in Europe before formal anti-dumping proceedings were opened. Interestingly, the speed of their response has made other European industries become more cautious about launching

anti-dumping actions (FT, 10.02.95). The European Motor Manufacturers' Association ACEA, for instance, refrained from such actions despite the evidence that Korean cars were being dumped on the European market. ACEA feared that anti-dumping complaints would prompt Korean car makers to set up assembly lines in Europe where local producers are still struggling to cope with the new capacity on the continents created by Japanese competitors. Given the large-scale investments recently made by Daewoo and the plans indicated by Kia and Hyundai to assemble cars and trucks respectively in Europe, this cautious attitude of ACEA apparently did not bear fruit.

Another inducement to Korean FDI has been the increased pressure imposed by EU authorities to further localize production activities by substantially raising local content requirements. As a result, the initial strategy of electronics firms to keep costs low by assembling imported inputs locally has become less adequate and has been replaced by a strategy to integrate operations to a larger extent into the European economy in the 1990s.

Also, a major change has been an active policy introduced by European governments to attract Korean firms. Even France which in the 1980s was known for its hostile attitude toward Japanese companies, currently competes with other potential host countries to attract Korean FDI. Most successful in this respect is the UK, however. By refraining from implementing EU laws - as those related to national minimum wages and maximum working hours - the UK has emerged as the most attractive destination in Europe offering comparatively low wages and flexible employment conditions. In addition, large subsidies are paid by regions to attract new companies. The Welsh authorities, for instance, paid LG about £200 million (or £30,000 a job) to locate in Wales (FT, 23.07.96). This, in combination with a continued increase in industrial wage levels in the home country have removed an important hindrance for Korean firms to invest in Europe. At present, labor rates in Korea equal or even exceed those in economies such as the UK, Northern Ireland and Portugal.

The second wave of Korean FDI in Europe is not merely a result of changes in locational conditions, however. The recent expansion of FDI coincides with a strategic reorientation that is taking place among Korea's leading companies. Until recently, many companies for their exports heavily depended on OEM contracts with leading industrial companies from other countries. OEM business refers to contractual agreements by which a foreign firm orders in volume products which the OEM supplier (a Korean firm) agrees to make according to specification. In other words, the production is under-taken by Korean firms whereas the marketing of the products is carried out by Japanese, American and European companies - under the latter's brand names. Although these OEM contracts have helped greatly in boosting Korea's exports in certain sectors and have also contributed to the competitive edges of these companies (primarily their manufacturing capabilities), the limitations of this mode of international business have increasingly become clear. Emerging competition from newly industrializing countries such as Malaysia and Thailand that also produce goods utilizing rela-tively mature technology has made the need to upgrade Korea's technological capabilities more imperative. Since OEM business puts the "burden" of R&D efforts with the buying company, Korean *chaebol* still considerably lag behind global leaders in many fields. Frontier technology is not readily available through arm's length transactions. Although strategic alliances have emerged as an increasingly important mode to generate new technologies, as opposed to "conventional" MNEs, only a limited number of Korean companies in a limited number of industries, for example, semi-conductors are technologically advanced enough to have something to offer *vis-à-vis* potential partners. Therefore, next to technologi-cal efforts carried out at home, the second wave contains an increasing number of strategic asset seeking investments meant to accumulate new firm-specific advantages in Triad economies (Dunning *et al.*, 1997).

In Europe, the privatization programs in the former East Block offer relatively cheap opportunities for Korean firms to enhance their technological capabilities by acquiring former state-owned companies. Samsung's picture tube factory (previously named "FGT") was acquired in former East Germany. Most active in this respect, however, has been Daewoo. By acquiring majority shares in Czech Avia and Polish FSC factories, for instance, Daewoo hopes to learn quickly how to build light trucks and vans. In addition, the various factories in Eastern Europe will provide substantial produc-tion capacity and extensive distribution channels, especially in Eastern Europe. An additional advantage is that many of the components of Daewoo cars in the future will be made locally, so that cars from these factories will be sold almost tariff-free in Western Europe. Daewoo has not limited its acquisitions to Eastern

Europe alone. In 1994, Daewoo Motor bought a technical design center in the UK where eventually 700 persons will work at the development of a new range of Daewoo cars. Another example of a strategic seeking investment was the acquisition in 1989 by Ssangyong Motor of British Panther Cars, a small producer of exclusive sports cars. Ssangyong bought the company primarily to gain access to European car technology. Soon after the purchase the assembly line was transferred to Korea while the R&D department remained in the UK.

Next to M&A activity, greenfield investments in Europe have also offered the opportunity to scan the local environment. LG Electronics Design Center in Ireland for instance taps from locally available knowledge to design products that are tailored to European lifestyles. Daewoo opened a development center in Germany where former engineers and designers of European car manufacturers are employed to design new engines.

The expanded investment activities in Europe also coincide with the desire among leading Korean companies to decrease their dependence on OEM contracts and build up strong own brand names instead. Samsung Electronics even pledged to reduce its OEM sales to zero in the near future. Daewoo initially produced cars in Korea in a joint venture with General Motors. This joint venture was dissolved in 1992 which freed Daewoo from the GM-imposed restriction to export cars under the Daewoo brand name. In an attempt to make up for the back-log the company had *vis-à-vis* other Korean and Japanese competitors, Daewoo in 1995 commenced aggressive advertising campaigns in Western Europe. Also Daewoo's sister company, Daewoo Heavy Industries which in the past sold more than 90 percent of its output to Caterpillar has switched its emphasis to own brand promotion after the contract ended. Similar increased efforts to strengthen their commercial capabilities are observed among other large Korean firms. To realize such goals, an extensive presence in important overseas markets is needed to build up their own extensive distribution network and improve brand awareness.

A final remark here concerns the investments made by smaller electronic components suppliers in the UK. The more offensive strategies conducted by the *chaebol* in Europe will undoubtedly draw complaints from local competitors, and eventually some form of regulation (such as stricter local content requirements) to obstruct the performance of these Korean firms might be taken. The attempts by Samsung, for instance, to convince component suppliers to join them in Europe should be seen in this perspective.

Brave or foolish?

How should we evaluate the ambitious plans of Korean companies for global expansion in view of their investments in Europe? The ambitions of the *chaebol* in some cases seem rather heroic. New investment plans are announced continuously, some of which the outsider finds difficult to rationalize. Samsung Motor, for instance, a company that still has to produce its first car (scheduled for 1998) has already set up their European headquarters in Frankfurt and has suggested that it may eventually build factories in Europe. Similarly, Daewoo which has hardly any experience in the semi-conductor business, has linked up with Texas Instruments for a US $1.2 billion semiconductor investment in Northern Ireland (*Financial Times*, 18 March 1996). Some of these ventures appear to be prompted primarily by the typical follower strategy that are so characteristic for Korea's oligopolistic industries. In some cases it may turn out that the actual amounts that will be invested are considerably lower than initially announced. This does not make these ventures less risky, however.

Moreover, most *chaebol* have daunting debt burdens and are among the largest borrowers of bank loans. As Samsung recently experienced, this keeps them dependent on good relationships with the Korean authorities.(9) The extremely high speed of interna-tionalization does not only imply that high financial risks are at stake. We saw already that, as opposed to Japanese companies, Korean firms did not have the time to build up the technological and commercial strengths needed to become successful overseas. In addition, the organization set-up of the *chaebol* in the past was not geared to deal with final consumers in European and American markets, but instead were used to do business with a limited number of industrial (OEM) clients. Companies like Samsung and LG there-fore recently introduced large-scale programs to prepare (Korean and non-Korean) managers for overseas positions.

Although pursuing all of these changes in such a short period may seem exaggerated, this behavior does not characterize these companies as brave or foolish. The foregoing clearly indicates how difficult it is to produce alternative strategies. Given the mounting pressure to open up its home markets, Korean firms will face increasing competition at home. The forming of regional trade blocks like the EU, NAFTA and APEC at the same time more or less pushes companies to be (physically) present in all these regions. These developments imply a major challenge for Korea where the discrepancy between early location advantages (such as cheap labor and a protected home market) and the firm-specific advantages needed to compete in the present global business environment becomes increasingly evident. It seems beyond doubt that the Korean economy must be upgraded further to more advanced, innovation driven and service-focused "Schumpeterian" industries that better match the new economic reality in which Korea wants to succeed, also in the (near) future. Unfortunately, this cannot be accomplished in a gradual manner but requires shortcuts instead.

A final question is how anxious should European companies be about the emergence of all these Korean companies? First of all, it seems that European companies are no longer in a position to play down the (potential) global role of Korean companies in important branches of industry. Especially the *chaebol* have access to large financial (government) sources to extend their presence in Europe considerably. Yet, all that glitters is not gold. In spite of their rapid expansion, most of these companies do have weaknesses, which put their present internationalization at risk. And it is exactly these weaknesses that offer possibilities to European business.

We know, for instance, that in some lines of business, the value added realized by Korean firms is relatively low. Although they are perhaps successful in terms of sales volume, the nature of these industries is still assembly types. In most cases, this is not merely the result of a rational "make or buy" decision. Often, the knowledge required to produce certain components is simply not available. This weakness causes many producers (of electronics and cars) to be strongly dependent on foreign sources, primarily Japan. This dependence on Japanese suppliers is an important and sensitive subject of debate in Korea.

This need for knowledge-intensive intermediate goods could mean an important stimulus for West European companies that, given the locational conditions in their home economies, in the future will have to shift the focus of attention to more knowledge-intensive industries. The cooperation between Korean and European firms need not be confined to the supply of intermediate goods, however. The joint development of new products could result from the combination of Korean financial resources and the European knowledge infrastructure available. In addition, more intensive cooperation programs can be achieved in marketing. Philips, for instance, cooperates with LG in marketing Philips products in Asia. Likewise, the lack of knowledge possessed by Korean firms about the European markets may be compensated by a European partner.

Such alliances as I have proposed here fit into the continued process of globalization of international business. Although there are obstacles to overcome, the present developments seem to offer opportunities both to Korean and European companies.

* Roger van Hoesel is researcher at the Tinbergen Institute, Erasmus University Rotterdam, The Netherlands.

Notes and references

1. UNCTAD estimates indicate that with regard to the European Union, more than half of inward investment originates in other EU member countries (UNCTAD, 1995). Taking this into account would imply that Korea's share as an *external* source of FDI is more sizeable than suggested in the text.
2. For a discussion on (very) early Korean outward investment, see for instance Jo (1981), Kumar & Kim (1984), Euh & Min (1986), Han & Brewer (1987). More recent developments are discussed in Lee & Lee (1992), Lee (1994) and van Hoesel (1994).
3. The trade sector (sales subsidiaries of Korean manufacturers and General Trading Companies) received another 32.2 percent.
4. In the case of Saehan, which established a large videotape plant in Ireland, an informal (family) link exists with Samsung since the company was established by the second son of the founder of Samsung.
5. These four groups account for no less than 60 percent of total Korean exports!
6. The share of other countries in Europe in the first half of the 1990s had gone down from 12.5 percent to 1.5 percent.
7. As a result, manufacturing wages went up with no less than 37.8 percent between 1986 and 1990.
8. Between 1986 and 1990, for instance, the Korean Won appreciated with 16.8 percent against the US Dollar.
9. After that Samsung's chairman Lee had labeled Korea's president Kim Young Sam as "second rate" and Korean politics as

"fourth rate" during a visit to China, government loans to Samsung companies were suddenly halted. As a result, the acquisition of a majority stake in American AST Research was jeopardised (*Volkskrant*, 13.09.95).

Bank of Korea (1996), *Overseas Direct Investment Statistics Yearbook*.

Dunning, J. H., R. van Hoesel and R. Narula (1997), "Explaining the 'new' wave of outward FDI from developing countries", in *International Business Review* (forthcoming).

Euh, Y.-D. and S.H. Min (1986), "Foreign Direct Investment from Developing Countries: the case of Korean Firms", in *The Developing Economies*, XXIV-2, June, pp. 149-168.

Financial Times (FT), various issues.

Han, C.M. and T.L. Brewer (1987), "Foreign Direct Investments by Korean Firms: An Analysis with FDI Theories", in *Asia Pacific Journal of Management*, Vol. 4 No. 2, January, pp. 90-102.

Hikino, T. and A.H. Amsden (1994), "Staying Behind, Stumbling Back, Sneaking Up, Soaring Ahead: Late Industrialization in Historical Perspective", in W. Baumol, R. Nelson and E. Wolff (eds.), *Convergence of Productivity: Cross Country Studies and Historical Evidence*, Oxford University Press: New York, pp. 285-314.

Hoesel, R. van (1994), "Taiwanese en Zuidkoreaanse multinationals (Taiwanese and Korean multinationals)", in *Economisch Statistische Berichten*, 26 January, pp. 86-88.

Jo, S.H. (1981), "Overseas Direct Investment by South Korean Firms: Direction and Patterns", in K. Kumar and M.G. McLeod (eds.), *Multinationals from Developing Countries*, Lexington Books: Lexington, pp. 53-77.

Jun, Y. and D. Yoon (1995), *An Exploratory Explanation of the Reverse Direct Investment: the case of Korean electronics industry*, paper presented at AIB Conference: Seoul.

Kumar, K. and K.Y. Kim (1984), "The Korean Manufacturing Multinationals", in *Journal of International Business Studies*, Spring/Summer, pp. 45-61.

Lee, K. (1994), "Structural Adjustment and Outward Direct Investment in Korea", in *Seoul Journal of Economics*, Vol. 7, No. 2, pp. 179-211.

Lee, C. H. and K. Lee (1992), "A Transition Economy and Outward Direct Foreign Investment: The Case of South Korea", in *Seoul Journal of Economics*, Vol. 5, No. 1, pp. 89-111.

Ozawa, T. (1995), "Structural Upgrading and Concatenated Integration; the vicissitudes of the Pax Americana in tandem industrialization of the Pacific Rim", in D. F. Simon, *Corporate Strategies in the Pacific Rim: Global versus Regional Trends*, Routledge: London, pp. 215-245.

UNCTAD (1995), *World Investment Report 1995*, UN: Geneva.

UNCTAD (1996), *World Investment Report 1996*, UN: Geneva.

Volkskrant, 13.09.95.

Appendix

Table 2: Production operations by Korean companies in Europe (Summer 1996)

Company name:[a]	Host country:	Products:	Initial year:	Investment:[b]	Share:
Daewoo	UK	VCRs	1988	US$M 42	100%
	France	Microwave ovens	1988	US$M 23	70%
	Belgium	Excavators	1990	US$M 10	100%
	France	Colour TVs	1993	US$M 37	100%
	France	Colour picture tubes	1993	US$M 150	100%
	France	Cathode ray tubes	1993	US$M 138	100%
	Poland	Cons.electronic products	1995	US$M 33	100%
	Poland	Vans, cars	1996	US$M 740	61%
	Poland	Cars	1996	US$bln. 1.1	60%
	Rumania	Cars	1996	US$M 156	51%
	Rumania	Ships	1996	US$M 53	51%
	Czech Republic	Light trucks, heavy vans	1997	US$M 200	50.2%
	UK	semiconductors (with TI)	ann.	US$bln. 1.3	na.
Hyundai	Belgium	Excavators	1995	US$M 10-15	100%
	Hungary	Trucks	ann.	na.	na.
	UK	Semiconductors	ann.	US$bln. 1.3	na.
LG	Germany	VCRs	1986	US$M 40	100%
	Italy	Refrigerators, freezers	1990	US$M 10	100%
	UK	Colour TVs, microwave ovens	1995	US$M 40	100%
	UK	- Semiconductors - CTV components	1996	US$bln. 2.65	100%
Samsung	Germany	Colour TVs	1982	US$M 2	100%
	Spain	VCRs	1990	US$M 2	100%
	UK	Colour TVs	1990	US$M 15	100%
	Germany	Colour picture tubes	1994	US$M 120	100%
	Portugal	Semiconductors (with TI)	1994	US$M 30	38%
	UK	Cons.electronic products	1994	US$M 700	100%
	Hungary	Colour TVs	1995	US$M 5	95%
	UK	Excavators	1995	US$M 15	100%
Carmen	UK	Car radios	1993	US$M 3	100%
Daeryung	UK	Satellite receivers	1996	US$M 26	100%
Dong Jin Precision	UK	Microwave oven components	1997	US$M 8	100%
Haitai	France	Car radios	1989	US$M 4	100%
Halla	UK	Earth moving equip.	1996	US$M 27	100%
Inkel	UK	Audio equipment	1990	US$M 3	100%
Kony precision	Ireland	Electronic components	1990	US$M 1	50%
Pacific	France	Cosmetics	1990	US$M 3	87.8%
Saehan	Ireland	Videotapes	1987	US$M 23	100%
Sammi	UK	Audio speakers	1993	US$M 3	100%
Shinho Electronic Telecomm.	UK	Computer monitors	1997	US$M 13	100%
Sunkyoung	UK	Magnetic tapes	1991	US$M 2	100%
Woo One	UK	Computer casings	1997	US$M 4	100%
YG-1	UK	Machine tools	ann.	US$M 13	100%
Young Shin	UK	Television casings	1995	US$M 9	100%

Fine Electromech.	UK	Coil components	1997		100%
Poong Jeon	UK	Wires and refrig. parts	1997	USSM 3 (together)	100%
Sung Kang Electromech.	UK	Cables	1997		100%

Sources: Bank of Korea, Financial Time
Notes: ann. announced; na.: not available
a. Since in some cases the subsidiaries are owned by various members of a business group, the names of the groups are mentioned here.
b. Amounts indicated to invest at start of venture, *viz.* sequential investments are not included.

Chapter 12

Helmut Schütte: "Regionalization of Global Thinking: Strategy and Organization of European MNCs in Asia"

Re-assessing Asia

Some European MNCs like Unilever, Cable & Wireless and Siemens were already represented in the Asia Pacific region a hundred years ago. Others had built up a number of offices and factories after WW II, but in the seventies and even eighties such activities were still considered fringe business run by "expatriates" dispatched to distant lands appropriately called the "Far East".

As a result, the presence of European MNCs in Asia is weak, both in terms of foreign investment in and exports to the region. While data on FDI and trade differ from source to source, there is agreement that European MNCs have neglected Asia in comparison with other parts of the world, and play a less important role in Asia than their American and Japanese equivalents (European Commission and UNCTAD, 1996; European Parliament, 1996; OECD, 1995). Various reasons have been posited for the slow response to the growing opportunities in Asia, including the preference given by European MNCs to the exploitation of opportunities arising from the European integration process and, more recently, the changes in Central and Eastern Europe.

An equally important reason for the low priority given to Asia in the past by the board rooms of European MNCs was the perception that Asia was too difficult in comparison with neighboring countries in Europe, the United States and even Latin America. The then booming Japanese market was perceived as closed, while Japanese competitors dominated the rest of Asia and started to threaten entrenched markets at home. The developing markets of Asia were considered not yet ready for sophisticated European products or else were riddled with corruption and red tape. Consequently, few European MNCs were committed to the region.

At the same time customers in Asia were increasingly demanding world class rather than outdated technology; local manufacturing and service capabilities rather than imported goods; and products and services adapted to Asia rather than global, i.e. standardized offerings. Operationally, MNCs saw their growth opportunities curtailed by their inability to recruit and retain top-notch Asian talents who refused to work for firms stuck in the managerial behavior of post-colonial times and which were not prepared to provide them with equal career opportunities.

Despite all of these problems sales and often profits grew, albeit from a very low base and accompanied by very low expectations. This was the reason why hardly anyone in the eighties realized that the traditional approach of European MNCs towards doing business in Asia no longer suited the speed with which the region was growing and changing. Low or moderate growth in sales, considered normal in Europe, meant losing market share in Asia's dynamic environment. Low profits were not, as it was often thought, the result of high entry costs, but rather signs of managerial under-performance when compared with the success of local, regional, and also Japanese and American competitors.

In the nineties consistently high growth in Asia had brought about volumes in demand for many product and service categories matching those of Europe and the Americas. Finally the prospects of continuing higher growth rates in Asia than in the rest of the world led to a major re-think of the position of Asia in the corporate portfolio. Hardly a week passes today without a major European MNC announcing its intention to double, if not triple its sales and investments in the region. Asia, excluding Japan, now becomes the primary investment priority, a "hot" destination compared to the Americas and Central and Eastern Europe(1)

(Arthur Andersen/Ministry of Economic Affairs of France, 1996, pp. 23 and 34).

The rush towards Asia since 1994 finally becomes visible also in export and investment statistics, and the first worries over the build-up of potential overcapacities surface. It was probably the emergence of China and the consequent realization that it may - after all - not be too late to jump on the Asian bandwagon that triggered this major reassessment. As a result, in many European MNCs, Asia has now become "strategically important". What, however, does this mean and what are the consequences?

The strategic importance of Asia

The strategic importance of a region is derived from its market size and potential as a source of sales and profits, the competitive threat emanating from competitors' activities in the region, and the availability of resources.

If GNP or GDP is taken as a proxy for the overall market size, Asia Pacific at the middle of the nineties represents about 25 percent of the world's output (The World Bank, 1996), i.e. 25 percent of all the opportunities in the world to make a sale or a profit. Within the next 10 or so years, the region will be equal in size to North America or Europe. As far as international trade is concerned, 24 percent of world imports go into the region already (World Trade Organization, 1995). Any firm claiming to have a global reach should ideally have already one quarter of its business in Asia. This may sound unrealistic as from a historical perspective firms tend to start growing in their home country, then expand into neighboring territories before exploring distant markets. However, most European MNCs are so far away from a regional alignment of their activities with market opportunities that their status as global players can hardly be confirmed (Figure 1).

The consequences of the under exploitation of Asian markets can be severe. Imagine if European rather than Japanese MNCs had taken over the markets for motorcycles, passenger cars and trucks in Asia ten to twenty years ago. Consider the case of Schindler, a fine Swiss manufacturer of elevators. It is second in the world (behind Otis), but only sixth in Asia (behind three Japanese manufacturers, Otis and one Korean firm). More than half of all elevators sold today are installed in Asia, and this percentage will probably rise. Everything else being equal, competitors better placed in Asia than

Schindler should grow faster than the Swiss firm. What is even more important, these other firms will probably reap profits more easily than Schindler. Fast growing markets rarely see the price battles and product proliferation that companies are exposed to when they fight for survival in stagnating markets, where gains for one firm lead to losses for another.

Figure 1   European MNCs in Asia

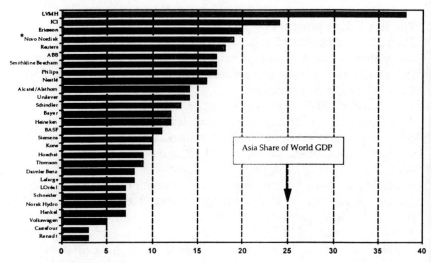

% of Sales in Asia Pacific (Source: Annual Reports for 1995)

*Japan only

Exploiting market opportunities in Asia, however, is only one side of the coin. The other is that slower growth and unsatisfactory profit performance in markets at home and insufficient participation in the growth of Asia can endanger the global market position in the long run. Often an expansion into the region can be justified only for strategic reasons, for example, to limit competitors' growth and profit opportunities, thereby denying them the opportunities for cross-subsidization and protection of their traditional markets closer home. This applies particularly to MNCs from Japan and more lately from Korea for whom the whole region meanwhile has become a profitable "home" market, allowing them to generate cash for expansion into Europe. It is at times of the announcement of their investments that Europeans realize how outdated the term "Far East" has become.

While market considerations have gained weight in strategic discussions of Asia, the possibilities to profit from Asia's resources have lost some of their attraction. Asia has plenty of natural resources, but few of them are proprietary or unique in the sense that they cannot be obtained outside the region. Its most valuable resources are its people, many of them prepared to work hard for long hours against low wages. But most of this cheap labor is unskilled and as such represents neither an attractive opportunity for cost savings nor a competitive threat for MNCs - except in very few industries such as shoes, garments and toys. Today's and tomorrow's technologies require skilled labor and management, good infrastructure and access to markets - all factor conditions not in abundant supply in Asia, and on their own not sufficient reason for an European MNC to move production to the region.

Pure offshore production has therefore lost its attractiveness. Exceptions to the general rule exist in special sectors such as computer parts and components in Taiwan or software production in India. And even in those cases, manufacturing can be outsourced, giving MNCs more flexibility and better opportunities for concentrating on their core competencies. However, cost advantages based on cheaper labor at all levels can often contribute to a competitive advantage when combined with a presence in the market, as companies such as Thomson in Singapore or Philips in Taiwan have experienced. Local manufacturing in a market not only reduces entry barriers, but also leads to better understanding of the market itself. The accompanying insider status - difficult to reach for firms exclusively involved in offshore manufacturing or import and sales activities - provides indirect marketing support.

Technology is another resource that can be accessed in Asia, so far primarily in Japan. Korea, Taiwan and Singapore are emerging as innovative places, particularly in the area of information technology (Hobday, 1995). The experience in strategic alliances with Japanese firms, is, however, not encouraging many European MNCs to seek further cooperative ventures with other Asian firms. American partners continue to be preferred for joint technological developments (Schütte, 1993, pp. 25-31).

The strategic importance of a region in terms of markets, competition and resources differs from MNC to MNC and even from business to business within the same firm. This is what makes it so irrational to prescribe Asia for everybody. In reality, however, most European MNCs have discovered that Asia is attractive for them, but that their assets and capabilities in the region are limited. In Europe, on the other hand, they are well established but for most industries this does not offer much hope for increased sales or profits.

Figure 2   Portfolio of Regions

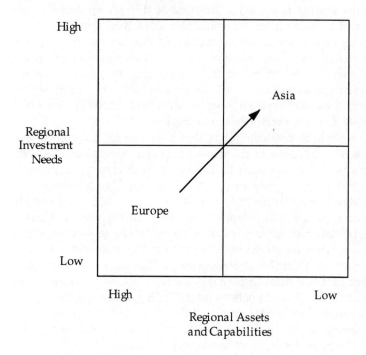

Consequently Europe's role is reduced to that of a cash-cow (Figure 2) - or even a dog - producing the money needed for investments in Asia: not an attractive proposition for managers in Europe already struggling to squeeze profits out of mature, embattled markets.

The divergent growth momentum in Europe and in Asia, however, makes a massive shift of funds inevitable. Even if Asian operations quickly show good returns on investments, the profits generated will not be sufficient to finance internal growth in the region, let alone new projects or acquisitions. Strong leadership is required in Euro-centric MNCs to boost their exposure to Asia when a substantial reallocation of resources is required.

Giving priority to Asia means changing the company status from that of an explorer or laggard to that of a mover or strategic investor as depicted in figure 3. Such a move is often preceded or accompanied by symbolic gestures like the holding of important meetings in the region, the presence of the chairman or major shareholders at a highly publicized inauguration of a new plant in Asia or the appointment of a board member as regional head - all actions designed to signal strong commitment of the MNC to Asia, and to give Asian managers and projects high visibility, both internally and externally.

Figure 3:   European MNCs in Asia

Stage	Explorer	Strategic Investor	Global Consolidator
Objectives	• Exploit Local Opportunities	• Build Regional Presence • Pre-empt	• Balance Global Portfolio
Operations	• Limited • Self-contained	• Regional Linkages • RHQs	• Global Linkages
Commitment to the Region	• Ambivalent	• Very High	• High

To implement the strategic reorientation, major steps have to be undertaken to develop a common regional perspective across countries and businesses, to upgrade the quality of managers involved in Asia, and to cope with the existence of a number of local partners and the resistance of subsidiary managers with limited interests in regional affairs. A truly regional presence has to be established and independent, country-based operations must be integrated to counter competition on a regional basis. Eventually a regional organization has to be set up to initiate change and co-ordinate operations. Without these moves, announcements of Asia being very important will remain just words, and managers, who have been dispatched from headquarters, will continue to see their own career lying elsewhere.

The need for a regional strategy

If Asia is supposed to receive a substantial boost, the first question to be asked is whether a special strategy for Asia will be needed. The intuitive answer is negative. MNCs have enough difficulties managing the trade-off between the pressures for global integration on the one hand, and the need to be locally responsive on the other (Prahalad and Doz, 1987, pp. 24-26) and thus shy away from further complications. What is acceptable and easily done is to divide global strategies up into different geographic sectors without adjusting them to different circumstances. This, however, cannot be counted as a truly regional strategy that would be distinct and different from the rest of the world.

Arguments in favor of a regional strategy for Asia would have to show that first, Asia is different from the rest of the world, and secondly, that the various parts of Asia are somewhat similar to each other. Only if both conditions are met, could a regional strategy be useful. The assessment of the situation has to be based on internal and external factors. Internal factors are firm-specific and depend on the resources available and the perceptions of the region at headquarters as well as the specific product markets in which the company competes. If the firm has not been successful in the region so far and resources for Asia are limited, Asia is often perceived as complex and psychologically distant. This alone may justify a specific regional strategy in order to break the vicious circle of failure and non-commitment. Equally, when products such as cosmetics differ considerably (whitening creams in Asia vs. tanning creams in Europe) a different strategy may be called for. In diversified MNCs this assessment can easily lead to a need for a regional strategy for certain businesses, but not for others. It makes finding a common strategic direction difficult, if not impossible.

Two external factors shape the need for a regional strategy and apply to almost all MNCs and businesses. The first refers again to the different growth dynamics in Asia and the rest of the world. Asia's economic development over recent decades is the result of the efforts of its entrepreneurs and managers whose mind-set thus far is almost exclusively shaped by success stories. Investing, acquiring, expanding, diversifying - thereby constantly taking risks and progressing - comes naturally in Asia. Growth of revenue and market share still come first, and the shortage of good and loyal staff is considered the most serious bottleneck. Contrast this with the thoughts going through the mind of a senior executive in Europe: restructuring, re-engineering, concentration on core businesses, cutting costs, and last but not least, down-sizing or getting rid of surplus staff.

Strategies born in and suitable for mature, slow-moving markets in Europe can rarely be expected to work in the fast-growing, rapidly changing environment of Asia in which growth is almost taken for granted. In the same way experienced managers coming from a predictable setting in Europe find it impossible to use their standard business approach to cope with the ambiguities and volatility of Asian markets. Yet these not only create uncertainties, but also surprising market opportunities for entrepreneurial executives.

Secondly, the region is becoming more integrated. Intra-Asian trade is increasing, as is intra-Asian investment, travel and cultural exchange. Contrary to Europe where politicians initiated the integration, governments are not the driving force behind this trend, but the business community itself, the Overseas Chinese and the Japanese MNCs in particular. Korean MNCs and bumiputra firms from Malaysia and Indonesia have also evolved into regional players. Their strongly centralized approach which varies little from country to country requires European MNCs to adopt a similarly regional approach. Equally, regional key account management is needed to deal with them as customers. The increasing integration of Asia also enables MNCs to rationalize production activities in order to exploit cost advantages across countries and to develop common marketing concepts adjusted to specific Asian needs and communicated through increasingly regional media.

Conceptually, a shift towards a regional strategy replaces the need for local responsiveness with that for regional responsiveness (Figure 4), and gives more weight to the pressures of regional responsiveness than to those for global integration. It is only justified when regional concerns are fundamentally different from global ones and therefore require a *modification* of management practices. Such a distinct strategy for Asia requires a different *thinking* mode compared to other parts of the world in terms of different mental models and different relationship paradigms (Lasserre and Schütte, 1995, pp. 44-46).

Figure 4   IR Grid for Regional Strategy(2) (Lehrer and Azakawa, 1995, pp. 3-4)

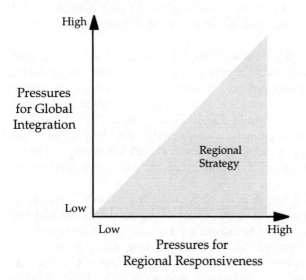

This does not suggest that local needs are becoming irrelevant, especially bearing in mind that the differences between the various Asian markets and business cultures remain large, certainly much larger than those between the various European countries. Local needs, however, have to be subordinated to regional concerns in the framework of regional strategies. In comparison with the difference between global and regional needs, the gap between regional and local responsiveness can be bridged by simple *adaptation* of management practices to different languages, institutions, legal frameworks and social codes. Responding to local needs may imply *acting* differently in the various markets, but still under the umbrella of one common Asian way of thinking.

The need for a regional organization
Leading on from the discussion of the need for a regional strategy is the question of a regional organization. This is normally understood to mean an additional administrative level in between global

headquarters and local subsidiary, though it need not be the case as we shall see below. The intuitive answer of managers concerned a t both ends will again be negative. Such an organizational solution is not in line with today's moves towards delayering and lean management.

Assuming that structure follows strategy (Chandler, 1962), there is no justification for a regional organization when there is no regional strategy. There are cases in which the regional organization was established with the task first of all to develop a regional strategy (Schütte, 1995), though this may be the exception rather than the rule. Regional organization in this context is defined as a regional headquarters (RHQ) to which authority is transferred to solve problems in the region which cannot be handled by the national units and otherwise would have to be dealt with and acted upon by headquarters. It actively manages the integration and coordination of activities of the MNC within the region, and represents the link between the region and headquarters - independently of its location. A representative office, a holding company set up for fiscal reasons or a regional organizational unit simply providing services and an infrastructure on behalf of headquarters could exist and be useful. However, such entities are not considered RHQs here.

Conceptually RHQs are justified when the pressures on the MNC for integrating its operations in the region are greater than the pressures for local responsiveness, as figure 5 shows. This implies that the benefits from regional integration must be higher than the cost of an RHQ as an additional organizational unit and hierarchical level, especially the cost associated with the loss of relative independence of the national units. The measurement of these costs is difficult, of the benefits practically impossible. This may be one of the explanations why RHQs of European MNCs in Asia have such a chequered track record and are largely unstable organizational phenomena. Their number is still low, but increasing. Most of the larger, diversified European MNCs with substantial operations in Asia have such an RHQ already established(3) (Schütte, 1996).

The roles of RHQs can be divided between those more directed towards headquarters and others more directly involved in regional operations. The first set of roles is concerned with strategy development and implementation in the sense of budgeting and control, strategic stimulation, intelligence gathering, new business development, and the bundling of otherwise fragmented demands from dispersed operations for resources or simply more attention from headquarters in competition with other regions. The second set of roles consists of raising efficiency and effectiveness through the pooling of resources, benchmarking and the spread of best practice and the coordination of activities across borders and business divisions. The aim of the latter set of roles is to achieve synergy's and consistency, and is integrative and administrative in nature (Lasserre, 1996).

Figure 5   IR Grid for Regional Organization

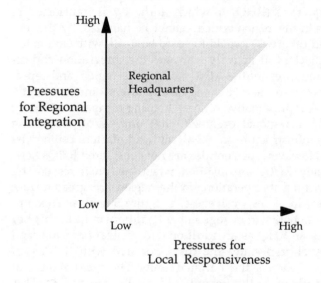

Pressures for
Local Responsiveness

Regional managers do not go unchallenged when carrying out their tasks. Corporate, business, functional and national unit managers feel that their influence and power over the activities in the region, or their specific territory in the region, is curtailed (see figure 6). Corporate managers fear that the region may go astray and therefore try to keep the RHQ in line with the other parts of the world. Business managers argue that product specific knowledge counts more than regional market know how; functional managers believe that their expertise is best leveraged across the world without any modification; and national unit managers maintain that their specific market is different from the rest of the region and the world, and should best be left alone(4) (Morrison, Ricks and Roth, 1991, and Blackwell, Bizet, Child and Hensley, 1992).

To overcome resistance from the various stakeholders, some European MNCs have decided to assign very senior executives to head their RHQs. In ABB, Schindler, Unilever and Volkswagen main board members have been appointed to manage the RHQ. Other MNCs have dispatched managers just one level below the board to direct the regional activities. Our data show that where less senior managers are transferred to the RHQ, they tend to be less effective. The actual leverage of an RHQ within the whole organization also depends on the overall organizational logic of the MNC. Where the businesses dominate in the board, and a geographic dimension is not represented, for example in a matrix structure, RHQs tend to be relatively weak.

Despite the emphasis in the management literature on processes rather than structure (Ghoshal and Bartlett, 1995), RHQs tend to stress authority and power, thus reinforcing the perception of an organization as a structure consisting of hierarchical layers. Those RHQs in which the national unit managers report to the RHQ, which in turn reports to headquarters, can be called vertical RHQs. In diversified MNCs this system is more complex as at least one further communication line (the "dotted" line) exists to a business division, but in principle hierarchical relationships continue to dominate.

The demand of business managers for greater powers of control is difficult to resist. Within the portfolio of a diversified MNC some businesses will be better off pursuing a global, others a regional strategy. Similarly, among those businesses for which a regional strategy is appropriate, some will require a high degree of integration and are therefore in urgent need of an RHQ, while others are better suited to the national unit approach. Rarely can a suitable strategy and organization in the region be found which fits all businesses of an MNC equally well. Unilever, for example, runs its chemical division on a global basis without the intermediary of an RHQ, while its main businesses (detergents, toiletries and food) are organized regionally. Rhone-Poulenc and ICI have separate RHQs for their various businesses, not all of them physically located in the same countries of the region. Synergies between businesses, already difficult to create in central RHQs, may become impossible to achieve when managers are based at different locations. There is also the danger that in the process of designing such organizations, too much complexity becomes too costly and cumbersome (Ghoshal and Nohria, 1993). As many MNCs have discovered, the problems related to the establishment and operation of a RHQ are nothing else than a microcosm of their overall problems of managing complexity!

Figure 6   Stakeholders in RHQs

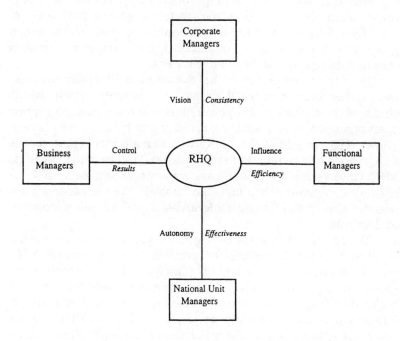

Two models of organization can be proposed to convert destructive conflicts into productive tension within the region. The first, the horizontal RHQ, operates on a consensus basis, with the authority of the RHQ dependent to some extent on the national units. In the extreme, the RHQ becomes the executing arm of the operating units in the region and can direct and control only with the consent of those governed. The second model, the virtual RHQ, also relies on input from national units, but an RHQ as a separate organizational unit with its own office and dedicated staff does not exist. The responsibilities and functions of the traditional RHQ are not abandoned, but are distributed to existing national units. As such, the RHQ continues to fulfill its tasks, though only in a conceptual sense through the activities of dispersed local/regional managers. These can take over additional responsibilities as regional business or functional managers, as in the case of the horizontal RHQ.

Attempts of this kind come close to what has been described as federalism in organizations combining the autonomy of individual organizational units with the scale benefits of coordination (Handy, 1992). Applied to the regional organization, the horizontal and virtual RHQs maintain the integrity of the national units, while at the same time unifying their activities for the common objectives of the region. They allow the local directors to become local barons or local heroes, while moderating their individualism through mechanisms that demand collegial approval and enforce close co-operation. Both models, however, lack mechanisms for conflict resolution among the various country units. Difficult or unpopular decisions are rarely made by consensus.

So far, it seems that none of the European MNCs in Asia has moved towards a more federalist organization in the region, though some firms have asked their managers in Asia to carry both regional and other responsibilities. "Wearing two hats" in these cases means, for example, being a member of an existing RHQ and at the same time of another unit, which may be a local subsidiary, a functional group such as an R&D center, or a business division/SBU.

The term "double-hatting" was probably coined by BP when it introduced such a system at the beginning of the 1990s. The MNC decided then that all managers should belong to profit centers, and that almost all purely staff functions would be eliminated. The resulting cost savings were significant but, what is more important, people began to find it easier to understand and appreciate each others' point of view. Wearing two hats became synonymous with having two perspectives, a welcome development in the MNC. An alternative route to double-hatting is the assignment of regional responsibilities for certain businesses or functional areas to senior managers who accept these tasks in addition to their continuing responsibilities as heads of national units. Some American MNCs such as Hewlett-Packard and Apple operate such a system in Europe (Doz and Ghoshal, 1994). Henkel has started applying this logic with the appointment of the senior head of their local Malaysian operations to a major regional responsibility without asking him to join the RHQ physically. Unilever in South East Asia brings senior managers regularly together in task force meetings to accelerate the roll-out of new products or practices.

To work well, the more senior managers in the region should know and trust each other, and the method of cooperation must be well established. This means that double-hatting is hard to achieve for relatively new regional organizations. As the regional networks of European MNCs in Asia mature, more of them can be expected to follow the example of longer established RHQs of American MNCs in Europe.

Asia as a region

By and large European MNCs use a broad definition of Asia, sometimes far exceeding the common understanding of what is represented by the region. Pragmatism seems to be the dominant principle when delineating borders. Distances and transportation links apparently matter more than political linkages and cultural similarities. While politicians and diplomats work on the ideas of the EAEC (East Asian Economic Caucus) and the expansion of ASEAN (Association of South East Asian Nations); on APEC (Asia Pacific Economic Cooperation) and ASEM (Asia-Europe Meeting) and place major emphasis on the economic benefits that accompany closer integration, managers in MNCs find these discussions rather irrelevant for their purposes.

If the core of Asia may be defined as Japan, the ASEAN 4 (Indonesia, Malaysia, the Philippines and Thailand), the NIEs or newly industrializing economies (Hong Kong, Singapore, South Korea and Taiwan), Vietnam and China, then almost all European MNCs take this definition as their base (Lasserre and Schütte, 1995, pp. 1-4). Australia and New Zealand are included in Asian territory, probably by default.

It is the extension to the West where MNCs differ in their interpretation of Asia. Heineken's Asian region represents the broadest scope and even includes Israel. For several other MNCs the Asian territory reaches as far as Pakistan. Most European MNCs now include India in the region, though not all are committed wholeheartedly. Several of them are starting to explore this market more seriously under the leadership of their Asian RHQs, but are uncertain whether to group this large country together with the other countries in the Asian region, or to create a new region called "South and Central Asia". Both BP and Unilever exclude

India from the ambit of their Asian region due to long-standing special relationships between national units and their headquarters.

The more broadly the region is defined, the more urgent is the question of whether a single regional strategy can do justice to the increasing variations in the region, and whether one regional organi-zation is able to exercise such a span of control. The answer is in the affirmative, at least in the sense that European MNCs try to operate on the basis of one Asia. Some MNCs, like BASF, however, have introduced sub-regions that then need to be coordinated, most likely by a board member at headquarters. The cost of managing this additional complexity has to be weighed against the potential costs of losing specificity and control.

European MNCs in Asia are exposed to a further issue, namely, the inclusion of Japan today or the inclusion of other major countries like China and India in the future, in a region otherwise consisting of small and medium-sized countries.

Discussion of the issue is difficult due to the often strong desire of the representative of a major country to follow a different strategy than the other countries and to report directly to headquarters rather than first to the RHQ. To reach an effective solution to the problem, two points must be taken into consideration. The first concerns the extent to which the specific country business is related to the region. Factors to take into account include, among others, differences in technical standards and the presence of regional customers. Secondly, the importance of the country operation itself for the global success or overall competitiveness of the MNC has to be determined.

The matrix in figure 7 takes the example of Japan and describes the effect of its inclusion in or exclusion from an MNC's Asian regional organization.

In the case of a close relationship between the country activities and the region, the units in Japan should be included in the region and be used either as service centers or to lead operations which depend on the overall importance of Japan. Both IBM and Procter & Gamble have chosen the latter solution and rely on their Japanese subsidiaries continually to create new ideas and products. If the local units in Japan are only loosely connected with Asia and are less important for the MNC's global success, they can be dealt with on a case by case basis. No strong argument speaks in favor of or against their inclusion in the region. However, when Japan is important, for example due to its market size or the technological capabilities of the local units, but is less related to the region, a separate strategy and organization are called for. BASF, Bayer and Hoechst have all opted for this solution.

China represents an even more complex case in that her scale and momentum are sufficiently great for her to be considered as a region in itself. She is closely linked with many other parts of the region, but for many MNCs China has not yet reached the stage technologically or in volume terms that she is important for global success. At the end of 1996, several MNCs had between 10 and 20 ventures in operation in the country and several more under negotiation. Under such circumstances the distribution of an MNC's activities across the whole Asian region is thrown out of balance.

Figure 7   The Role of Japan in Asia

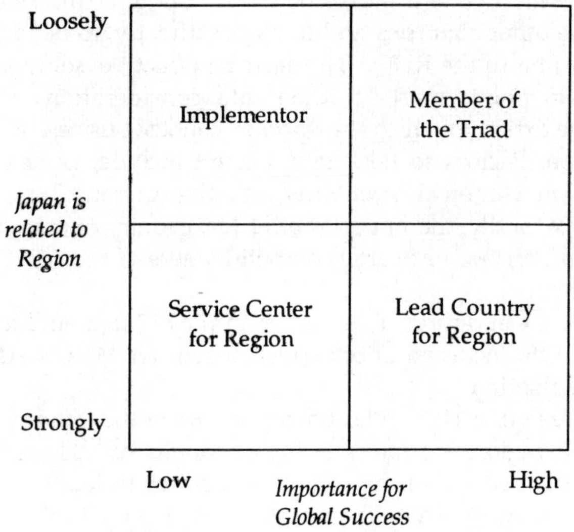

	Low	High
Loosely	Implementor	Member of the Triad
Japan is related to Region	Service Center for Region	Lead Country for Region
Strongly		

Importance for Global Success

The formation of a China holding company as a new legal entity adds to the uncertainty over the organizational treatment of the country. If the various China ventures are first bundled under a

China office which in turn reports to an RHQ which in turn reports to headquarters, lines of communication clearly become too long. If all these ventures report to the RHQ directly, it will turn into a disguised China office itself. The alternative is to establish a direct link between the China office and headquarters - a clear signal that a common regional strategy and a unifying regional organization for Asia are coming to an end.

In sum, Europe's MNCs are rising to meet the opportunities which Asia's markets offer. But the shift towards Asia brings unexpected problems which are rooted in the strategic and organizational complexities of large firms. There is no end in sight to the new challenges for European MNCs in Asia.

* Hellmut Schütte is Affiliate Professor of International Management, INSEAD, Euro-Asia Centre, Fontainebleau, France.

Notes and references

1. European MNCs consider investments in other European countries still equally important. This contrasts with American and Asian MNCs which consider Asia an absolute, unrivaled priority.
2. Figures 4 and 5 are based on the integration/responsiveness grid of Prahalad and Doz which was then further developed to include a regional component by Lehrer and Asakawa.
3. These statements as well as others given below are based on a comprehensive, yet unpublished study of *Regional Headquarters of Multinational Corporations* by Schütte. RHQs of 30 MNCs were explored in-depth, 15 of which were from Japanese MNCs for Europe, 15 of Western MNCs for Asia. Among the 15 Western MNCs 12 were from Europe.
4. Resistance to the establishment of RHQs is, however, not a typical Asian phenomenon.

Arthur Andersen, Ministry of Economic Affairs of France (1996) *International investment towards the year 2000.*

Blackwell, N., Bizet, J.-P., Child, P. and Hensley, D. (1992) Creating European organizations that work. *The McKinsey Quarterly*, 2, pp. 31-43.

Chandler, A.D. (1962) *Strategy and Structure: Chapters in the History of the American Industrial Enterprise.* MIT Press, Cambridge, Mass.

Doz, Y. and Ghoshal, S. (1994) *Organizing for Europe: One Size Does Not Fit All!* Working Paper, INSEAD.

European Commission and UNCTAD (1996) *Investing in Asia's Dynamism - European Union Direct Investment in Asia.* ECSC-EC-EAEC, Brussels/Luxemburg.

European Parliament, Directorate General for Research (1996) *The Dynamics of Economic Change in Asia - Implications for Trade and European Union Presence.* Working Paper W-12, pp. 3-96, External Economic Relations Series, Luxemburg.

Ghoshal, S. and Bartlett, C.A. (1995) Changing the Role of Top Management: Beyond Structure to Processes. *Harvard Business Review*, 73, 1, pp. 86-96.

Ghoshal, S. and Nohria, N. (1993) Horses for Courses: Organizational Forms for Multinational Corporations. *Sloan Management Review*, 35, 2, pp. 23-35.

Handy, C. (1992) Balancing Corporate Power: A New Federalist Paper. *Harvard Business Review*, 70, 6, pp. 59-72.

Hobday, M. (1995) *Innovation in East Asia - The Challenge to Japan.* Edward Elgar, Aldershot.

Lasserre, P. and Schütte, H. (1995) *Strategies for Asia Pacific.* Macmillan, Basingstoke.

Lasserre, P. (1996) Regional Headquarters: The Spearhead for Asia Pacific Markets. *Long Range Planning*, 29, 1, pp. 30-37.

Lehrer, M. and Asakawa, K. (1995) *Regional management and regional headquarters in Europe: A comparison of American and Japanese MNCs.* Working Paper, INSEAD.

Morrison, A.J., Ricks, D.A. and Roth, K. (1991) Globalization versus regionalization: Which way for the multinational? *Organizational Dynamics*, Winter, pp. 17-29.

OECD (1995) *Foreign Direct Investment, OECD Countries and Dynamic Economies of Asia and Latin America.* OECD, Paris.

Prahalad, C.K. and Doz, Y. (1987) *The multinational mission: Balancing local demands and global vision.* The Free Press, New York.

Schütte, H. (1993) *Competing and Co-operating with Japanese Firms.* USJP Occasional Papers, Harvard University, Cambridge, Mass.

Schütte, H. *Regional Headquarters of Multinational Corporations.* (forthcoming 1997)

Schütte, H. (1995) Henkel's Strategy for Asia Pacific. *Long Range Planning,* 28, 1, pp. 95-103.

Schütte, H. (1996) *Between Headquarters and Subsidiaries: The RHQ Solution.* Paper presented at the EIBA Conference, Stockholm, December 1996.

The World Bank (1996) *World Development Report 1996.* Oxford University Press, New York.

World Trade Organization (1995) *1995 International Trade: Trends and Statistics,* World Trade Organization, Geneva.

Chapter 13

Gioia Marini and Jan Rood: "The Embarrassment of Choices? The US between Europe and the Pacific Rim"

The collapse of the Soviet Union fundamentally altered the geostrategic realities underpinning post-World War II American foreign policy. This tectonic shift changed in particular the position of Western Europe, which until then was the main confrontation line of the bipolar world political system. Given this new setting, it was only natural that the Europeans reacted with alarm to Secretary of State Warren Christopher's November 1993 statement to the Senate Foreign Relations Committee that "[n]o area of the world will be more important for American interests than the Asia-Pacific region."(1) Christopher's remark moreover came on the eve of the APEC-Seattle summit, at which the seventeen states that participated in this forum, according to President Clinton, were to lay the foundations of a "new Pacific community", representing the most dynamic part of the world economy and more than half of world trade and world production.

To many - both within the United States and amongst its allies - Christopher's statement and the Seattle Summit were evidence of a *Pacific drift* in American foreign policy: a fundamental shift in priority from Europe to Asia-Pacific. "America's chilly message for Europe", according to the *Herald Tribune* (16 November 1993) was that the US had converted from a "European power" into a "Pacific power".

At that time there were many reasons for the Europeans to fear the eventuality of such a development. Not only did they have serious disagreements with the US about the war in Bosnia and the conclusion of the GATT-Uruguay negotiations on world trade, but to an American president whose main foreign policy aim at the time seemed to be the pursuit of American economic interests in the world, the prospect of an exclusive partnership with the emerging markets of Asia must have appeared too attractive to refuse.

If this reorientation of American foreign policy were to occur, it would mean the end of the special relationship which to a large extent had defined Western Europe's post-war position. To Europeans, Christopher's remark reinforced their impression that a rebalancing of power, position and prestige was taking place at the expense of Western Europe. It emphasized that in a world in which competition among nations had shifted from the political-military field to the field of technological sophistication and domination of markets, Europe was losing the battle. Without any exclusive relationship or political leverage of its own toward Asia, Europe was being pushed to the periphery of world affairs. But most signifcantly, Christopher's statement was seen as a signal that the Atlantic was widening and that the security links between the US and Europe were loosening. No longer the focal point of the bipolar confrontation, Europe had apparently lost priority in the American geopolitical calculus. And this at a time of growing concern in Europe about stability in Central and Eastern Europe and the former Soviet Union and an increasing fear that a US withdrawal might once again reduce this region to chronic conflict and instability.

Four years later, as a result of the conclusion of the Uruguay Round, the American participation in IFOR and the agreements about a new set-up of NATO, the worst fears about an American disengagement from Europe seem to have worn off. But amongst American foreign policy makers and analysts there is an ongoing discussion about the need for a reappraisal of American foreign and security policy toward the Asia-Pacific region. In a recent report, for instance, Douglas Stuart and William Tow posit that the rise of Asia will force the US to assign this region a greater weight, "as opposed to the Cold War practice of treating Asia-Pacific as an adjunct to the US global campaign of anti-communist containment".(2) And in a recent study by the *Council on Foreign Relations* called "Redressing the balance", it is recommended that "US lead-

ership activism in Asia needs to be heightened - commensurate
with the importance of the region".(3)

This chapter will examine the impact of the rise of Asia on
the American geostrategic calculus. What is the position of Europe
in the US strategic framework compared to that of Asia? Is a shift
in the strategic orientation of the US away from Europe towards
Asia likely? Does America have a choice between the two or is this
a false premise?

On "grand strategy"

To determine whether the US really has a choice, we should first
examine the goals of American foreign and security policy. A fash-
ionable view nowadays is that American foreign policy is in a state
of disarray as a result of the end of the Cold War; that it lacks
vision, priorities, and therefore predictability. The US may be the
only superpower, but without the Soviet Union as a challenger and
opponent, it is a superpower without a mission. George Bush's
concept of "a new world order" was meant to fill this ideological
vacuum, but the complexities of the post-Cold War world disorder
were revealed to his successor in a painful manner in the streets of
Mogadishu. Since then American foreign policy has been swayed by
the issues of the day.

This view is contested by Michael Cox as being based on an
overestimation of the historical consistency of American foreign
policy, an underestimation of the impact of the end of the bipolar
confrontation and a denial of the continuity in American external
policies. In fact, he posits, the goals of American foreign policy
"have not changed as much since the end of the Cold War as some
analysts imply". In his view American external policy is still
driven by the following aims:

- "to reduce foreign policy costs where possible;
- to encourage the broad historical movement toward democratic
  capitalism around the world;
- to compete more effectively in the world economy;
- to deter aggression by maintaining a reasonable military capability;
- to underwrite the balance of power in both Europe and Asia;
- (...) to ensure the United States remained the dominant actor in
  the international system".(4)

What has changed is the relative weight of some of those aims. One example is the case of the promotion of democracy, human rights and the market economy, where the demise of communism created greater room for an active policy to further those principles. A clear shift in emphasis can be seen in the greater interest of the Clinton administration in the economic dimension of foreign policy. During the Cold War, America's security concerns clearly superseded its economic interests. The United States tolerated the often-discriminatory trade practices of its allies and guaranteed them access to its profitable markets, in the hope that economic prosperity would provide the political stability needed to ward off communist insurgencies. The post-cold war Clinton Administration, by contrast, has placed America's first priority on its economic interests. Elected on a mandate to revive the US economy, Clinton shifted the focus of American foreign policy from geostrategic matters to economic concerns, or what he calls "economic security".(5) This is apparent in the creation in 1993 of a National Economic Council, designed to mirror the National Security Council, and in the high profile of the US Trade Representative. Indeed, if there is one characteristic of Clinton's foreign policy that distinguishes him from his predecessors, it is the prominent role that trade policy has assumed.(6)

Recent events in Bosnia-Herzegovina, Chechnya, and the Taiwan Straits, however, have served to remind the Clinton administration of the continuing relevance and importance of military security concerns. So, despite this "Clintonmania" concerning economic matters, the foreign policy agenda is still dominated by the familiar problems of maintaining regional stability in Europe, Asia and the Middle East, of the relationship with the former Soviet Union, and of the need to strike a good balance between resources and commitments.

The most important change in America's external policy does not concern its aims, but rather its strategy. As "the first post-Cold War President of the United States"(7), Bill Clinton was from the outset faced with the overriding need to construct a credible, new national security strategy. It is obvious that it takes time for such a strategy to emerge; it will evolve only gradually. It requires a thorough re-examination of America's global interests by policy makers, military officials and experts, legislators, and the general public, as well as the forging of a rough consensus in the direction of the strategy.(8) Moreover, it is shaped by domestic and international events and trends as much as by policy makers.

The debate about the need for and the elements of what is called a "new grand strategy" centers on the question to what extent the US in a more complicated world with more diffuse security risks must act as the world's policeman. Should it pursue a policy of noninterventionism, act on an *ad-hoc* basis through a policy of "balancing", or should it be permanently involved in security affairs through a framework of multilateral alliances?(9) Although this debate is continuing, the main elements of America's post-Cold War strategy are slowly beginning to emerge. In general, external policy has become more minimalistic and unilateral; i.e. more remote and selective with regard to interventions, less supportive of multilateralism (in particular the United Nations) and more explicitly geared to America's (social-economic) self-interest. Leadership is still the aim of America's foreign policy, but the outside world must now pay a price for it. In this respect the end of the cold war, though, has been more an accelerator than a rupture in the development of foreign policy. For the transformation of the US from a benign hegemon to a more selfish nation already started in the seventies.

Europe and the end of the Cold War
The concern of Europeans about a "Pacific drift" in America's foreign policy can only be understood within the context of the end of the Cold War, and its effects on the position of Western Europe. From the fifties onwards, NATO and the presence of American troops on European soil were the clearest expression of the American commitment to European security. Through its policy of extended nuclear deterrence the US acted as the protector of Western Europe against the hegemonic aspirations of the Soviet Union. The presence of this common enemy created a common interest between both sides of the Atlantic. With the collapse of the Soviet Union, this common interest disappeared. In the absence of a direct threat to the territorial integrity and security of Western Europe, the American and West-European security interests no longer coincided. Instead, their interests were diverging. This was the view at the time of Christopher's remarks about the importance of Asia. There was a strong feeling in Europe that as a result of the diverging security interests, the Atlantic relationship had already lost its foundation and that both sides would inevitably drift apart.

There was also a real fear the transatlantic economic relationship would become a source of friction and further disintegration. Here, too, the impact of the end of the Cold War should not be underestimated. During the period of bipolar confrontation the need to maintain political and military unity put a break on economic conflicts between the US and Europe. "A common purpose held the allies together even when their economic, political or even military interests temporarily diverged", according to Philip Gordon.(10) The end of the Cold War, however, meant that for the US, there was no longer any reason to subordinate economic interests to strategic objectives. On the contrary, in a period of "economization" of international relations, the economy, instead, came more and more to the forefront. Clinton's emphasis on American economic interests presented a real risk of escalation of economic conflicts, which could further damage the Atlantic relationship, and "spill-over" into the security field.

The Transatlantic connection, therefore, was threatened from two interrelated perspectives: the lack of a common security challenge and the risk of an escalation of economic problems. From this perspective, a disengagement between the US and its European allies was inevitable. But has the Atlantic really widened? Or are we instead witness to a difficult but still successful adaptation of both sides to the requirements of the post-Cold War world? What interests might the US have in Europe that would keep it engaged?

Still a "European power"?

The first thing which should be kept in mind is that it is not the first time that there is discussion and doubt about the cohesion of the Atlantic alliance, in particular the American commitment to Europe. Crises, confrontations and conflicts have been an integral part of the post-war Euro-American relationship. Henry Kissinger, for instance, wrote in 1965 already about "the troubled partnership": an alliance which was to fall victim to tensions and conflicts between its members about responsibilities and NATO's strategy. He referred in particular to the ongoing debate about the alliance's nuclear strategy.(11) In the sixties, moreover, the inflationary spill-over of American domestic and monetary policies and foreign policy put great strain on American-European cooperation, especially the relations with France and Germany. The seventies showed a list of confrontations and conflicts about "burden sharing" within NATO, trade frictions concerning agriculture and steel, differences of opinion on the Middle East, energy policies and the optimal mix of *détente* and deterrence towards the Soviet Union, especially the need for modernization of theater nuclear forces. The Year of Europe, proclaimed by the then foreign secretary Henry Kissinger in 1972 as a benchmark of American foreign policy, turned out to be a complete failure.

The eighties and nineties were no exception to this rule of Transatlantic disarray. In 1987, François Heisbourg wrote an article under the title "Can the Atlantic alliance last out the century?" His answer was that "[a]s a result of a number of recent developments the Alliance is now exposed to a new, more diffuse peril: senility, possibly leading to death from natural causes ... it faces the possibility of gradual, spontaneous disintegration after a period of growing incoherence".(12) And in 1992 in a follow-up article he added: "[w]hat in 1987 was a largely hypothetical question (...) has now become an urgently practical issue".(13) Reality seemed to serve him, when in 1993 the prospect of a failure of the Uruguay Round on trade liberalization led to lively speculation about a falling apart of NATO. From this perspective, the least that might be expected is that the loss of the Soviet threat and the specter of intensifying economic competition would put the Atlantic cohesion to the test.

Still, though, there are important factors which, from a structural point of view(14), make a prolongation of America's involvement in Europe more likely than a further disengagement. First, although the threat of a massive Soviet attack has disappeared, the US still has a vital interest in preventing the rise of a dominant power on the European continent and in maintaining peace and stability in this region. This requires the US to stay actively involved in European security. The US, in other words, is still part of the European balance of power and therefore a "European power" beyond the Cold War. As Richard Holbrooke recently wrote:

> "The United States has become a European power in a sense that goes beyond traditional assertions of America's 'commitment' to Europe. In 21st century, Europe will still need the active American involvement that has been a necessary component of the continental balance for half a century. Conversely, an unstable Europe would still threaten essential national security interests of the United States. This is true after as it was during the Cold War".(15)

To function as a "balancer", US involvement is not only necessary to counter the remaining power of the former Soviet Union, to control the risk of nuclear proliferation in this area and to manage the process of transformation in Eastern Europe, but also to guarantee a political order within which a reunited Germany can peacefully coexist. In this sense, the latent function of NATO and of US participation during the Cold War era - i.e. the intra-alliance pacification - has become more important, but now on an all-European level. Secondly, from an American perspective, Western Europe, in particular through the NATO-infrastructure of bases and command facilities and the equipment prepositioned on European soil, functions as a sort of forward base for American operations in other parts of the world, especially in the Middle East (e.g. during the Gulf war). Maintaining this investment in "military hardware" is of vital importance to the US as a global power.

Thirdly, although the US-EU economic relationship is plagued by conflicts, crises and from time to time even (the threat of) trade wars, there is also a strong economic interdependency between both sides of the Atlantic. Both in terms of imports and exports Asia-Pacific has become more important to the US than trade with the European Community. Within the increasingly triadic pattern of trade flows between the US, Europe and Asia Pacific, the Transatlantic trade relation has been relegated from first place until the beginning of the eighties to third position at present. The reason for this of course is the import and export potential generated by the fast economic growth of the East Asian economies. But from a "qualitative" point of view, there still is a very strong and, according to some, more stable trade relationship between the US and Western Europe than between the US and the Pacific area. While US trade with Asia is in deficit and has become the source of much political tension, transatlantic trade is, and has been, much more balanced. But if other dimensions of the international economy are taken into account, then also from a quantitative point of view US-EU relations are still very substantial. Western Europe is by far the most important investor in the US as is the US in Western Europe, and the degree of technological cooperation and participation in joint development programs is much more intense between European and American firms than between the US and Asia. In a recent study it was concluded that: "the link between Europe and the United States is central to US economic relationships. In most areas, relations with Europe are much more important quantitatively than are similar relations with Asia. The evidence strongly suggests that this will remain true well into the next century."(16)

Fourthly, the US cannot afford to disengage from Europe because important American interests may be affected as a result of the course and outcomes of the European integration process. This is obvious in the case of security cooperation among the Europeans, which on the one hand is a precondition nowadays for continued American involvement in European security, but which on the other hand may complicate America's role as a European and world power. The integration process may also have a substantial impact on the economic position of the US as a trading nation, and now the creation of a single European currency as an alternative and competitor to the dollar is likely to have an even greater impact on the US's global economic position. For both security and economic reasons, therefore, the US has an interest in maintaining some influence on the European integration process.

Finally, the US is the one and only remaining superpower. But in this ever more complicated and interdependent world political and economic system, even the US must depend on reliable allies in order to realize its goals and commitments. It is fair to assume that compared to other possible alliances, the US-EU relationship is a potentially "winning coalition", and that Western Europe is America's most stable and "natural" partner:

> "US-EU relations are stronger and more institutionalized than relations between any other major players in international politics. US-EU political relations are themselves multidimensional: they are rooted in strong cultural, historical and economic ties."(17)

Not only do they have a history of institutionalized cooperation in the field of security through NATO, but, perhaps even more important, they have a common history. Both the US and Western Europe laid the foundations of the post-war political and economic order, and still share more or less the same views about the future of the world political and economic order. In this perspective, transatlantic cooperation could function as the "anchor" for further collective management of the world political and economic system, in accordance with US and European interests.

In accordance with this view, Christoph Bertram in a recent publication even defends the thesis that America's future role as a world power depends upon its relationship with Europe; emphasizing the position of the US as a "European power":

"For the United States (...), the relationship with Europe will be the litmus test of its future world role. Europe is the main, if not only, anchor tying the United States to extra-hemispheric international order. The anchor may not hold. Americans may become tired of a Europe absorbed with its own identity but continuing to need the involvement and perhaps the deterrent of the United States to prosper in peace. But if that happens, the United States will be saying farewell not only to Europe but to international commitments as well".(18)

The US as an "Asian power"

Given the strong historical, economic and military ties between the US and Europe, can one really claim that the US is becoming increasingly an Asian power? The first point that should be stressed is that the US, notwithstanding the suggestion of a "Pacific drift", has been an "Asian power" for a long time already. American involvement in Asian/Pacific affairs even precedes US intervention in Europe during the First World War. Three of the last four major wars in which the US was involved were fought out in this region: the Second World War, the Korean war and the Vietnam war. In addition, the US has long-standing bilateral security links with South Korea, Japan and Taiwan, through which it would inevitably become involved in a conflict on the Korean peninsula or between China and Taiwan. Finally, already before the "hype" about the Asian economic miracle started, American prosperity had become increasingly dependent on economic developments in Asia.

The second point is that in Asia, as in Europe, the end of the Cold War had a potentially damaging impact on regional security and stability. It removed the threat of a menacing superpower; but more importantly, it meant the sudden disappearance of the American military's *raison d'être* in Asia, making a US withdrawal from the region a real prospect. Again, this phenomenon applies to both Asia and Europe, the important difference being that while the United States remains firmly tied institutionally to European security through NATO, in Asia such a transpacific security arrangement is lacking. There the US based bilateral alliance system is the only viable security structure, and most analysts agree that any alternative to this framework will take time to evolve. So, while Europeans worry about a Pacific drift, Asians fear an imminent Pacific withdrawal of the US; a fear most pronounced among those Asian states who believe that without the Americans a fierce balance-of-power struggle might break out among the major Asian powers.

In the case of Asia too, therefore, there is reason to ask what the American interests in the region are and why these interests, as scenario of a "Pacific drift" suggest, might be taking on more importance. The main argument for such a drift is the rise of Asia-Pacific as the fastest growing and most dynamic part of the world economy. Many studies show that the center of economic activity and gravity in the world is shifting from the Atlantic towards this region. Already now the economic weight of Asia is comparable to that of the EU and North America. The high growth rates of emerging markets in Asia, which are expected to persist well into the next century, dictate that Asia's relative share in world production and trade will increase further and that the economic balance of power will therefore continue to tilt towards the Pacific. According to some estimates, Asia's share in world product may even rise to 40 to 50 percent during the first decades of the next century.(19) The same studies show that as a result of this shift in the balance of economic power, by the year 2020, five of the seven largest economies (and seven of the ten largest) will be in Asia.(20)

The economic rise of Asia is reflected in the growing importance of Asia to the US. The link between America's economic well-being and its ties to the Asian economies have only become more crucial. Asia is America's most important trading partner, with the volume of US-Asian trade in goods (excluding services) outstripping transatlantic trade as early as 1978. In many strategic sectors, in particular aircraft and telecommunications, exports to Asia have become vital for the American economy. At the same time, several Asian countries - notably Japan, China and the four tigers - have emerged as America's main competitors in a number of economic sectors. A large part of the persistent US trade deficit is caused by the imbalance in US-Asia trade, especially in manufactured goods. The economic manifestation of Asia, in others words, is both an opportunity and a threat to the United States.

The economic rise of Asia cannot be separated, however, from America's role as a stabilizer in the region. According to Joseph

Nye, political stability has been, and remains to this day, a fundamental prerequisite for economic growth in Asia. In an article in *Foreign Affairs*, he asserted that America's military presence in the region provided this stability for the past fifty years, and emphasizes that the US is committed to continue doing so. The rationale behind this policy is that American businesses can only profit in Asia if it is a stable, and therefore prospering, region.(21) Most analysts would agree with Thomas Duesterberg that "an active policy of economic engagement in Asia probably cannot succeed if the United States fails to play an active role in the security arrangements of the region."(22) Active American involvement in regional security is thus an American economic interest. Moreover, continuing engagement in Asian security affairs offers the additional gain of political-strategic leverage that can be used to enhance American economic opportunities in the region. At the Seattle summit of APEC leaders in November 1993, President Clinton made this link between American security and economic interests clear when he stated that the US does "not intend to bear the cost of [its] military presence in Asia, and the burdens of regional leadership, only to be shut out of the benefits of growth that stability brings."(23)

The US and Asian security
But apart from the economic "spill-over" of the American role as a stabilizer in Asia, the US also has a number of strategic interests in the region, which may be threatened by certain events. Firstly, there is the real risk of imminent instability and conflict in Asia/Pacific. Secondly, if a hegemonic challenger to the US were to arise, it would most likely be an Asian power.

The first cause of possible instability in Asia is to be found in the shifting power balances within the region and the rise of "new" regional and great powers. According to many observers, with the end of the Cold War and as a result of its fast economic growth, Asia has entered a period of "unstable equilibrium."(24) As Paul Kennedy points out in his seminal work *The Rise and Fall of the Great Powers*, uneven economic growth rates of countries eventually result in shifts in the political and military balance of power.(25) In Asia, where the economies continue to grow at rapid and divergent paces, the regional balance of power is shifting and has yet to stabilize. In view of the prediction that Asia will be the fastest-growing region well into the next century(26), it is possible that the region's power balance will remain in a state of flux for some time to come. Such periods of shifting power balances are inherently unstable.(27) If history serves as a lesson in this respect, one cannot find much comfort in the fact that "of the six dyadic relationships among the current four great powers (US-Japan, US-China, US-Russia, Japan-China, Japan-Russia, Russia-China), *none* has been consistently stable, and *all* have eventuated in combat at some point in this century."(28) In describing the current political-strategic security environment in Asia, François Heisbourg for instance notes that "the parallel with pre-1914 Europe appears to be uncomfortably strong".(29) As in Europe in that period, Asia is now confronted with the rise of a number of regional and competing powers, among which a stable framework of political relations has yet to crystallize. In view of the region's lack of an effective multilateral security framework, this observation is particularly worrying.

There is, moreover, certainly no dearth of unresolved conflicts in Asia, which could potentially destabilize the entire region. According to the Stockholm International Peace Research Institute, Asia has even the highest number of border disputes and territorial claims in the world.(30) Many of the Southeast Asian nations are still in the process of negotiating their borders with their neighboring countries. Both the China-Taiwan issue and the future of the Korean peninsula have yet to be resolved. A final security danger that could destabilize much of Northeast Asia is a disintegrating China. The number of potential conflicts in Asia is even more alarming in the light of recent increases in the region's defense spending. Between 1990 and 1993, China expanded its defense budget by 20.6 percent (experts believe this official figure is much lower than *actual* spending)(31) South Korea by 13.6 percent, Taiwan by 20.3 percent, Japan by 38.2 percent, and Indonesia by 34.5 percent. While it may still be too early to speak of a regional arms race, this sort of development only exacerbates the suspicion and tension that already exists within the region. In addition there is the risk of a spread of weapons of mass destruction, in particular nuclear weapons. The United States has a long-standing interest in discouraging countries from developing or acquiring such weapons, both for its own security and for the sake of global stability. This has been one of the central tenets of American post-Cold War defense strategy and has become more prominent as a result of the collapse of the Soviet Union. The proliferation of weapons of mass destruction is a global security concern. US policy in this area does not focus exclusively on Asia, but with five potential nuclear powers in the region (China, Russia, India, Pakistan, and North Korea) Asian nuclear matters may come to dominate the agenda.(32)

The second security issue the US has in Asia concerns the rise of new great powers. It is conceivable that China or Japan will in the near future develop into the dominant power in Asia. Indeed, the countries most likely to pose a hegemonic challenge to the United States in the near future - China, Japan, and Russia - are all in East Asia.(33) According to Richard K. Betts, "A China, Japan, or Russia that grows strong enough to overturn a regional balance of power would necessarily also be a global power that could reestablish bipolarity on the highest level".(34) The rise of a hegemon in Asia is for the United States both a regional security issue and a possible threat to its global position. The most important question for American policy makers therefore is: what sort of relationship will a future Asian hegemon have with the other Asian powers and with the United States?

One foreign policy option for the United States is to try to re-sist any challenge to US hegemony. Such thinking was evident in the policy debate that emerged in Washington immediately fol-lowing the collapse of the Soviet Union. Charles Krauthammer claimed in 1992 that "now is the unipolar moment" and that "[t]here is but one first-rate power and no prospect in the immediate future of any power to rival it."(35) He argued that the United States is the only great power willing and able to keep the interna-tional system from degenerating into chaos, and that Americans have a duty to fulfill this global role. More recently, Zalmay Khalilzad comes to the same conclusion that American leadership is the best option for the United States and for the international community.(36) Samuel Huntington argues in a similar fashion, focusing on the threat posed by Japan to America's power and the need for the United States to protect its predominant position.(37)

US policy makers steer clear of declaring themselves in favor of unipolarity (for obvious reasons), but a leaked Pentagon document of 1992 reveals important evidence of the dominant line of think-ing. The Defense Planning Guidance (DPG) for Fiscal Years 1994-99 stated that:

"Our first objective is to prevent the re-emergence of a new rival, either on the territory of the former Soviet Union or elsewhere, that poses a threat on the order posed formerly by the Soviet Union. This...requires that we endeavor to prevent any hostile power from dominating a region whose resources would, under consolidated control, be sufficient to generate global power...Our strategy must now refocus on *precluding the emergence of any potential future global competitor..*"(38)

Although the report was later altered to avoid international embarrassment, it gives a clear indication of the preference for maintaining the US position of leadership within the American defense community. A more realistic approach, however, would be to accept the inevitability of the rise of new great powers in the region and of the emergence of a multipolar constellation. This is in accordance with Christopher Layne and Kenneth Waltz, who have argued that unipolarity is unsustainable because of the natural, systemic inclination of less-powerful states to coalesce against a dominant power in order to balance it.(39) Instead of trying to resist its own relative decline, this would require the US to try to manage this process, in order to prevent the rise of a belligerent challenger or of a regional struggle for leadership.

American interests in Asia-Pacific
There are, thus, strong arguments for the US not to disengage from Asia. Firstly, the overriding American economic interest is to take advantage of Asia as an "engine of growth" for the US economy. As Joseph Nye remarked: "[t]o cut ourselves off from such an area of economic dynamism would be foolish strategy indeed."(40) More specifically, it is in the American interest to prevent the emergence of an intra-Asian trade bloc, to further liberalization of trade and investment in the region and to counter illegal activities in the field of intellectual property. Those aims are reflected in the Clinton Administration's aggressive trade policy towards Asia, most notably in its active engagement in APEC as a means of ensuring that the US is not excluded from Asian economic affairs(41) and in its bilateral and unilateral policies towards specifically Japan and China, in order to open their markets to American products.(42)

Secondly, a regional military conflict would necessarily involve the United States, in particular through its defense treaties with Japan and South Korea and its relationship with Taiwan, but also through its security links with the Philippines, Australia and New Zealand, and Thailand. American officials have repeatedly sought to reassure their Asian allies that the US stands firmly behind these security pacts. Failure to uphold them in a moment of crisis would deal a serious blow to American credibility both in the region and worldwide. Moreover, a US withdrawal from the region could trigger an increase in instability. With three major powers (China, Japan, and Russia) and several emerging powers (India, Indonesia, a united Korea), there is a substantial risk that a departure of American troops would be followed by a fierce leadership struggle.

Thirdly, assuming that a competing great power will most likely come from this region, the US has no other choice than to be actively involved in this area, primarily to protect its allies and to maintain regional stability. In this sense, according to Richard Betts, there is a strong similarity with the American objectives in Europe: "[i]f the rationale behind US interventions and peacetime presence in Europe in this century was to prevent a hostile power [i.e., the USSR] from dominating a vital center of the world's wealth, productivity, and markets, the same logic should apply in East Asia."(43)

Finally, in order to be able to realize its interest the US will increasingly need the cooperation of other countries and will therefore be dependent on their policies. This applies in particular to Asia. The economic rise of this region and the emergence of new great powers from Asia will in time inevitably lead to more influence on world affairs or a greater demand for such influence. From this perspective, it is in the American self-interest to develop its partnership with Asian countries.

Is there a choice?

Does the next American president have a choice between Europe and Asia? The answer is no, if he wants to maintain the US position as a global power. The US derives this position from her ability and willingness to act on a global scale. In other words, her status as a global power requires her to be both a European and an Asian power and to accept the responsibilities which follow from the position of a great or global power. Therefore, the suggestion of a shift in American foreign policy priorities from Europe toward Asia is based on a simplistic view of world politics and American interests. As Gordon points out:

"It is important to dispel the notion that the United States must make a choice between regions or allies. Good foreign relationships and trading partnerships are not a zero-sum game, and there is no reason why a country cannot have good relationships with several countries at the same time."(44)

This is not meant to suggest that the position of Europe within the American strategic calculus has not changed. It has, but this is mainly the result of the end of the Cold War and not a kind of mechanical effect of the economic rise of Asia. Moreover, the changing geopolitical position of Europe constitutes, at least partly, a "normalization" of international relations. Indeed, "[i]n retrospect, it is striking how focused Washington was on Europe" during the Cold War.(45) The end of that era had to lead to a 'relaxation' of US policies towards its main ally: a return to more normal relations. This also explains why in the case of Europe there has been a much more substantial reduction in military personnel (Table 1).(46) But, again, this is no evidence of a Pacific drift. Moreover, the initiatives for a new Transatlantic framework - whether it is TAFTA, a new Transatlantic Charter or a Transatlantic Union(47) - which are in particular supported in the US, underline the continued American interest in Europe.

So, events until now do not support the alleged drift in American foreign policy away from Europe toward Asia. US-European relations have "normalized"; a process which took place independent of developments in Asia. Yet, in view of the economic rise of Asia, the emergence of new great powers and the risk of regional instability, it is likely, and perhaps even inevitable that during the next decades in response to this shift in the world's relations of power, the relative weight of Asia-Pacific in the American strategic calculus will increase. In accordance with a "push-and-pull" perspective of international politics, the US may be *forced* to turn its attention more toward Asia, both for reasons of profit and of conflict (within Asia and between Asian countries and the US). It may be questioned, however, whether Europeans should oppose such a development. A *relative* shift of American foreign and security policy may be the reflection of differentials in security demand. The difference between Asia and Europe being, that whereas Europe is in the middle of a process of adjustment to the post-Cold War era - first with German reunification and then with negotiations to bring its Central and Eastern European neighbors into the fold of the European Union and NATO - Asia, as was argued, in an unstable state of flux. Moreover, while, according to Richard K. Betts, in Europe "[o]ne of the reasons for optimism about peace (...) is the apparent satisfaction of the great powers with the status quo"(48), the same cannot be said of Asia. For these reasons the Asian demand for American engagement in security affairs may be stronger than in Europe. In this view, it even might be in the European interest to support America's involvement in Asia and to encourage American leadership in maintaining stability in this region. For, in the end, a stable and prospering Asia is also in the interest of Europeans.

Finally, in the long term the real question is not whether the US will turn towards Asia, but whether she will be able to maintain her position as a global power and act accordingly. This question can only be answered from a broader "systemic" view of the strategic setting for US external policies. This setting is/will be characterized by:

1. the rise of new great powers and a multipolarization of the international system;
2. a regionalization of economic activities and political responsibilities;
3. a further relative "decline" of the American capacity and ability to manage the international political and economic system.

These factors point to the emergence of a more complicated international system, with greater room for maneuver for regional powers and rising challengers and a greater risk of instability. Given this reality, what kind of strategy will the US adopt in order to be able to cope with this strategic environment? Will it pursue a flexible policy of balance of power or a policy of permanent alliances? In the end, the ability to develop a policy of alliances boils down to the classical tension between commitments and decreasing resources in a more complex world political system. This is the proper perspective to discuss the US position towards Asia and Europe.

* Gioia Marini was until April 1996 a research-assistant at the Institue of International Relations, Clingendael, The Hague. Jan Rood is director of studies at this institute. A first outline of this

chapter was presented during the workshop on *International rela-tions and security in Pacific Asia*, The Netherlands Institute for International Relations, 2 and 3 April 1996. A first version of this chapter was published in: Marianne van Leeuwen en Auke Venema (eds.), *Selective engagement; American foreign policy a t the turn of the century.* The Hague: Netherlands Atlantic Com-mission/Netherlands Institute of International Relations "Clingendael", 1996, pp. 113-132.

Notes and references

1. See: *US Department of State Dispatch.* 22 November 1993, vol.4/47, pp. 797-799. Christopher made similar remarks on two earlier occasions, on 15 and 17 November, 1993.
2. Douglas T. Stuart en William T. Tow, *A US Strategy for the Asia-Pacific; Building a Multipolar Balance-of-Power System in Asia.* London: IISS, 1995 (Adelphi paper 299), p. 66. Also: Kishore Mahbubani, "The Pacific Impulse". In: *Survival.* 37(1995) Spring, pp. 105-120.
3. Council on Foreign Relations, *Redressing the Balance; Ameri-can Engagement with Asia.* New York, 1996, p. 8.
4. Michael Cox, *US Foreign Policy after the Cold War; Super-power without a Mission?* London: Pinter/RIIA (Chatham House Papers), 1995, p. 121.
5. Stuart and Tow, p. 25. The increasing importance of economic matters is stressed *inter alia* in: Edward Luttwak, "From geo-politics to geo-economics: logic of conflict, grammar of com-merce". In: *The National Interest.* no.20 (Summer 1990), pp. 17-23; and Samuel Huntington, "Why International Primacy Mat-ters". In: *International Security.* vol.17(1993) 4, pp. 68-83.
6. This new focus on trade is a recognition of the increasingly significant role that US exports play in promoting economic growth. The percentage of exports to GDP in the United States has risen steadily over the last decade to reach almost 12 per-cent in 1993. At a time when domestic demand is dampened by ongoing efforts to balance the budget and by the global eco-nomic slowdown of the 1990s, exports have become the most promising source of growth for the United States. The Clinton Administration seems to realize that "growth in the United States in the medium term will depend a great deal on contin-

ued growth in US exports, so a sustainable growth and job creation agenda requires an active trade-enhancing component."
See: Thomas J. Duesterberg, "Trade, Investment, and Engagement in the US-East Asian Relationship". In: *The Washington
Quarterly*. vol.17(1994) 1, p.74.

7.   Ronald D. Asmus argues that although George Bush was
      President when the Soviet Union collapsed, "the real debate
      over future US national security strategy did not really take
      place in the final years of the Bush Administration". See
      Ronald D. Asmus, *Future US Defense Policy Toward Europe:
      The New Politics and Grand Strategy of European-American
      Relations*. Santa Monica, CA: RAND Corporation, 1993, p. 22.

8.   John J. Komhout, e.a., "Alternative Grand Strategy Options
      for the United States". In: *Comparative strategy*. 14(1995), pp.
      362-364.

9.   See *inter alia*: David M. Abshire, "US Global Policy: toward
      an Agile Strategy". In: *The Washington Quarterly*. 19(1996),
      pp. 41-61; Hans Binnendijk en Patrick Clawson, "New strategic
      priorities". In: *The Washington Quarterly*. 18(1995), pp. 109-
      126; John Lewis Gaddis, *The United States and the End of the
      Cold War*. New York: Oxford Univ.Press., 1992; Joseph Joffe,
      "'Bismarck' or 'Britain'?: toward an American Grand Strategy
      after Bipolarity". In: *International security*, 19(1995)4, pp. 94-
      117. Komhout, pp. 361-420.

10.   Philip H. Gordon, "Recasting the Atlantic Alliance". In:
      Survival. 38(1996), p. 34.

11.   Henry Kissinger, *The Troubled Partnership; a Re-appraisal of
      the Atlantic Community*. New York: McGraw-Hill, 1965.

12.   François Heisbourg, "Can the Atlantic Alliance Last Out the
      Century?" *International Affairs*, 63(1987)3, p. 413.

13.   François Heisbourg, "The European-US Alliance: Valedictory
      Reflections on Continental Drift in the Post-Cold War Era". In:
      International Affairs. 68(1992), p. 666.

14.   I.e., a perspective in which the long-term positions and inter-
      ests of the parties are taken into account instead of their daily
      conflict and squabbling.

15.   Richard Holbrooke, "'America' a European power". In: *Foreign
      Affairs*. 74/2(1995), p. 38.

16.   See: Robin Gaster and Clyde Prestowitz, *Shrinking the Atlan-
      tic; Europe and the American economy*. Washington: North
      Atlantic Research, Inc., 1995, p. iv.

17. John Peterson and Hugh Ward, "Coalitional Instability and the New Multidimensional Politics of Security: a Rational Choice Argument for US-EU Cooperation". In: *European Journal of International Relations*. 1(1995)2, p. 146. Also: John Peterson, *Europe and America; the Prospects for Partnership*. London/New York: Routledge, 1996 (sec.ed.); Miles Kahler and Werner Link, *Europe & America; a Return to History*. New York: Council on Foreign Relations Press, 1996.

18. Christoph Bertram, *Europe in the Balance; Securing the Peace Won in the Cold War*. Washington: Carnegie Endowment, 1995, p. 3.

19. See e.g.: OECD, *Long-term Prospects for the World Economy*. Paris: OECD, 1992; OECD, *Linkages: OECD and Major Developing Economies*. Paris: OECD, 1995; World Bank, *The East Asia Miracle; Economic Growth and Public Policy*. Washington: World Bank, 1993.

20. See in particular: "War of the Worlds: a Survey of the Global Economy". In: *The Economist*. 1 October 1994.

21. Joseph Nye, "The Case for Deep Engagement". *Foreign Affairs*. vol.74 (1995) 4, pp. 90-102.

22. Duesterberg, 1994, p. 84.

23. Cited in Stuart and Tow, p. 48. ("Remarks to the Seattle-APEC Host Committee, 19 November 1993")

24. Paul Dibb, *Towards a New Balance of Power in Asia*. London: IISS, 1995 (Adelphi Paper no. 295), p. 53. See also: Gerald Segal, "How Insecure is Pacific Asia?". In: *International Affairs*. 73(1997), pp. 235-250.

25. Paul Kennedy, *The Rise and Fall of the Great Powers*. New York: Random House, Inc., 1987, pp. 436-46. Also: Stuart Harris, "The Economic Aspects of Pacific Security". In: M. Howard, et al., *Asia's International Role in the Post-Cold War Era*. London: IISS, 1993 (Adelphi Paper no. 275), pp. 14-30.

26. OECD, 1992.

27. According to Robert Gilpin, the disequilibrium resulting from such power shifts can only be resolved through war. As he writes: "[t]hroughout history the primary means of resolving the disequilibrium between the structure of the international system and the redistribution of power has been war, more particularly, what we shall call a hegemonic war". Robert Gilpin, *War and Change in World Politics*. New York: Cambridge University Press, 1981, p. 197.

28. Richard K. Betts, "Wealth, Power, and Instability: East Asia and the United States after the Cold War". In: *International Security.* Vol.18,(1993/94)3, p. 46.

29. François Heisbourg, "A Secure Future for East Asians Supposes Collective Tending". *International Herald Tribune,* 2 March 1994.

30. Cited in Dibb, p. 52.

31. China is particularly keen to modernize its navy and boost its blue-water capabilities. Partly in response to these moves on the part of Beijing, Southeast Asian nations have stepped up their own defense spending and last year "overtook the Middle East as the world's third largest weapons market after the US and Europe". Edward Luce and Ted Bardacke, "Fear of Beijing Fuels ASEAN Arms Spending". *The Financial Times.* 28 February 1996. ASEAN nations bought $9 billion worth of weapons, representing 22 percent of world sales.

32. See Stuart and Tow, pp. 21-22.

33. Betts, p. 48.

34. Betts, p. 74. According to James R. Lilley, China is certainly the nation most likely to emerge as Asia's hegemon: "China senses an unprecedented opportunity for improving its regional position - the former Soviet Union crumbled, the United States appears to have strong withdrawal impulses, and Japan remains restrained by its own pacifist mood and continuing US military presence on Japanese islands". James R. Lilley, "American security in Asia". In: *Global affairs.* vol.8(1993)4, p. 75.

35. Charles Krauthammer, "The Unipolar Moment". In: Graham Allison and Gregory F. Treverton (eds.), *Rethinking America's Security: Beyond the Cold War to New World Order.* New York: W.W. Norton & Company, 1992, p. 296.

36. Zalmay Khalilzad, "Losing the Moment? The United States and the World after the Cold War". In: *The Washington Quarterly,* vol.18(1995)2, pp. 87-107.

37. Huntington, pp. 68-83.

38. Quoted in: Robert Jervis, "International Primacy: is the Game Worth the Candle?". in: *International Security.* vol.17(1993)4, pp. 53-54 and p. 59 (Italics added).

39. Christopher Layne, "The Unipolar Illusion: Why New Great Powers will Rise". In: *International Security.* vol.17(1993)4, pp. 5-51; Kenneth N. Waltz, "The emerging structure of inter-

national politics". In: *International Security*. vol.18(1993)2, pp. 44-79. See also: Jervis, pp. 52-67.
40. Nye, p. 93.
41. *Inter alia* to counteract the Malaysian proposal to create an "East Asian Economic Caucus", with an exclusively Asian membership.
42. An intra-Asian conflict moreover might disrupt trans-Pacific and intra-Asian commerce by effectively closing off important commercial waterways (if the conflict takes place on the seas) or by increasing exporters" risks to the point where trade becomes prohibitively expensive.
43. Betts, p. 46. See also: Paul R.S. Gebhard, *The United States and European Security*. London: IISS, 1994 (Adelphi Paper no. 286), p. 8.
44. Gordon, p. 39.
45. Gregory F. Treverton, "America's Stakes and Choices in Europe". In: *Survival*. vol.34(1992)3, p. 121.
46. Table I: US Military Personnel in Europe and Asia, FY 1988-94 (in thousands)*

	Europe	*East Asia/Pacific*
1988	356	141
1989	341	135
1990	310	119
1991	285	105
1992	205	98
1993	166	99
1994	128	98
Total reduction:	**228**	**43**

* Due to the American people's demand for a so-called peace dividend, President Bush introduced in the early 1990s significant cuts in American troops stationed in Europe and in Asia. The Clinton Administration's "Bottom-Up Review of Defense Needs and Programs" further reduced the number of overseas US forces.

47. See *inter alia*: Thomas J. Duesterberg, "Prospects for an EU-NAFTA Free Trade Agreement". In: *The Washington Quar-*